MW01620880

Glory of the World

contradicts long-held assumptions on his own work and aspirations. His description of Hofmann's abstract painting *Gloriamundi* (1963; fig. 2, p. 111) gave this book and the exhibition its title, *Glory of the World*, as well as its focus on the force that abstract painting continues to command.

I came to this study of Color Field painting from multiple experiences and perspectives. As the Curator of The Mark Rothko Foundation, New York (1980–85), I had the unique opportunity to immerse myself in the Foundation's extensive holdings of the artist's works and unpublished writings, as well as conduct interviews with many artists who were friends with him. Although Rothko was considered a forerunner of Color Field, he rejected all classifications by art movement, including Color Field. I also have had the distinct honor of working with Frank Stella on two major exhibitions. *Frank Stella at Two Thousand: Changing the Rules*, which focused on the direction his work took in the 1990s (Museum of Contemporary Art North Miami, 1999). The catalogue for this exhibition published his writings of the decade, including "Bombs Away: Hans Hofmann at 2000." *Frank Stella: Experiment and Change* (NSU Art Museum Fort Lauderdale, 2017) was an extensive retrospective, which juxtaposed Stella's work in a non-chronological arrangement that revealed the conceptual and formal links between his ongoing experimentations with painting. The process was illuminated by the first in-depth installation of his study works and models. I was additionally fortunate to work with Helen Frankenthaler on a survey of her paintings on paper that I organized in 2003 (Museum of Contemporary Art North Miami). This experience provided essential insight into her paintings and Color Field.

My discussions with Eric N. Mack (b. 1987) in 2021, in conjunction with the presentation at NSU Art Museum of his solo exhibition (curated by Ashley James for the Brooklyn Museum), and for the group exhibition *Lux et Veritas* I organized for NSU Art Museum (2022), were especially beneficial to the development of *Glory of the World* as his work and perspective helped crystallize my own thoughts about Color Field. I thank him for his openness and his generosity towards the artists who preceded him.

Other unique opportunities guided my study of Color Field painting. I would like to acknowledge those who supported my early work on Mark Rothko, including the late art historian Irving Sandler, and his wife the eminent Medieval art historian Lucy Sandler who was my mentor at New York University, as well as my husband James Clearwater for encouraging me to embark on this path as Curator of The Mark Rothko Foundation, and the Foundation's President, the late Ambassador Donald M. Blinken for providing me unprecedented access to Rothko's work and writings. Frank Stella has been a constant source of inspiration for me and I express my deep appreciation to him for his generous participation in this project. His wife, Dr. Harriet McGurk has been steadfast in her assistance for which I am most thankful. Thanks also go to Paula Pelosi for her assistance on my research on Stella over the years. Only an artist with Larry Poons' energy could have produced such forceful works as his Throw paintings. It was a great treat to work with him and his wife Paula De Luccia. Peter Bradley offered essential insight into his work and the history of *The De Luxe Show*, he organized in Houston in 1971, as well as his account of his close relationship with Greenberg and Rothko. I am appreciative of art historian Karen Wilkin as an essential resource on Color Field and also thank Douglas Baxter, Sabrina Blaichman, Nicolas Graille, Sarah Greenberg, Alex Grimley, Lauren Poster, Marc Selwyn, and Victoria K. Woodhull for their insights and assistance with my research.

This exhibition could not have been accomplished without the generosity of the collectors who loaned extraordinary works to this exhibition. I am in awe of David Mirvish's single-minded dedication to Color Field, begun when he opened his gallery in Toronto at the age of 18, and which he has sustained as a collector with his wife Audrey to this day.

Introduction and Acknowledgments

Glory of the World: Color Field Painting (Early 1950s to 1983) focuses on mid-twentieth century Color Field painting from the perspective of the artists' ambitions for the future of abstract painting. Color Field was not an art movement, rather it was a cohort of like-minded artists who began painting at a time when the dominant art historical narrative of modern art as a series of progressive advances still held sway. For these artists, modern painting meant being committed to abstraction. While the American Abstract Expressionists cleared a path for this postwar generation to forge ahead with abstract painting, their achievements naturally challenged the next generation of artists to create abstraction anew. These artists' experimentation with non-traditional painting mediums and methods and probing of conventions of painting led to unprecedented works.

This book is based on the exhibition of the same title at NSU Art Museum Fort Lauderdale (November 21, 2023 – August 25, 2024). The arrangement of the paintings in the exhibition was devised to heighten their direct confrontation with the viewer and focus attention on the moment when Color Field was new. The physical relation of these paintings to the viewer is critical to their impact and meaning. The extensive installation photographs in this book provide a semblance of this important physical correspondence between painting and viewer. One of the most rewarding observations of this exhibition, was the way viewers responded to these paintings without the mediation of formalist theory. Where critics such as Clement Greenberg applauded these artists for reducing the tactile quality of painting through the stain painting technique and limiting the spatial illusions in order to reinforce the flat picture plane, viewers responded to these paintings' thrilling optical depth in person. They experienced an overwhelming sense that they could physically feel and explore this space through their eyes. This response, in fact, corresponded with the artists' intent. As Frank Stella recently stated to me, Color Field was never about color, it was about finding a real and believable space in painting.

The supplemental text in this book reprints articles representing a selection of views of critics and artists regarding Color Field painting. Art historian and curator, William S. Rubin's "Younger American Painters" (January 1960) prompted Clement Greenberg's rebuttal "Louis and Noland" (May 1960). Both writers debated the criteria by which to judge these new paintings, while artist Frank Bowling in "It's Not Enough to Say 'Black Is Beautiful'" (April 1971) proposed that the focus of criticism should be on the artist's intention, which, in regards to the Black artists he discussed, embraced the coded meaning of their materials and images. Alex Greenberger's interview with artist Eric N. Mack revisits the relevance of Bowling's essay to a new generation of Black abstract artists in "Artist Eric N. Mack on a 1971 Frank Bowling Essay About Black Art: 'He's Arguing for the Importance of Innovation'" (April 23, 2021). Stella, in "Bombs Away: Hans Hofmann at 2000" (1999),

Contents

Glory of the World
Color Field Painting
(Early 1950s to 1983)

NSU Art Museum Fort Lauderdale
November 21, 2023 – August 25, 2024
Curated by Bonnie Clearwater

Glory of the World: Color Field Painting is sponsored by Suzi and David Cordish, Stephanie and Howard Krass, the Jerry Taylor and Nancy Bryant Fund of the Community Foundation of Broward and Four Seasons Hotel and Residences Fort Lauderdale.

Major support for NSU Art Museum Fort Lauderdale is provided by the David and Francie Horvitz Family Foundation Endowment, the City of Fort Lauderdale, Wege Foundation, Community Foundation of Broward, Lillian S. Wells Foundation, the Broward County Cultural Division, the Cultural Council, and the Broward County Board of County Commissioners, and the State of Florida through the Division of Arts and Culture and the National Endowment for the Arts.

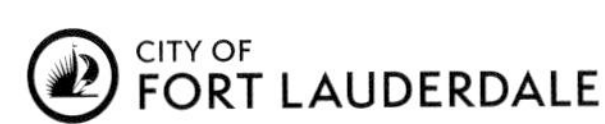

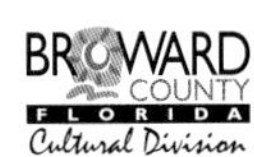

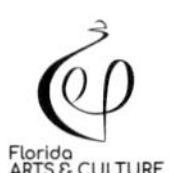

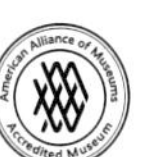

Bonnie Clearwater

Glory of the World

Color Field Painting (Early 1950s to 1983)

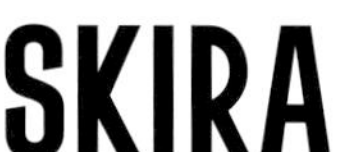

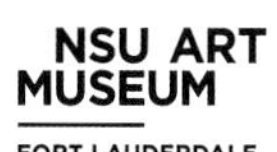

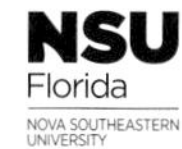

His first-hand knowledge of these artists and their work was invaluable for this project, as was the access he and Audrey provided to their collection. The Mirvish Collection is unique in its mix of family and associates who make the study and loans of the work an enjoyable experience. I express my appreciation to the participation of Hannah Mirvish, Richard Conway, Laurel Purvis, and the very knowledgeable and diligent Collections Manager Eleanor Johnston. Other major loans were made by Jill and Jay Bernstein, Beth Rudin DeWoody, Karma Gallery, Jumaane N'Namdi and N'Namdi Contemporary Art, Miami, S. Donald Sussman, and other private collectors who prefer to remain anonymous, for which I am most grateful. Thanks go to Todd Levin for coordinating the loan of Alma Thomas' painting and Beth Stub, Hauser & Wirth, New York, for assisting with the loan of Ed Clark's painting. Appreciation is also extended to Skira for editing, designing and publishing this beautiful book and to Steven Brooke for the installation photography.

The museum's entire staff has contributed enormously to the successful organization and presentation of this exhibition and book, including the curatorial staff consisting of Exhibition and Collection Manager, Jordyn Newsome, who expertly coordinated the loans, shipping and installation of the exhibition, and transcribing the articles reprinted in this book, Rebecca Vaughn, Registrar, the Bryant-Taylor Curator Ariella Wolens and Caroline McNabb, Assistant Registrar, for assisting with research, Cathie Conn for proofing the articles for reprint, Oliver Loaiza, Head Preparator/Technician, for coordinating the installation and supervising the art handlers, and Charles Ross for his assistance with exhibition design. I acknowledge Primary Art Services for their expertise in installing the monumental paintings in the exhibition. The museum's education staff headed by Lisa Quinn, The Lillian S. Wells Education Curator, along with the Education staff Michael Belcon, The Wege Foundation Assistant Curator, Susan Giradi-Sweeney, and Tristen Trivett developed compelling educational content and oversaw countless exhibition tours with the museum's dedicated corps of Docents for school groups and adults. Thanks also go to Marketing and Communications Manager, David Guidi, and Glickman Media for producing video content to augment the visitor experience. Lisa Kasten, Event Manager, coordinated and supervised multiple events, with additional support from Christina Benedictsson, Executive Assistant, Elisabeth de Lapresle-Wennberg, Major Gifts Officer, and Ferida Mamatkazina, Development Associate.

An exhibition and book of this magnitude could never have been undertaken without major support. I am deeply grateful to Suzi and David Cordish, the family of Linda Frankel, Francie Bishop Good and David Horvitz, Stephanie and Howard Krass, the Jerry Taylor and Nancy Bryant Fund of the Community Foundation of Broward, and Four Seasons Hotel and Residences Fort Lauderdale for ensuring this project's success.

Special thanks go to the museum's extraordinary Board of Governors, chaired by Michelle Howland, and Nova Southeastern University for their continued and enthusiastic support.

Bonnie Clearwater
Director and Chief Curator
NSU Art Museum Fort Lauderdale

GLORY OF THE WORLD **COLOR FIELD PAINTING**

Bonnie Clearwater

Glory of the World: Color Field Painting (Early 1950s to 1983)

Frank Bowling
Peter Bradley
Jack Bush
Ed Clark
Helen Frankenthaler
Sam Gilliam
Adolph Gottlieb
Hans Hofmann
Morris Louis
Al Loving
Robert Motherwell
Kenneth Noland
Jules Olitski
Larry Poons
Frank Stella
Alma Thomas

Glory of the World

"Ambition!" It was "ambition," Larry Poons repeatedly insisted in an interview with art historian Karen Wilkin, that defined a cohort of postwar American artists who committed themselves to abstract painting in the mid-twentieth century.[1] These artists were not so much personally ambitious, rather they were ambitious for their paintings and the future of abstract painting.

American art at mid-twentieth century was ambitious. The first generation of Abstract Expressionists (Barnett Newman, Willem de Kooning, Adolph Gottlieb, Franz Kline, Robert Motherwell, Jackson Pollock, Mark Rothko, and Clyfford Still, among others) had broken new ground with their paintings in the late 1940s and early 1950s, which attracted the global recognition that eluded previous generations. In 1949, *Life* magazine catapulted Pollock's career when it hailed him as "the most powerful painter in America" in a feature story that included photographs of the artist stretched over a large canvas on the floor as he vigorously dripped and splattered paint onto its surface.[2] Pollock's renown helped to raise his contemporaries out of obscurity. Then as now, controversy fueled publicity. Most significantly, in May 1950 a group of eighteen abstract painters and ten sculptors sent a letter to the president of New York's Metropolitan Museum of Art, protesting against the planned exhibition *American Painting Today, 1950*, on the grounds

that the jury selecting the artists would be biased against their work. The letter was published on the front page of *The New York Times* on May 22, 1950, and their protest was memorialized in the iconic "Irascibles" photograph of eighteen of the artists that appeared in *Life* magazine's January 15, 1951 issue.[3] While the Metropolitan Museum of Art missed the mark in 1950 to feature these artists, other museums took early risks in showing these maverick Americans' work, including the Museum of Modern Art and The Jewish Museum in New York, San Francisco's California Palace of the Legion of Honor, San Francisco Museum of Modern Art, and the Art Institute of Chicago. Although the Whitney Museum of American Art championed the nation's artists, a number of the Abstract Expressionists had a love-hate relationship with the institution that traced back to the 1930s when its exhibitions favored figurative Social Realist painters. By 1960, the Metropolitan Museum of Art caught up with the times, hiring Henry Geldzahler right out of Harvard graduate school as its first curator of Modern Art.

Even the French magazine *Art d'aujourd'hui* took notice, devoting its June 1951 issue to painting in the United States. It included an article by Michael Seuphor on the New York art scene, thought to be the first "written sympathetically and understandably" by a European on avant-garde American artists.[4] Seuphor, who traveled from Paris to New York during the winter of 1950–51 to research his article, marveled at the astonishing growth of Manhattan and its art world, remarking, "It is only in the past five or six years that modern painting has begun to live. I mean it has entered the ranks of society, it is talked about."[5] This article was also published in *Modern Artists in America No. 1* (1951), which was intended as the first volume of biennial publications documenting modern art in the United States. Its editors, artists Robert Motherwell and Ad Reinhardt, along with Museum of Modern Art Librarian Bernard Karpel, aimed to record developments as objectively and directly as possible while they were happening. This included the transcript of the artist-led discussions at New York's Studio 35 presented in 1950, in which the artists attempted to define their "community" and their work.[6] Motherwell described the challenge the artists faced: "to re-invent painting, its subject matter and its means, is a task so difficult that one must reduce it to a very simple concept in order to paint for the sheer joy of painting, as simple as the Madonna was to many generations of artists in the past."[7] Unlike the artists of the past, the Abstract Expressionists had no "inherited iconography." Consequently, Motherwell and several of his peers, including Gottlieb, Newman, and Rothko, invented their own images that they could repeat with variations in order to concentrate on the act of painting itself.[8]

The second generation of Abstract Expressionists (including Norman Bluhm, Grace Hartigan, Al Held, Joan Mitchell, and Milton Resnick, among others) continued on the same track, pursuing the more painterly gestures associated with de Kooning and Franz Kline. In 1958, Alfred Barr, Director of New York's Museum of Modern Art, exclaimed that he was anxiously awaiting a rebellious new generation of artists to emerge and challenge the status quo, only to discover soon after this pronouncement that a new generation had already appeared on the scene, and he quickly embraced artists such as Jasper Johns and Frank Stella.[9] Unlike the first generation of Abstract Expressionists who generally were unified in their commitment to abstract painting, these up-and-comers splintered off along multiple paths that led to Color Field painting, Minimalism, Neo-Dada, Op art, Performance art, and Pop art, to name a few.

The focus here is on the American artists who are often identified as Color Field painters. It is by no means a comprehensive list of Color Field painters as this, in itself, is impossible due to the fluid and expansive nature of this classification. This cohort of artists chose their art historical family based on their own proclivities and pursuits. Their shared

interests coalesced in a direction that critics attempted to describe and define. A cohort, however, is not an art movement and hardly any of the artists defined their work as Color Field. Yet critics, art dealers, and art historians continually seek to classify artists working within a temporal moment in ways that would define their commonalities. Color Field, or Post-Painterly Abstraction, as influential critic Clement Greenberg coined it, typically minimized the brushy gestures associated with the Abstract Expressionists, and de Kooning in particular. Other similarities are these paintings' large, and even immense scale, that situates the viewer within their fields; allover compositions that activate the painting's entire surface so that all elements, including the white areas of unpainted canvas, exist on the same plane and are of equal importance; and a lively pictorial space forged by color, shape, and pigment rather than through the use of perspective, light-and-dark modeling, or figure/ground relationships. There are no hard-edge lines in Color Field painting. Rather, these paintings are comprised of masses of colored shapes and exposed raw canvas that abut, intersect, overlay, or blend into one another. Even the most geometric bands of Noland and Stella's paintings are not hard-edged as the artists allowed the diluted paint to bleed at the perimeter of the bands.[10] These artists' commitment to the primacy of abstract painting led them to experiment in ways that ultimately challenged the conventions of painting itself.

The title, *Glory of the World*, takes its cue from Stella's writings on the influential abstract painter and teacher Hans Hofmann's painting *Gloriamundi* (1963; fig. 2, p. 111), in which he states, "We revere Hofmann … for proving that the straightforward manipulation of pigment can create exalted art … Glory of the world this painting surely is, and glory of the world his painting surely was and is."[11] Like Hofmann, Color Field paintings arouse a sense of wonder and discovery.

The time frame of this study extends from the early 1950s, when Helen Frankenthaler's stain paintings opened up the possibilities of abstraction to a new generation of artists, to early 1980s with the rise of Neo-Expressionism, which infused the medium with a new sensibility that seemed antithetical to Color Field painting.[12] This trajectory allows viewers the opportunity to follow the continued experimentation of these artists as they broke new ground in painting.

American-Type Painting

While the Color Field artists were forging their own pictorial language, critics and curators were devising methods to articulate these paintings' novel characteristics. The artists did not always agree with the critics' conclusions, and often were at odds with them; nevertheless, their critical analyses held sway for decades.

Critics Harold Rosenberg and Greenberg offered two opposing assessments of the first generation of Abstract Expressionists that established the parameters for the future of abstract painting in America. In his famous essay, "The American Action Painters," published in 1952, Rosenberg observed "at a certain moment the canvas began to appear to one American painter after another as an arena in which to act—rather than as a space in which to reproduce, redesign, analyze or 'express' an object actual or imagined. What was to go on the canvas was not a picture but an event." Moreover, he noted, these new creations were liberated from value judgements, including "political, aesthetic, moral."[13] Greenberg wrote his foundational essay, "American-Type Painting" (first published in 1955 in the *Partisan Review*) as a rebuttal to Rosenberg. Greenberg aspired to establish a rigorous criteria by which to gauge the success of these developments as part of an art historical lineage that was traceable to the dawn of modern art. For Greenberg, aesthetic judgements were not subjective as each medium was governed by the internal logic of

its formal properties. He suggested that the success of a painting could be evidenced by the degree by which it furthered the medium toward its purest elements. For Greenberg, "pure" painting meant eliminating anything that was extraneous to the medium itself, including the figure and narrative. It meant avoiding creating illusory pictorial space as it contradicted the flatness of the surface of the painting, which was the single characteristic that was unique to the medium.

In "American-Type Painting" Greenberg made the bold prediction that modernism was far from running its course and that painting, in particular, would continue "to work out its modernism with unchecked momentum because it still has a relatively long way to go before being reduced to its viable essence."[14] Greenberg could make this statement with full confidence as he already encountered new works in 1952 by the young New York artist Helen Frankenthaler, who succeeded in pushing painting towards what he considered the next step in its evolution, by staining paint right into the fabric of raw, unprimed canvas so that it fused with the support itself rather than sit atop the surface. Although he did not mention Frankenthaler by name in this essay, her soak-stain painting technique must have been upper most in his mind for he erroneously described how Rothko's abstract paintings of broad fields of color looked as though he allowed the paint to soak into the canvas "to get a dyer's effect and avoid the connotations of a discrete layer of paint on *top* of the surface," even though he admitted that he knew Rothko did not actually stain the canvas but achieved this effect through scumbling colors on top of each other.[15]

Greenberg and Rosenberg's essays on the Abstract Expressionists offered two opposing paths for artists to follow—the Action Painting of de Kooning or the formal direction Greenberg proposed, which had the benefit of holding out the promise of future innovations yet to come. By the early 1950s, the gestural painting associated with Action Painting seemed manneristic and derivative. Where most artists of Frankenthaler's generation chose to follow in de Kooning's footsteps, she saw opportunity and potential in Pollock's paintings that led to her own breakthrough in 1952.[16] Pollock's exhibition at the Betty Parsons Gallery in 1950 was a revelation and final liberation for Frankenthaler. What interested her most about Pollock's big paintings was not necessarily the technique, but "the fact that they seemed to have been born or happened all at once in that size," instead of it looking as though they were "made in steps or labored, even though it might have taken weeks or months" to paint.[17] Pollock's line was fluid as well as calligraphic, and it expanded to define the contour of the shape. He primarily used enamel paint, which he allowed to stain the canvas, splatter, drip, and puddle. Frankenthaler's appreciation of Pollock's painting coupled with an intense period of painting with watercolor led to her leap with *Mountains and Sea* (1952; fig. 5, p. 113), which she created through the soak-stain painting technique by which she poured greatly diluted paint onto raw, unprimed canvas rolled out on the floor. Unlike Pollock's more visceral and tactile paints, Frankenthaler's process allowed the fluid pigment to bleed into the canvas' weave. By staining her paintings with thinned pigments, Frankenthaler transformed Pollock's line into pure color and form.

Greenberg recognized *Mountains and Sea* as a breakthrough and enthusiastically brought people to see the painting in Frankenthaler's studio. Among them were Kenneth Noland and Morris Louis from Washington, D.C. Seeing *Mountains and Sea* was a revelation to the two artists, who were grappling with their own experimentations with abstract painting. This watershed encounter inspired them to create their own colorful stain-painted abstractions. Frankenthaler herself was not present on this occasion, which is significant to note as Louis and Noland saw the end result of her process, instead of a demonstration of her process. This first impression was mediated through Greenberg rather than through the absent artist. As Noland later remarked in 1966, Frankenthaler

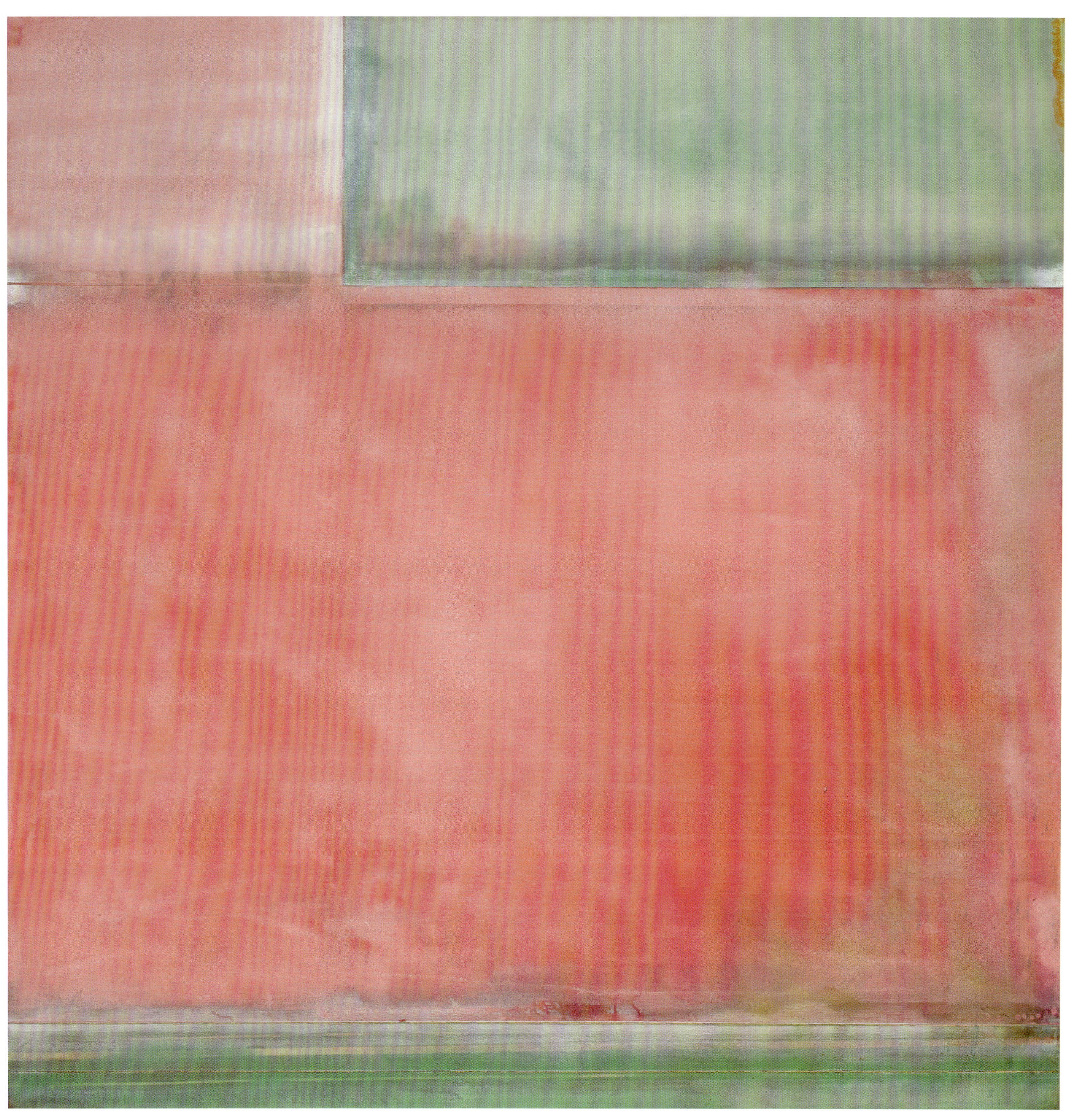

Frank Bowling
1 **Yonder II, 1972**
Acrylic on canvas, 68½ × 68½ in. (174 × 174 cm)
Collection of Beth Rudin DeWoody

Peter Bradley
2 **Belle Coast, 1973**
Acrylic on canvas, 51⅝ × 74⅛ in. (131.1 × 188.3 cm)
Courtesy of the artist and Karma

FOLLOWING PAGES

Peter Bradley
3 **Stormy Weather III, 1975**
Acrylic on canvas, 44⅛ × 80⅛ in. (112.1 × 203.5 cm)
Courtesy of the artist and Karma

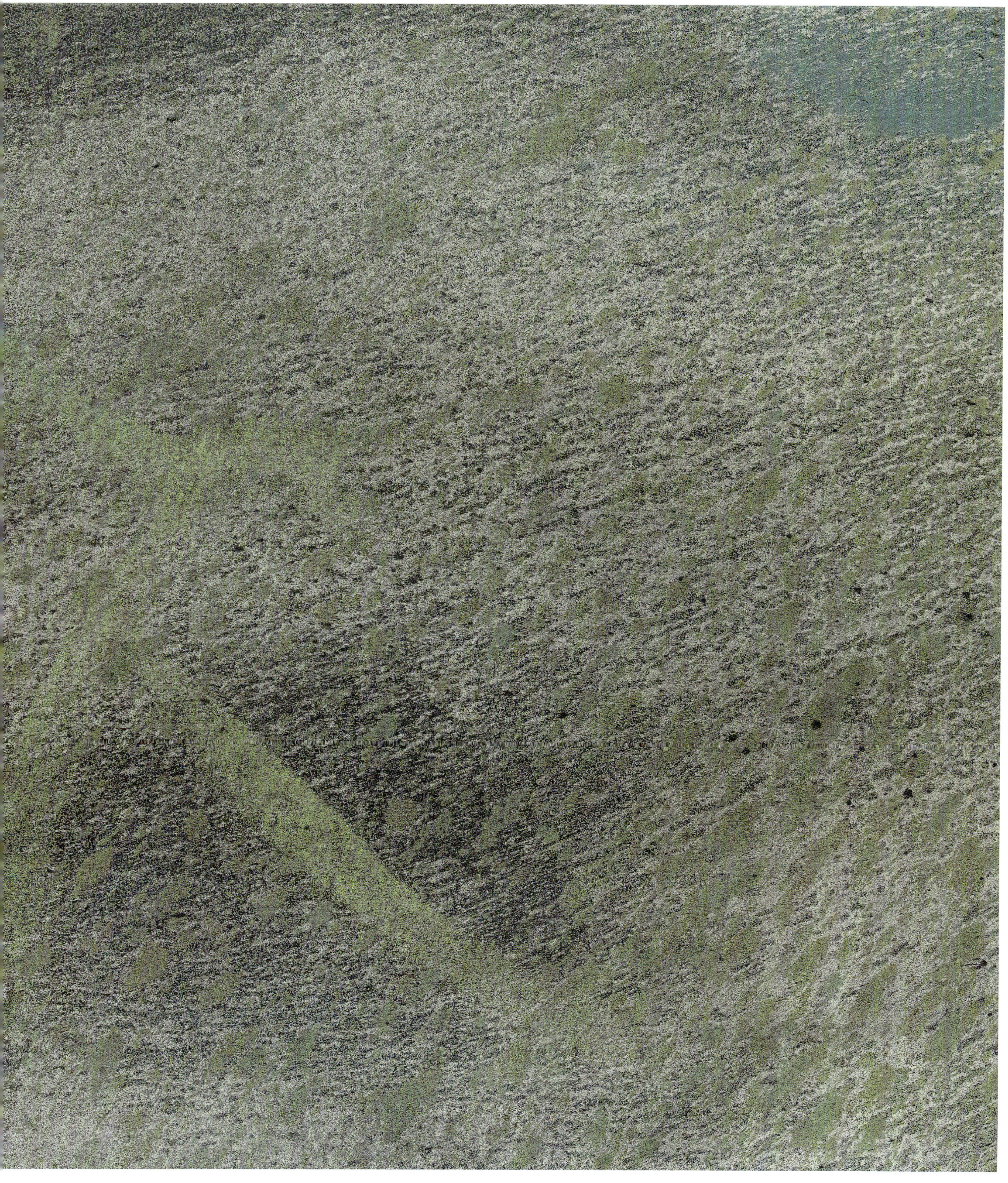

Jack Bush
4 **Red Column #2, 1963**
Oil on canvas, 84⅛ × 69½ in. (213.7 × 176.5 cm)
Audrey and David Mirvish, Toronto

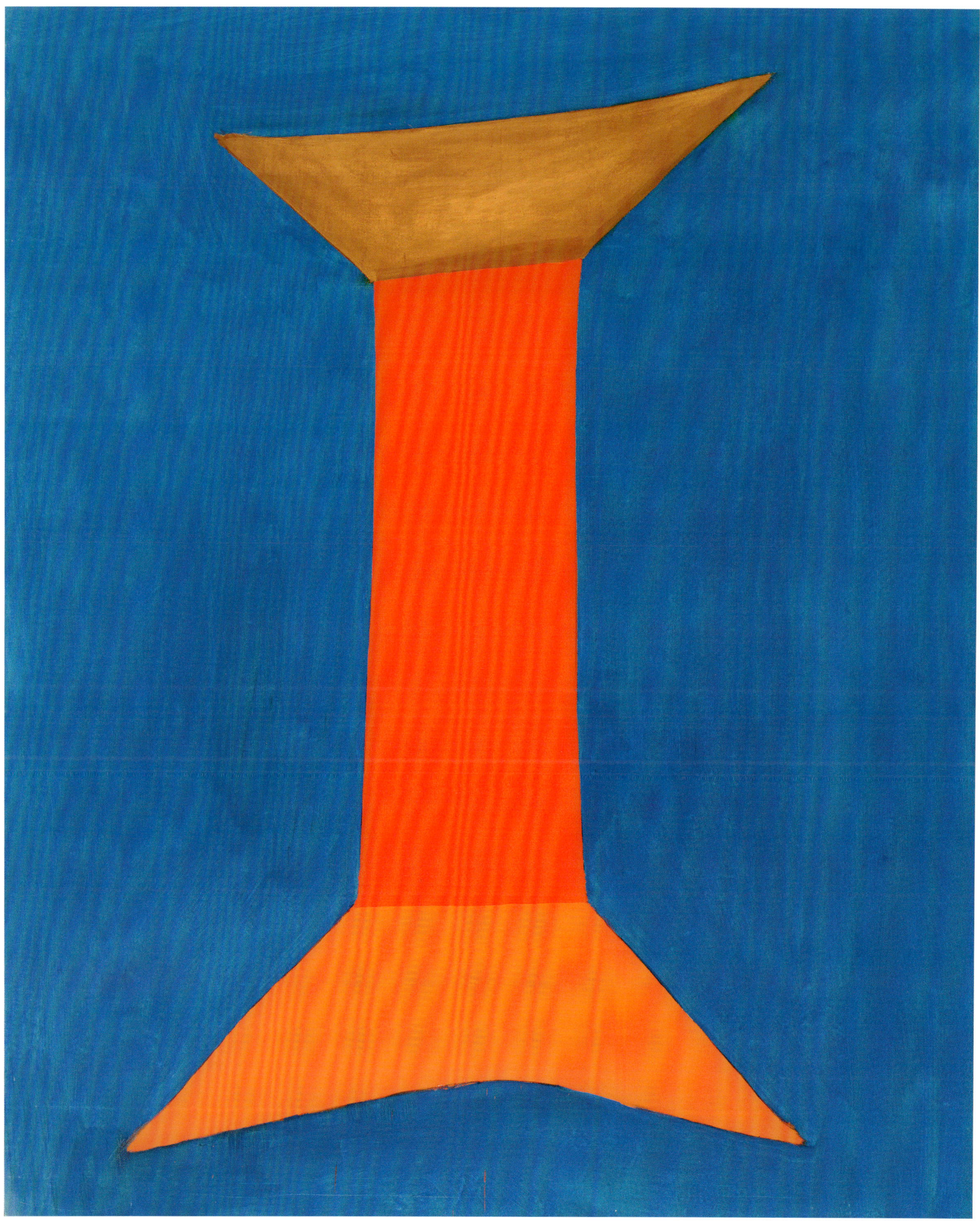

Jack Bush
5 **Pinched Orange, 1964**
Oil on canvas, 87 × 70 in. (221 × 177.8 cm)
Private Collection

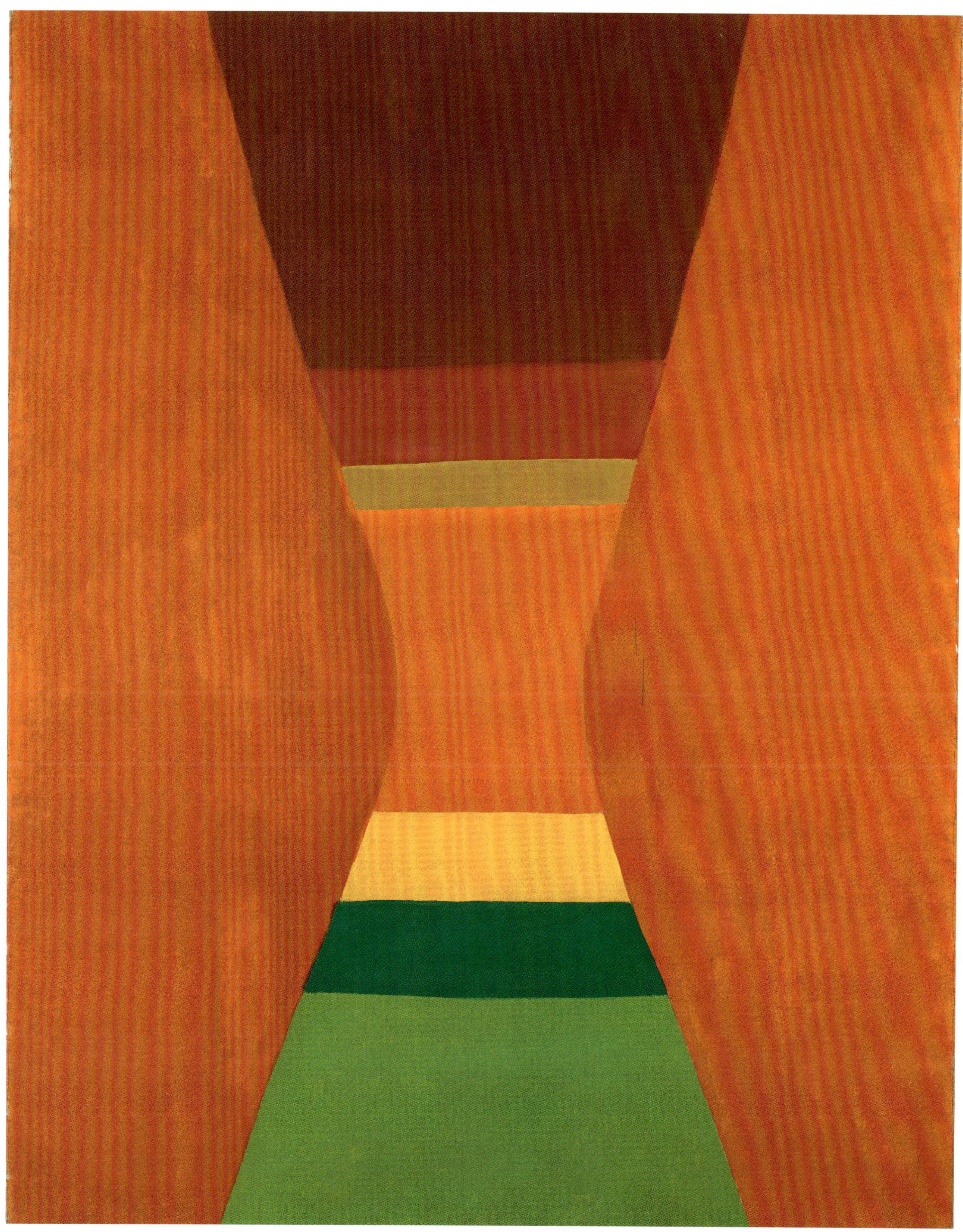

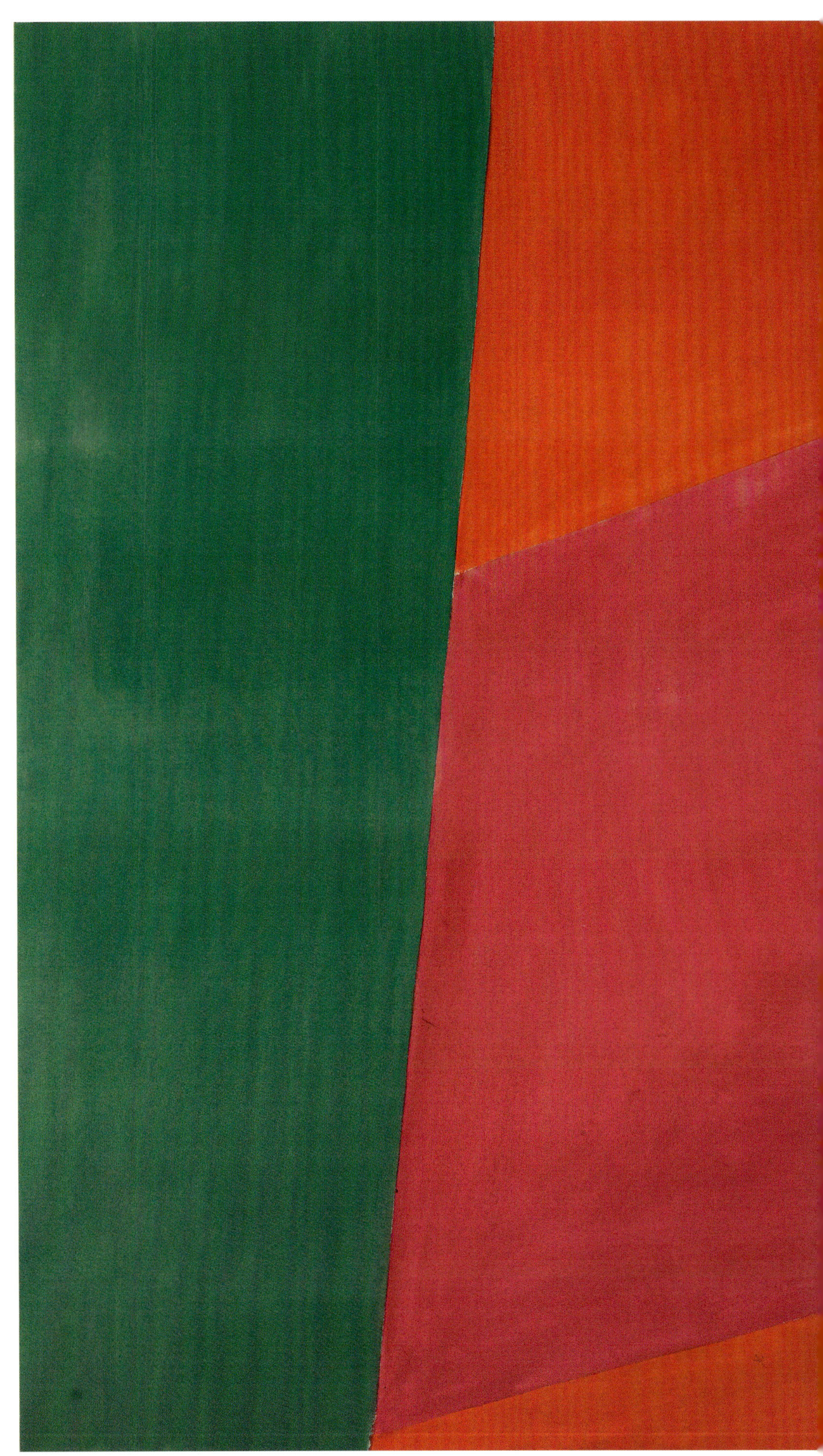

Jack Bush
6 January Reds, 1966
Oil on canvas, 79½ × 116½ in. (201.9 × 295.9 cm)
Private Collection

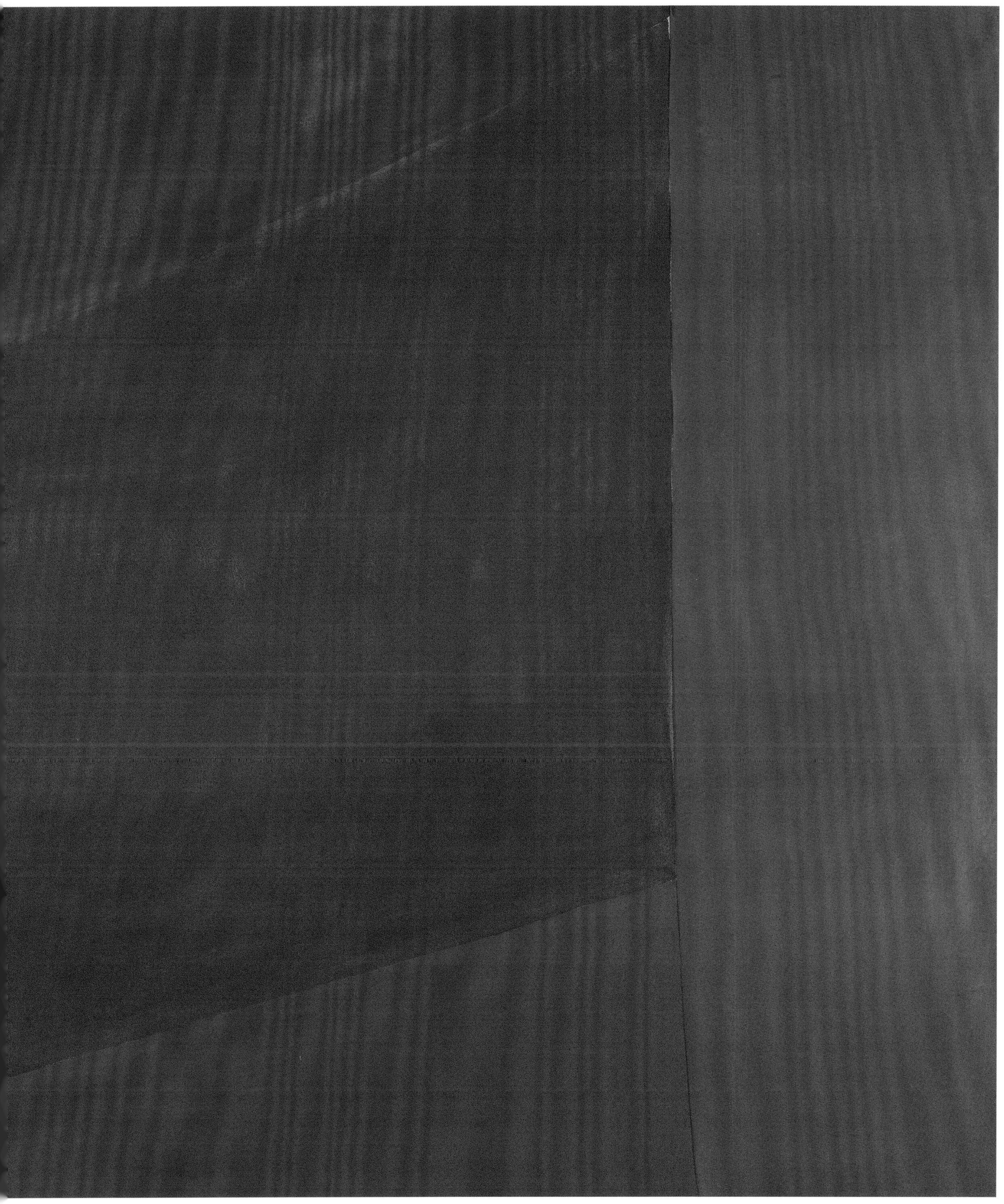

was the first artist he and Louis had seen who was influenced by Pollock without being derivative. He was struck by how her stain painting "looked free and open and unencumbered by a lot of the clichés of painting at that time, and it looked very chancy."[18] In Noland's estimate, Frankenthaler achieved the creation of "a one-shot painting," meaning it looked like the entire painting was made very quickly without modification, much like Pollock's late stained black paintings in which black enamel stained directly into the raw canvas so that the gesture "immediately welded and froze."[19] Frankenthaler's successful adaptation of the way Pollock painted on raw unstretched canvas was also liberating for Noland and Louis as it freed them from working on a rigid rectilinear structure. As Noland remarked, "Just to be able to handle the canvas as a free thing instead of a support or a wall was a very revealing thing."[20]

After their initial encounter with *Mountains and Sea*, Louis and Noland set about experimenting both collectively and individually over an extended period of time with deconstructing the conventions of painting and trying out new techniques. By the latter part of the decade, the pair felt they had finally broken new ground—Noland with his series of concentric circles (pl. 23, p. 64, and pl. 24, p. 65) and Louis with his Veil paintings stained with diaphanous layers of pigment (pls. 16–19, pp. 48–55). As Noland noted, the appeal of stain painting was the way it led the eye to follow one color as it flows into another, and then into another by juxtaposing degrees of transparency and luminosity, and the modulation of warm and cool colors. The process causes the different colors to have an accumulation of "pulses" that give the painting its "general resonance."[21]

Despite championing Frankenthaler's painting, Greenberg's published writings on her work was limited to an oft quoted article on Louis and Noland in *Art International* (May 1960), in which he singled out the two other artists as candidates for major status.[22] This article was written in reaction to art historian William Rubin's article "Younger American Painters," published in a previous issue of *Art International* (January 1960), which weighed in on the work of many of the young artists active on the New York scene.[23] Like Greenberg, Rubin, who became a major force in the art world as long-time Chief Curator and subsequently Director of the Department of Painting and Sculpture of New York's Museum of Modern Art (1968 to 1988), sought to identify the innovators among the new young American artists and establish a criteria by which to evaluate their work. Rubin proffered some complimentary comments about Frankenthaler's paintings and was impressed by how her "picture is 'provoked' as much as 'painted.'" He also remarked that "the beauty of Frankenthaler's unassertive canvases lies ... in their breadth and airiness," but he was dismissive of her achievements for lack of being "accompanied by a sense of deep meaning in what is said." Rubin's assessment prompted Greenberg to break with his restraint regarding writing about Frankenthaler (due to a sense of probity as the two had previously been romantically involved)[24] to establish for the record (a point he previously often made in conversation) that Frankenthaler played a seminal role as a major influence on Color Field painting by opening up the potential of Pollock's paintings.[25] He ascribed a deeper meaning to her painting by demonstrating that her soak-stain technique was not a means to relinquish control of the painting, rather it contributed to the advancement of abstract painting because "the more closely colour could be identified with its ground the freer it would be from the interference of tactile associations. The way to achieve this colour identification was by adapting watercolor technique to oil and using thin paint on an absorbent surface" so that pigment and canvas became unified "like a dyed cloth."[26] In the same article Greenberg asserted that Louis' "first sight of middle-period Pollock and a large and extraordinary painting done in 1952 by Helen Frankenthaler called *Mountains and Sea*" led him "to change his direction [from Cubism] abruptly."

Greenberg's mention of Frankenthaler in the *Art International* article was brief but central in establishing the importance of her soak-stain painting technique and place in art history. A few months after Greenberg's article was published, Louis stated in an interview in the *Washington Post* that Frankenthaler "was a bridge between Pollock and what was possible."[27] In order to justify his heralding of the Color Field paintings of Louis and Noland, Greenberg needed to demonstrate that they directly descended from Pollock (who the critic had championed), through Frankenthaler's innovation. Greenberg encouraged Frankenthaler to keep making paintings like *Mountains and Sea*, but she remarked later in life that "it was impossible … while I might take off from there, I couldn't repeat it."[28] Frankenthaler was only 23 when she painted *Mountains and Sea*, but the soak-stain painting technique became the overriding characteristic that defined the significance of her work. In fact, she never considered herself a Color Field artist. Although spreading diluted pigment into the unprimed canvas helped open new areas of exploration for other artists, it was only one of many ways she continued to apply paint. For her, "meaning" did not come from technique alone, but also from the way miraculous acts of painting can move and inspire both the viewer and herself.[29]

When Color Field Painting Was New

Frank Stella has remarked that artists face two fundamental problems: "One is to find out what a painting is and the other is to find out how to make a painting."[30] What to paint could be a harrowing decision when anything is possible. Although Color Field painters share many commonalities, the artists followed their own distinct paths in resolving this dilemma. They all started from the position that the American Abstract Expressionists or "Painterly Painting," as Greenberg termed it, had broken new ground in art.[31] Most of the Abstract Expressionists took over twenty years to move through the various phases of discovery from Realism to Surrealism and biomorphic abstraction to finally arrive at the creation of distinctly new images, pictorial space, and visual impact in the late 1940s. Their thrust towards abstraction, contrary to formalist theory, had little to do with reducing painting to its essence. Rather, it was aligned with their search for universality in art, which at their formative stage was a response to world events. Newman, for instance, equated the dominant figurative style of American Regionalism in the early 1940s with the nation's isolationist tendency, which was dangerous because it is the result of the "same intense, vicious nationalism," that gave rise to "Hitlerism."[32] Figurative art and even the symbolic and biomorphic forms that replaced the figure were impediments to the universality these artists hoped to achieve in their work through abstract painting.

While the Abstract Expressionists cleared a path for the subsequent generation to forge ahead with abstract painting, their achievements also challenged the younger artists to investigate unconventional ways of painting and develop their own pictorial language that would create abstraction anew. Experimenting with different mediums and methods of painting, and introducing fresh insights into their probing of the conventions of painting led to unprecedented works.

Although their roots were in Abstract Expressionism, most of the Color Field artists attended art schools in the United States and abroad (many benefitting from tuition provided by the G.I. Bill for veterans after World War II) where art history and the analysis of the great art of the past was part of the curriculum. Their ambition drove them not only to absorb the lessons of the old and modern masters but to surpass them by creating paintings the likes of which had never been seen before.[33] Whereas Pablo Picasso and Cubism set the pace for previous generations of modern American painters, Color Field artists were enamored of Henri Matisse's mastery of color. In their competitive spirit,

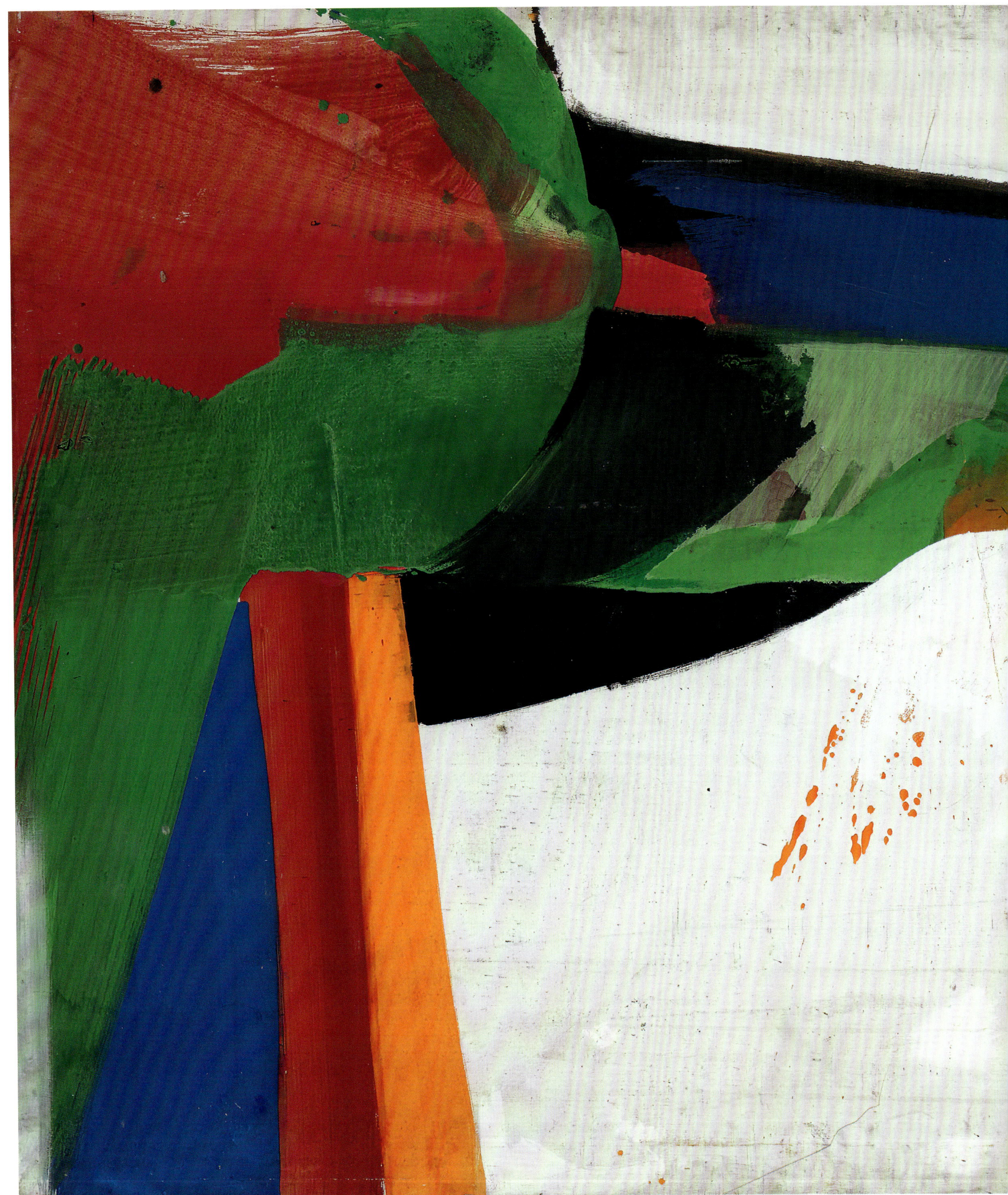

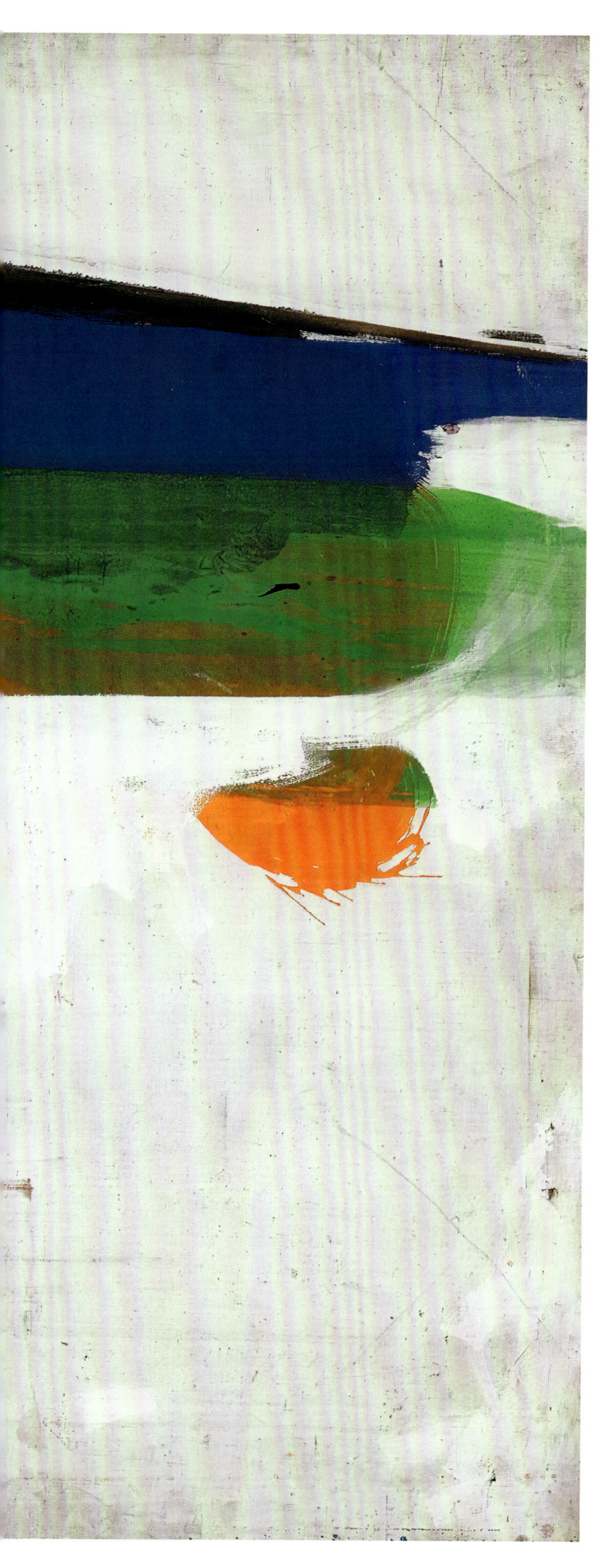

Edward Clark
7 **Paris series, 1966**
Acrylic on canvas, 60 × 77 in. (152.4 × 195.6 cm)
Courtesy of The N'Namdi Collection

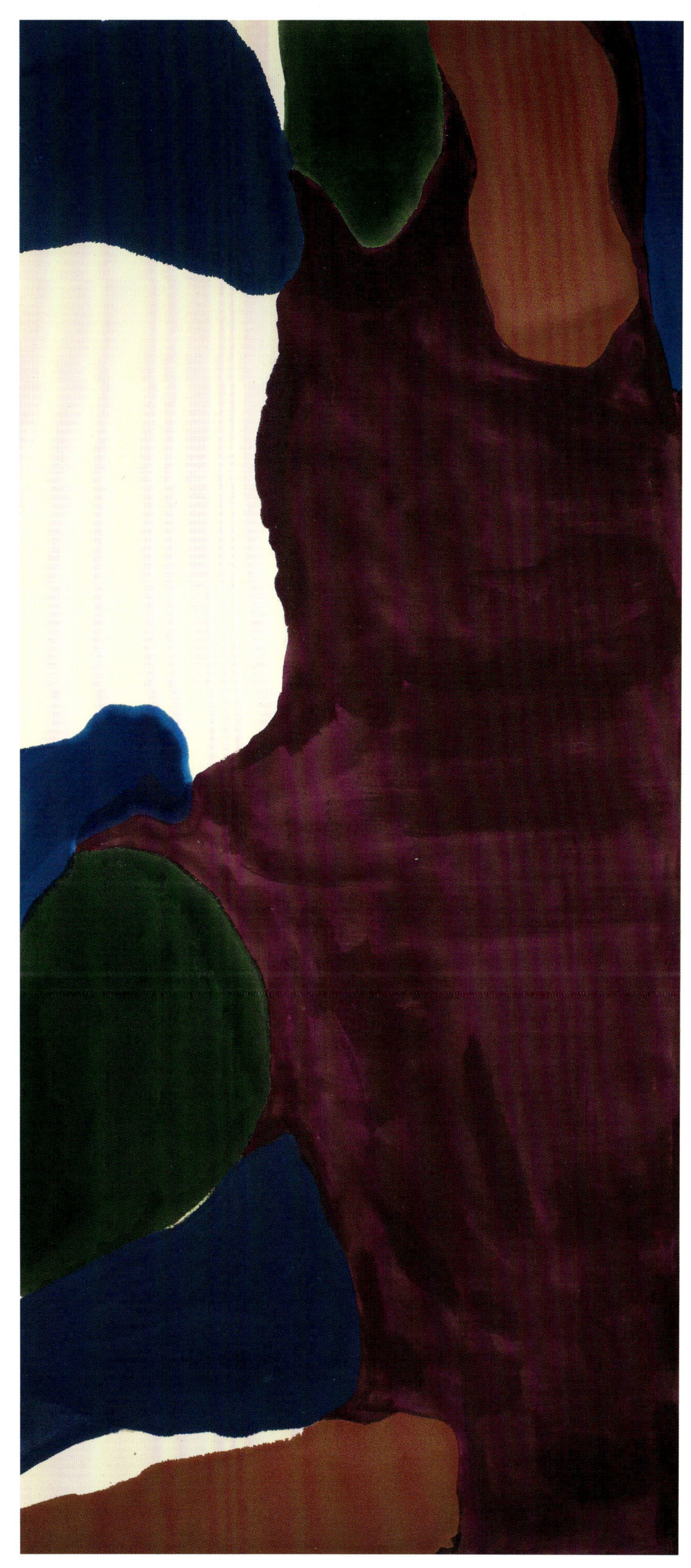

Helen Frankenthaler
8 **Wine Dark, 1965**
Acrylic on canvas, 102 × 45½ in. (259.1 × 115.6 cm)
Private Collection

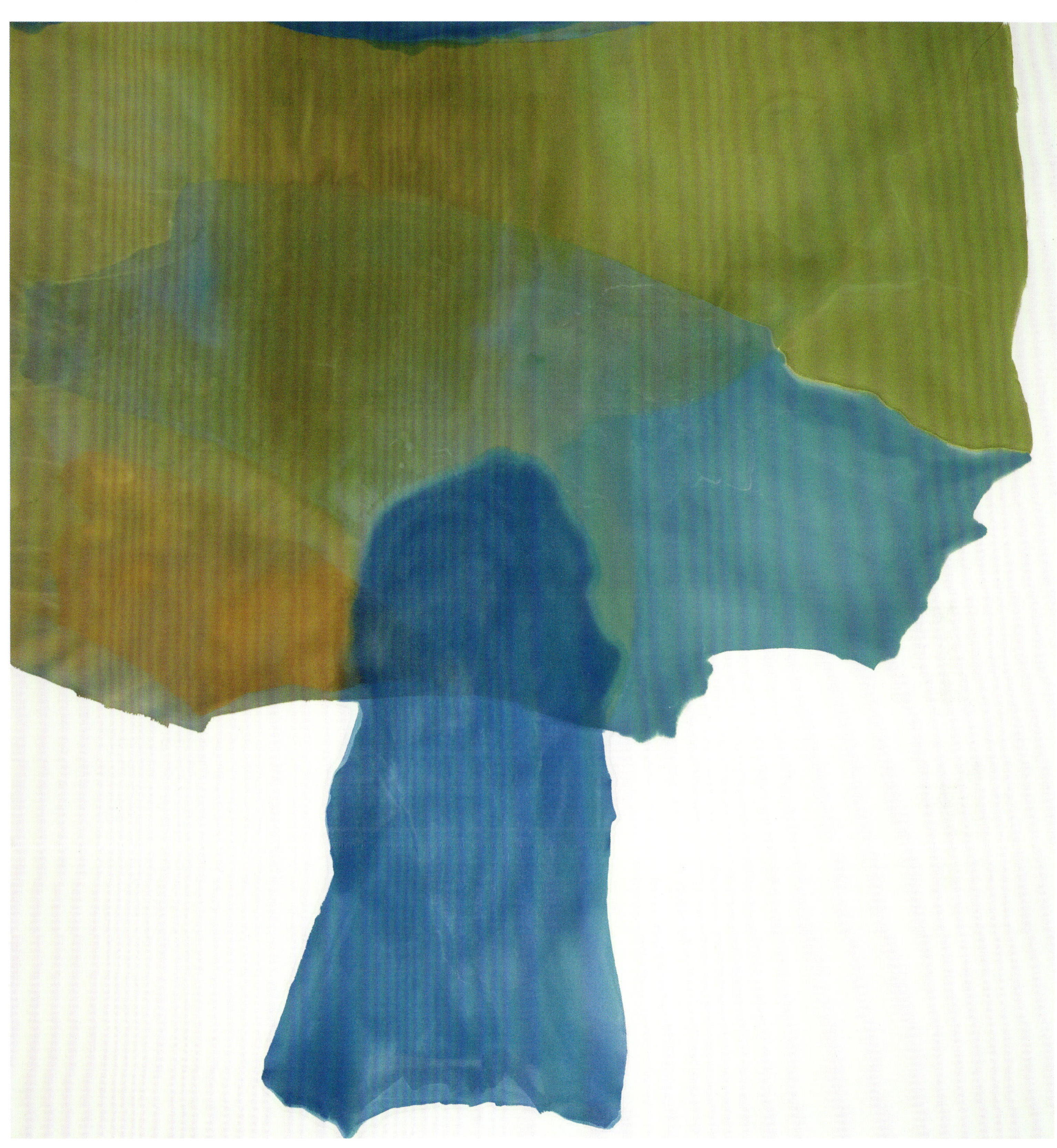

Helen Frankenthaler
9 **Signal, 1969**
Acrylic on canvas, 102 × 99 in. (259.1 × 251.5 cm)
Private Collection

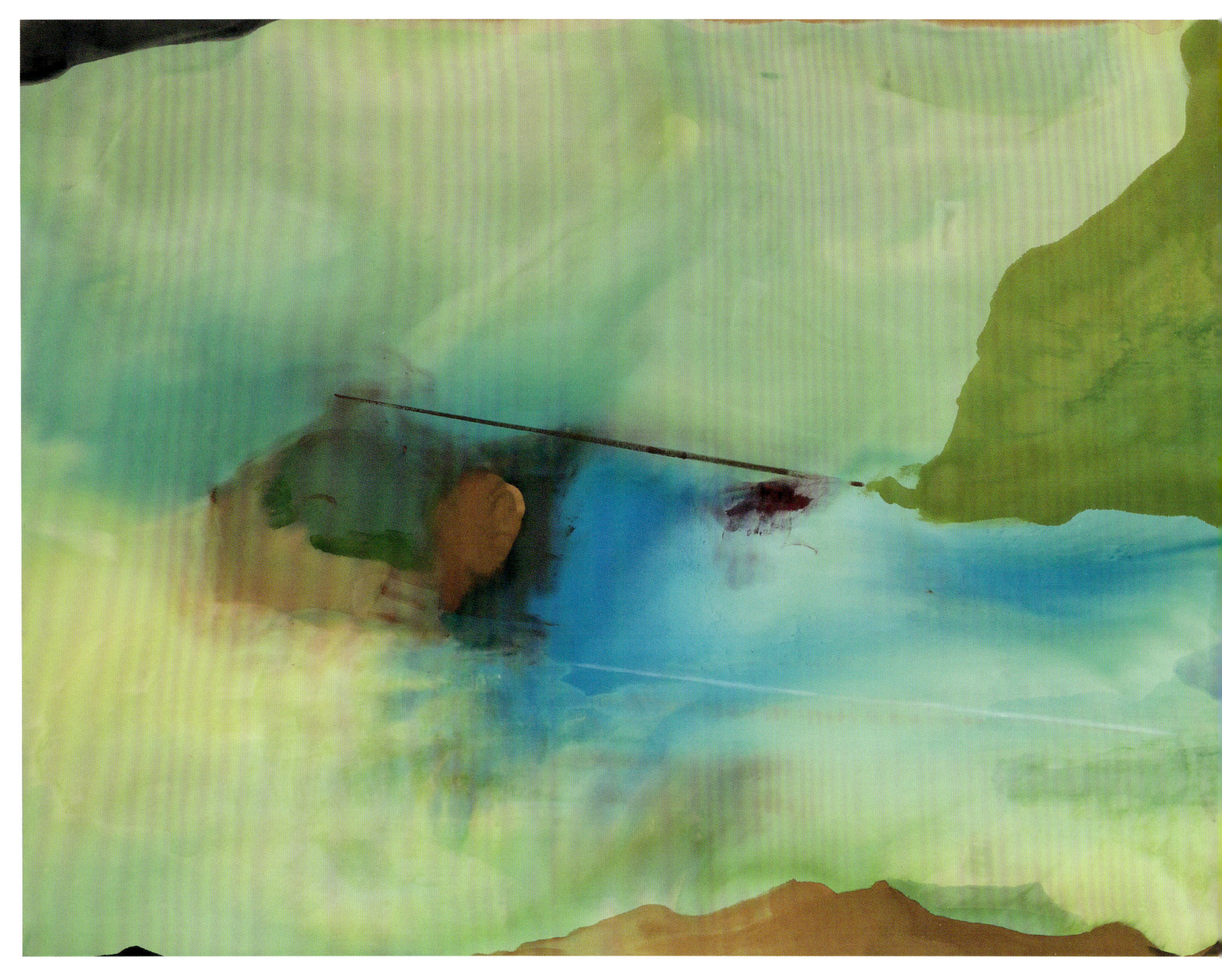

Helen Frankenthaler
10 Hint from Bassano, 1973
Acrylic on canvas, 85 × 227 in. (215.9 × 576.6 cm)
Audrey and David Mirvish, Toronto

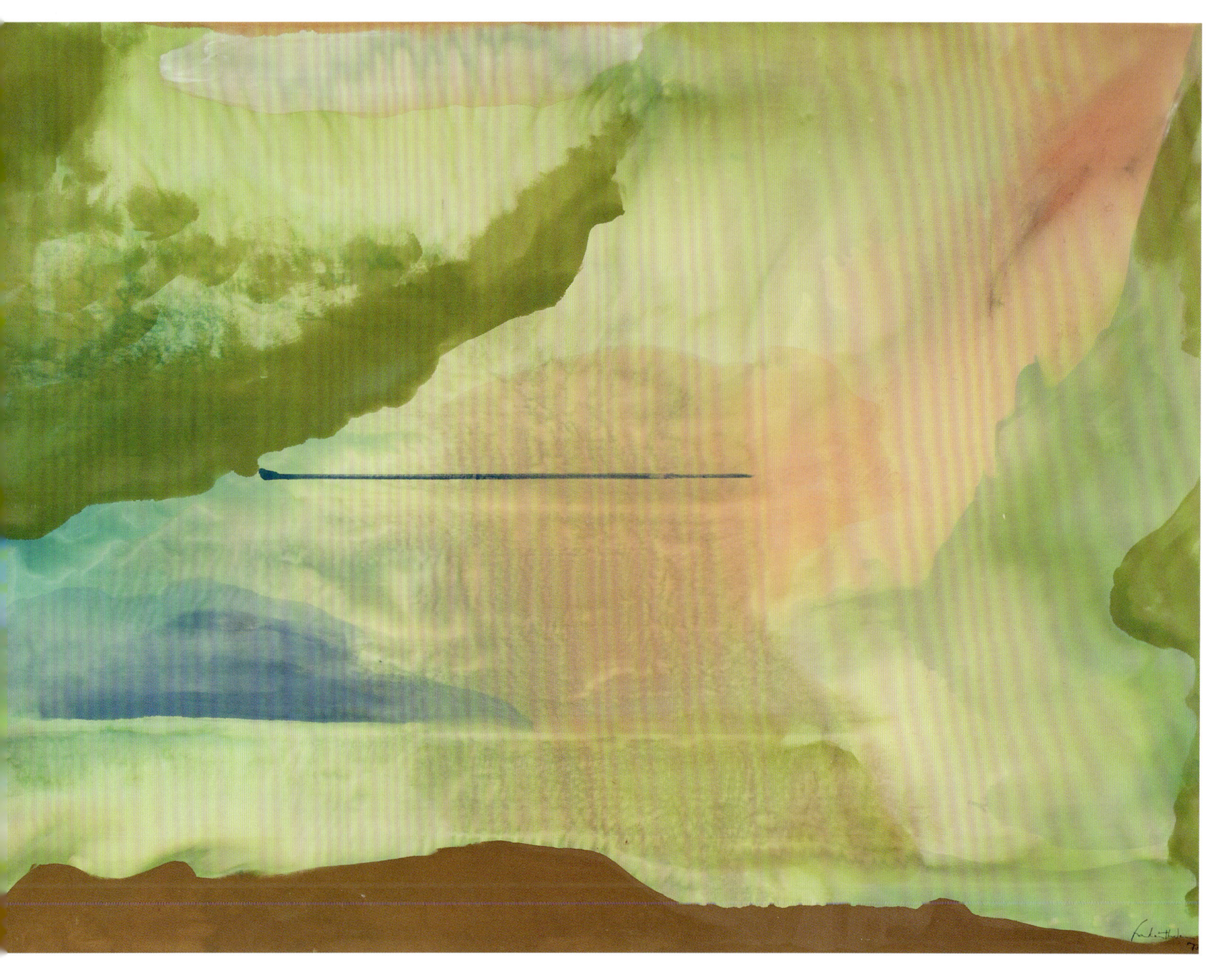

Sam Gilliam
11 **Idylls I, 1970**
Acrylic, metallic paint, crayon, and synthetic cable on unstretched canvas, 76 × 61 in. (193 × 154.9 cm)
Private Collection

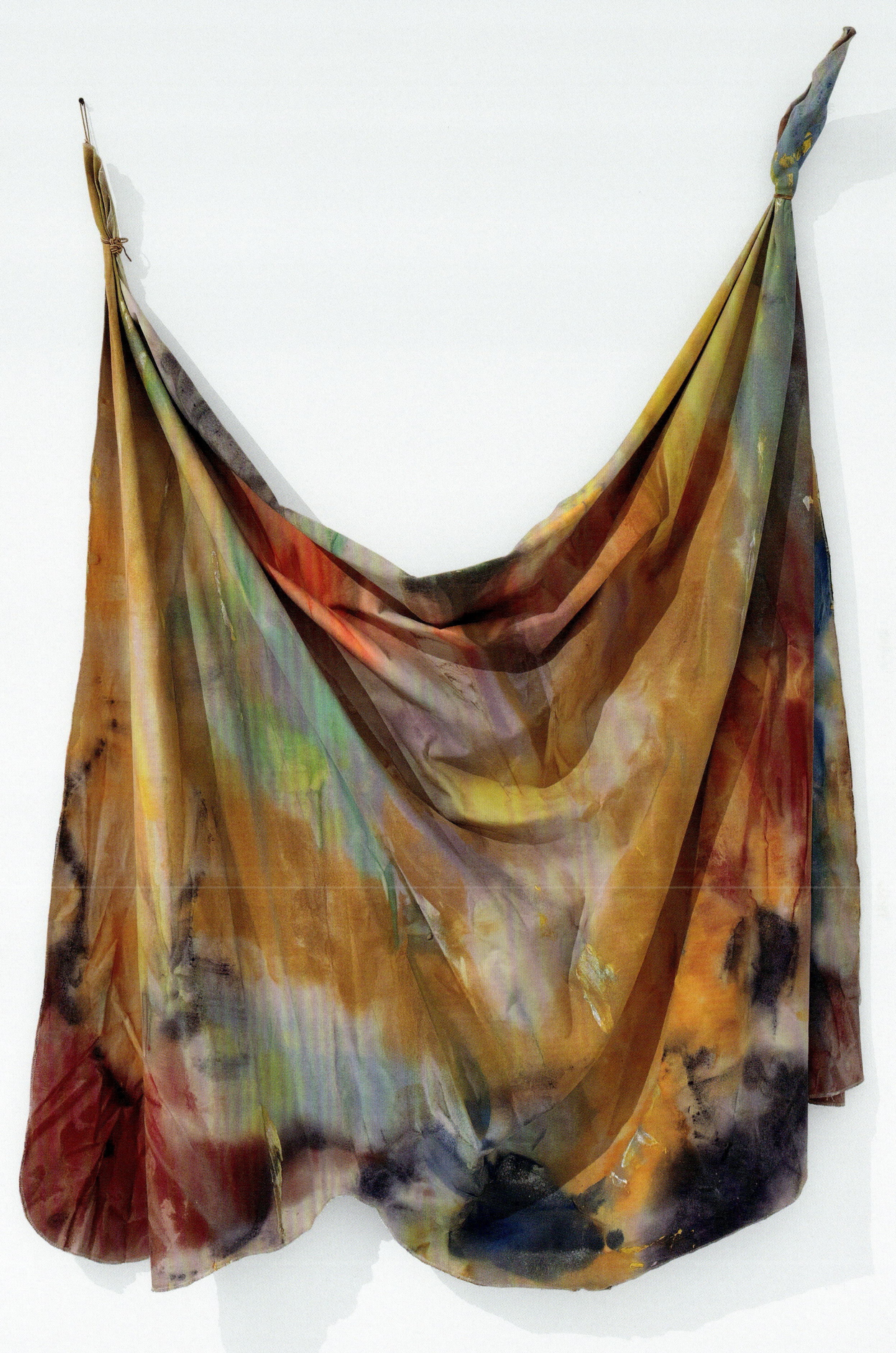

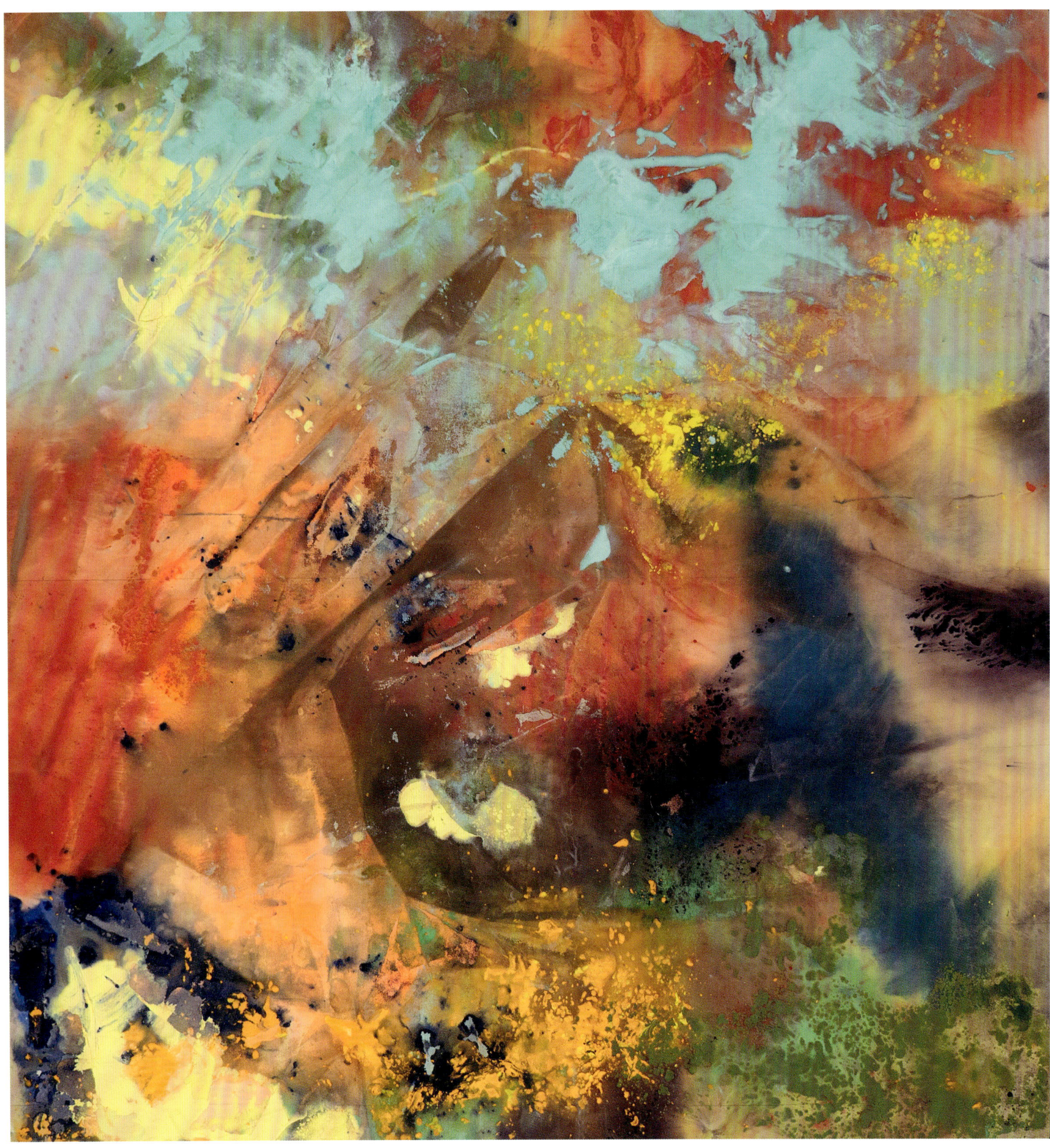

Sam Gilliam
12 **Cordial I, 1972**
Oil on canvas, 76 × 73 in. (193 × 185.4 cm)
NSU Art Museum Fort Lauderdale,
gift of Dr. and Mrs. Henry R. Hope

Sam Gilliam
13 **Clear Around, 1973**
Acrylic on canvas, 52 × 48 in. (132.1 × 121.9 cm)
Collection of Beth Rudin DeWoody

FOLLOWING PAGES

Adolph Gottlieb
14 **Green Turbulence, 1968**
Acrylic on canvas, 94 × 157 in. (238.8 × 398.8 cm)
Private Collection

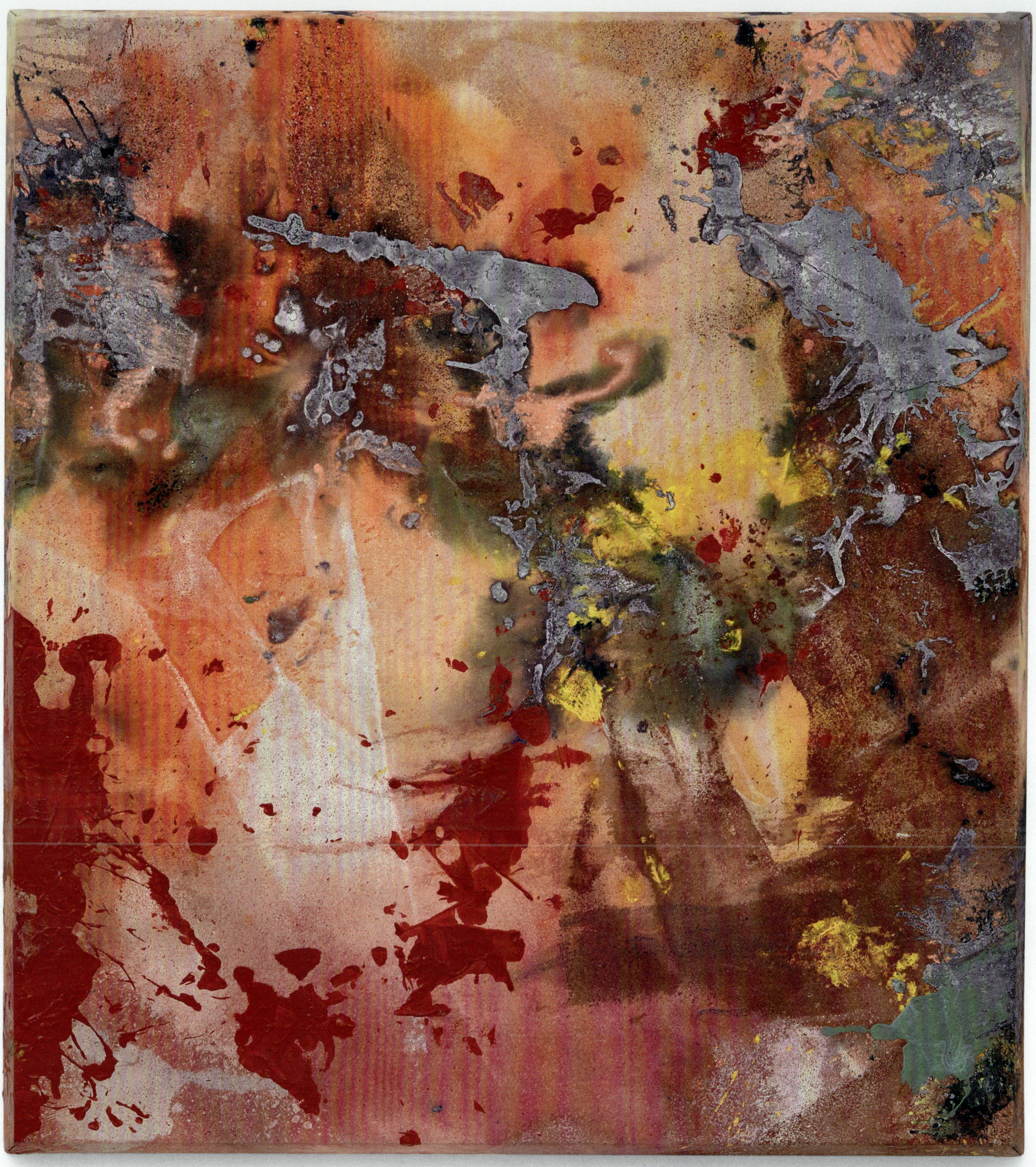

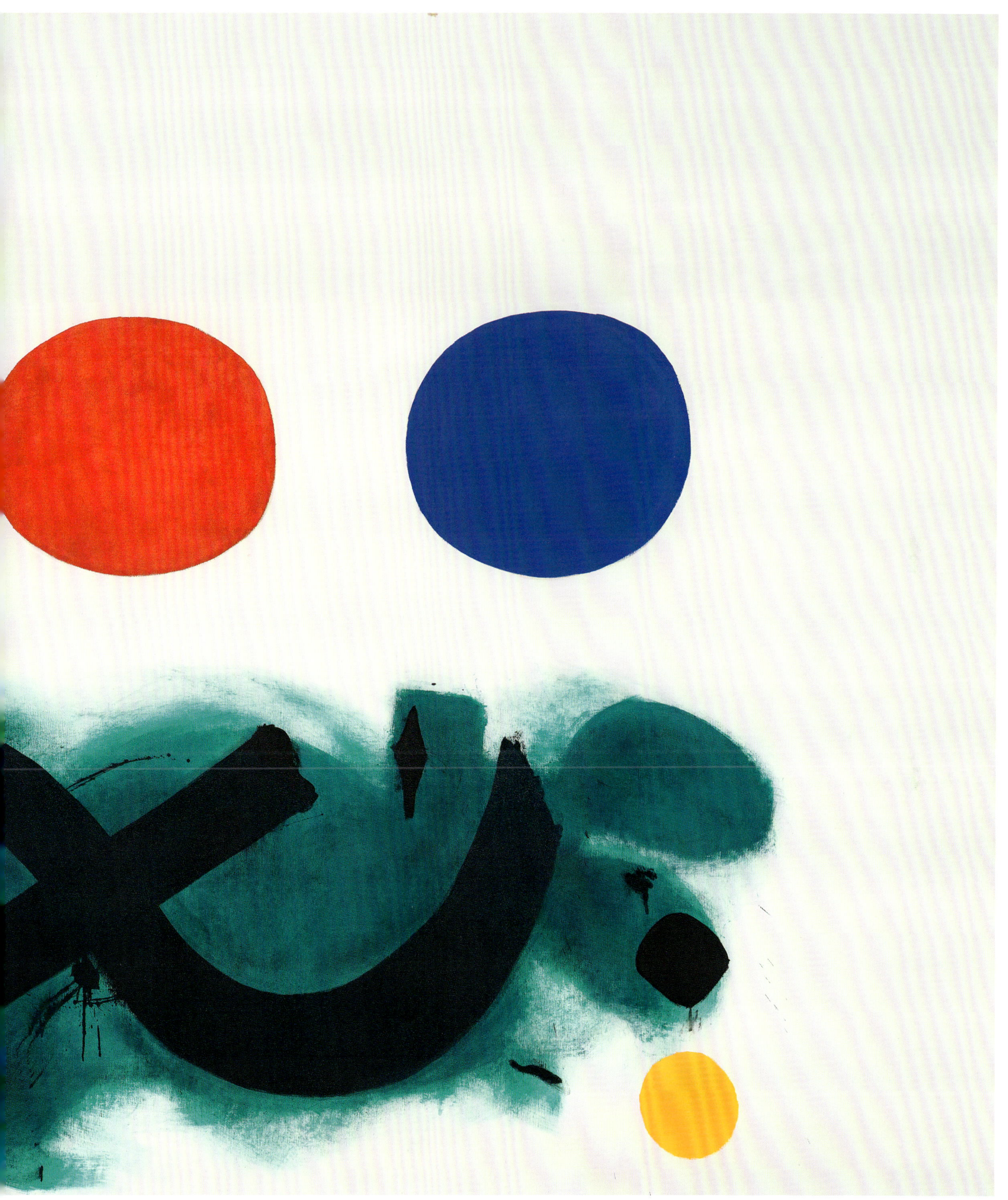

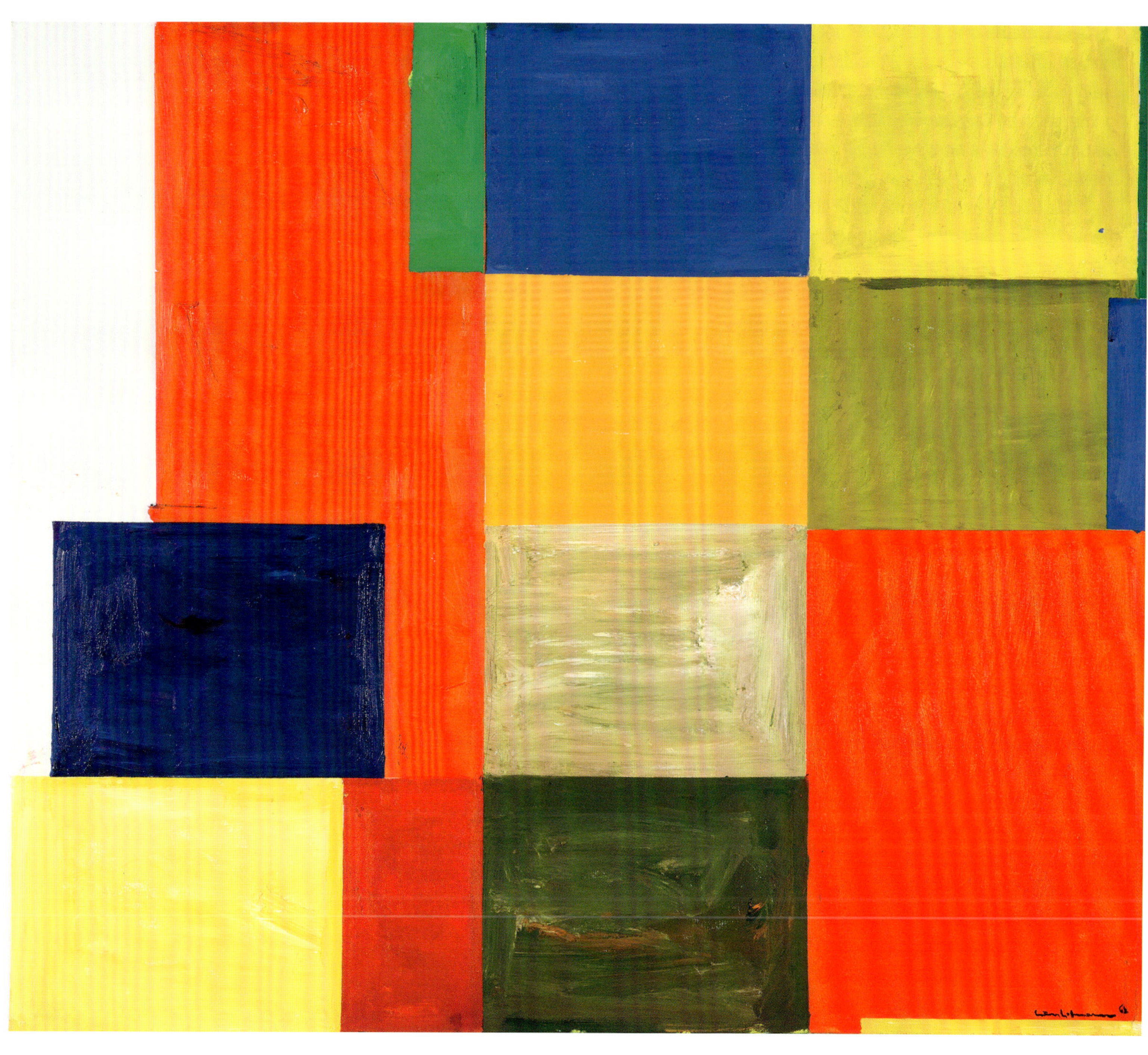

Hans Hofmann
15 **Iris, 1964–65**
Oil on canvas, 72 × 84 in. (182.9 × 213.4 cm)
Private Collection

Morris Louis
16 **Beth Peh, 1958**
Acrylic resin (magna) on canvas,
91¼ × 133 in. (231.8 × 337.8 cm)
Private Collection

FOLLOWING PAGES

Morris Louis
17 **Gothic, 1958**
Acrylic resin (magna) on canvas,
91¼ × 145½ in. (231.8 × 369.6 cm)
Private Collection

Morris Louis
18 **Lamed Gimel, 1958**
Acrylic resin (magna) on canvas,
89 × 146¾ in. (226 × 372.7 cm)
Private Collection

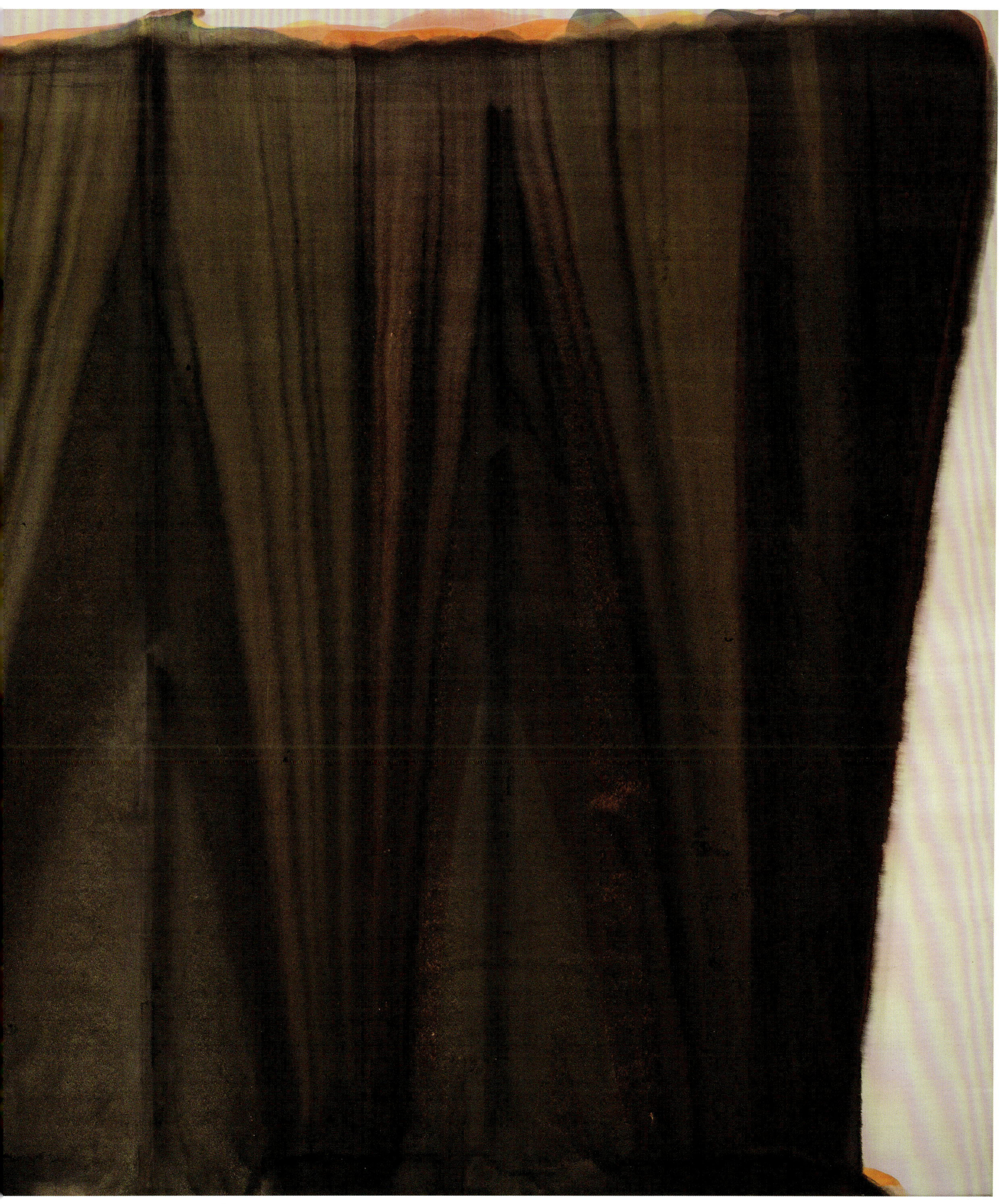

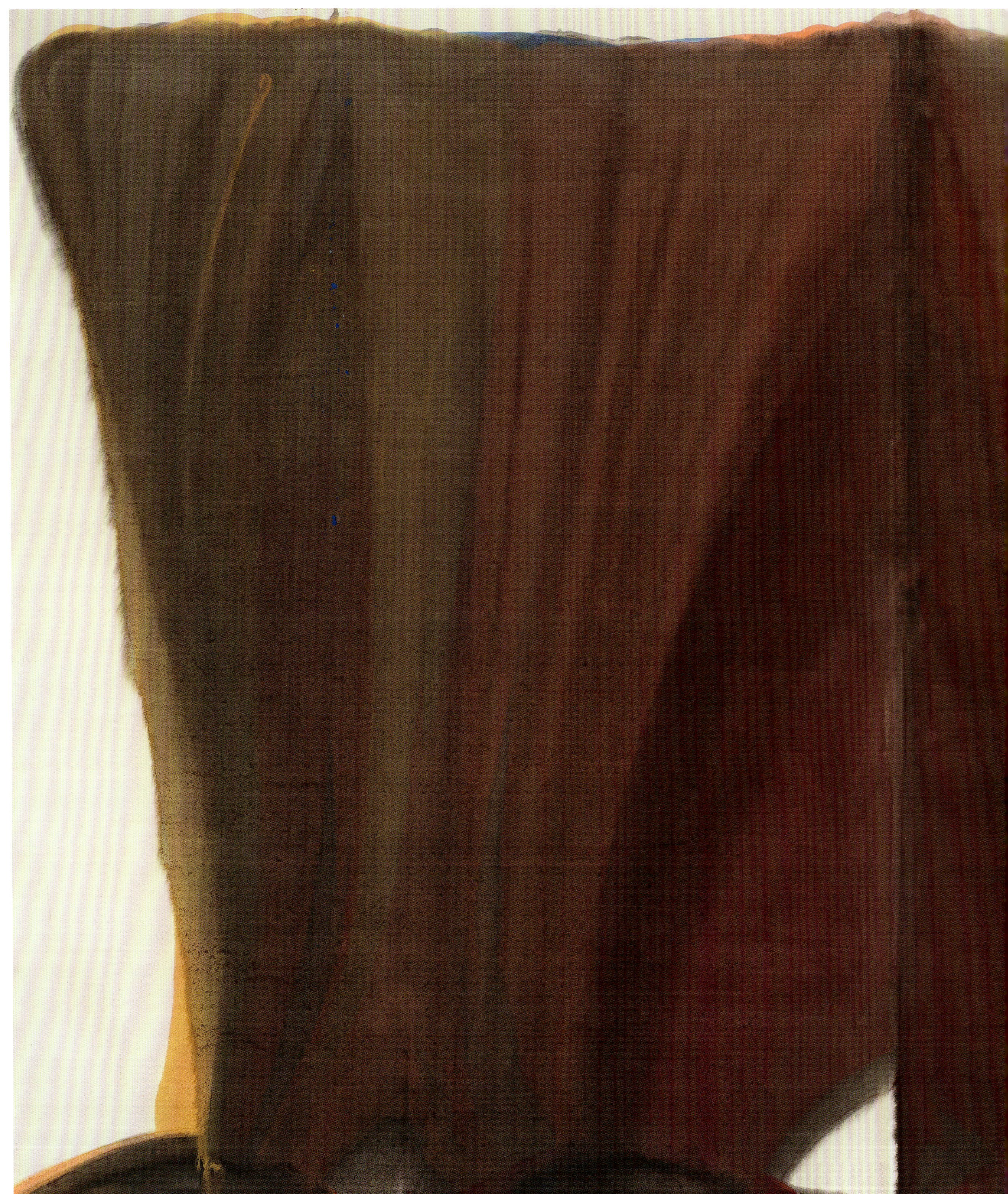

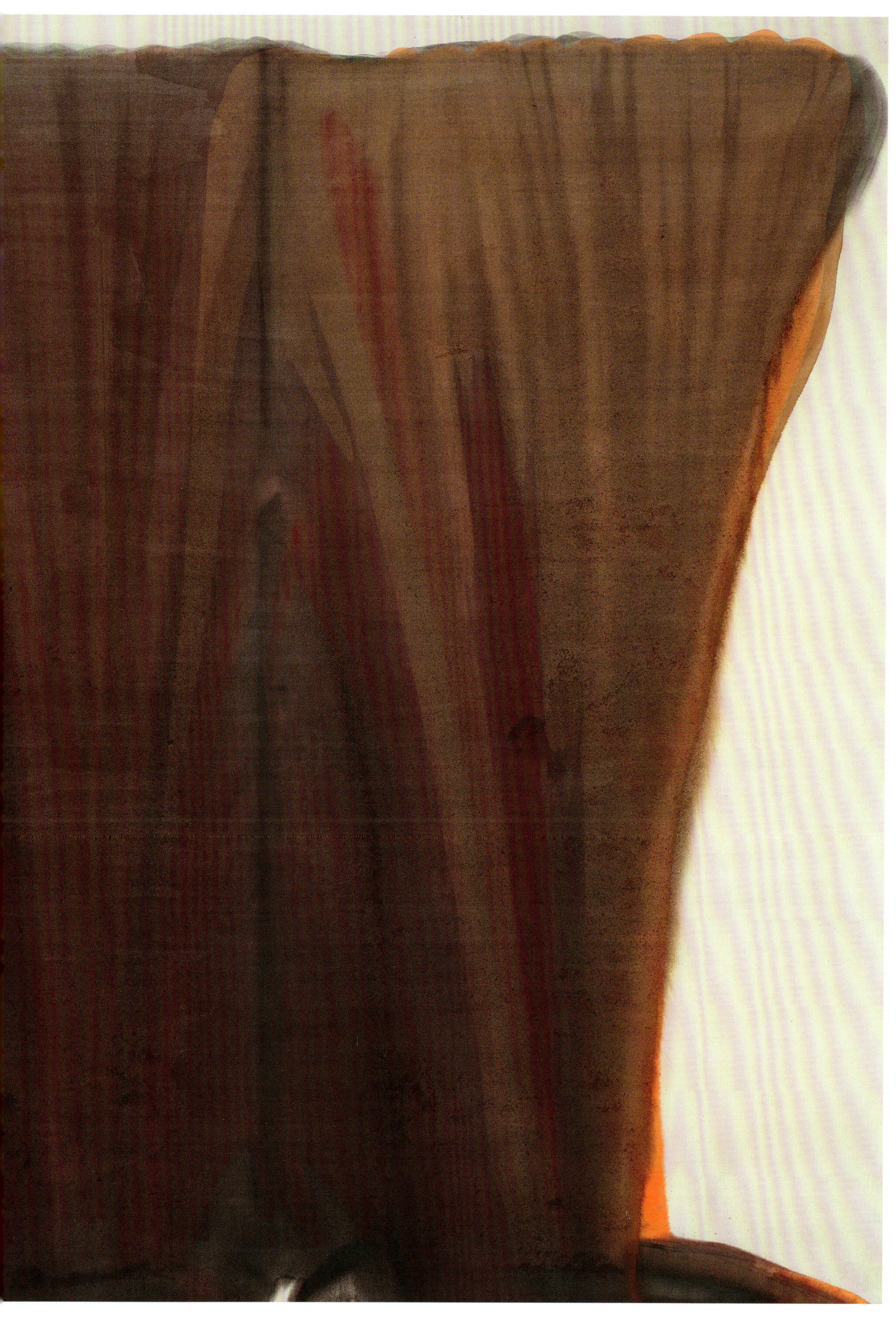

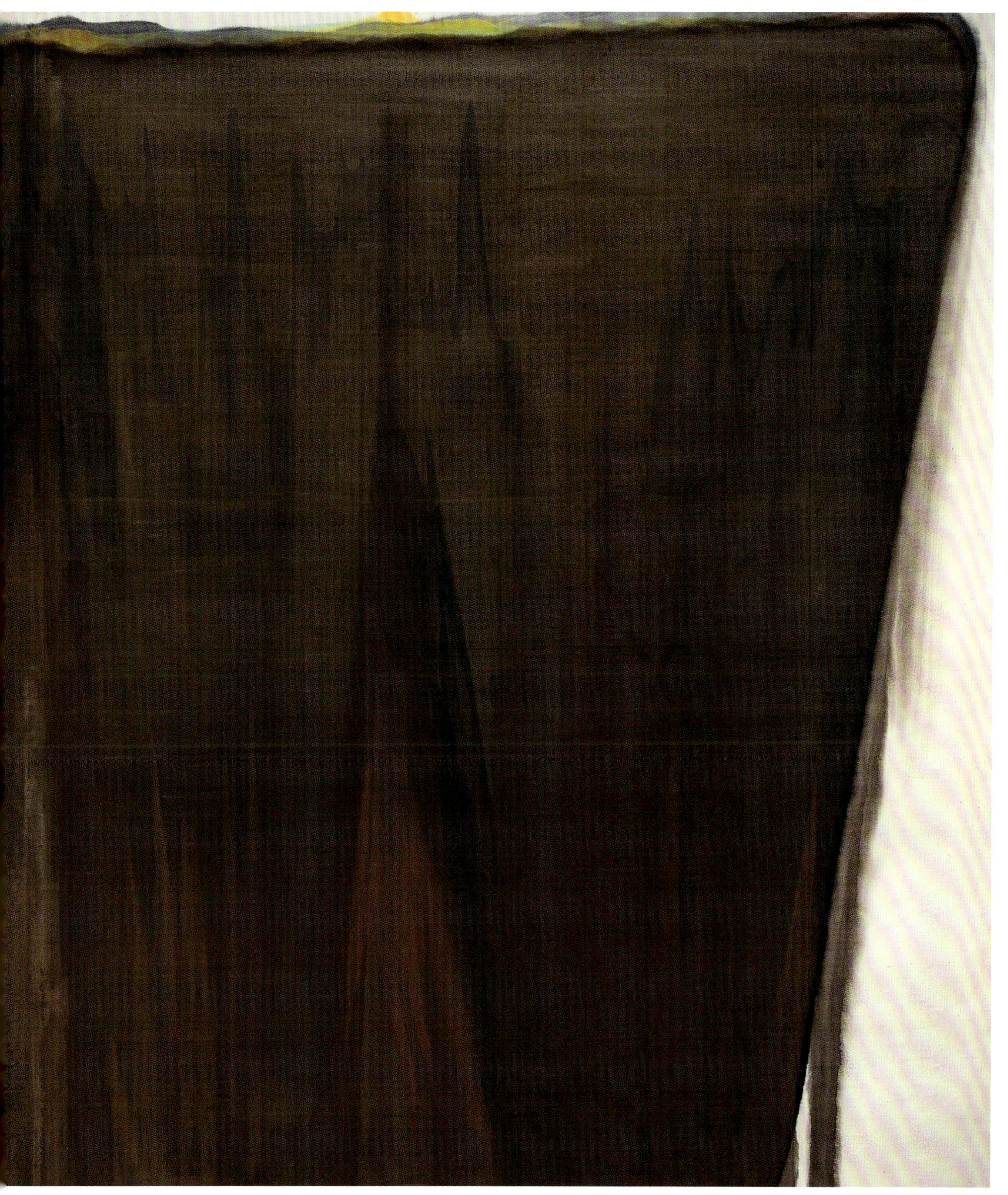

Morris Louis
19 **Curtain, 1959**
Acrylic resin (magna) on canvas,
91½ × 140¼ in. (232.4 × 356.2 cm)
Audrey and David Mirvish, Toronto

FOLLOWING PAGES

Morris Louis
20 **Beta Psi, 1960–61**
Acrylic resin (magna) on canvas,
102¾ × 194⅜ × 1½ in. (261 × 493.7 × 3.8 cm)
Audrey and David Mirvish, Toronto

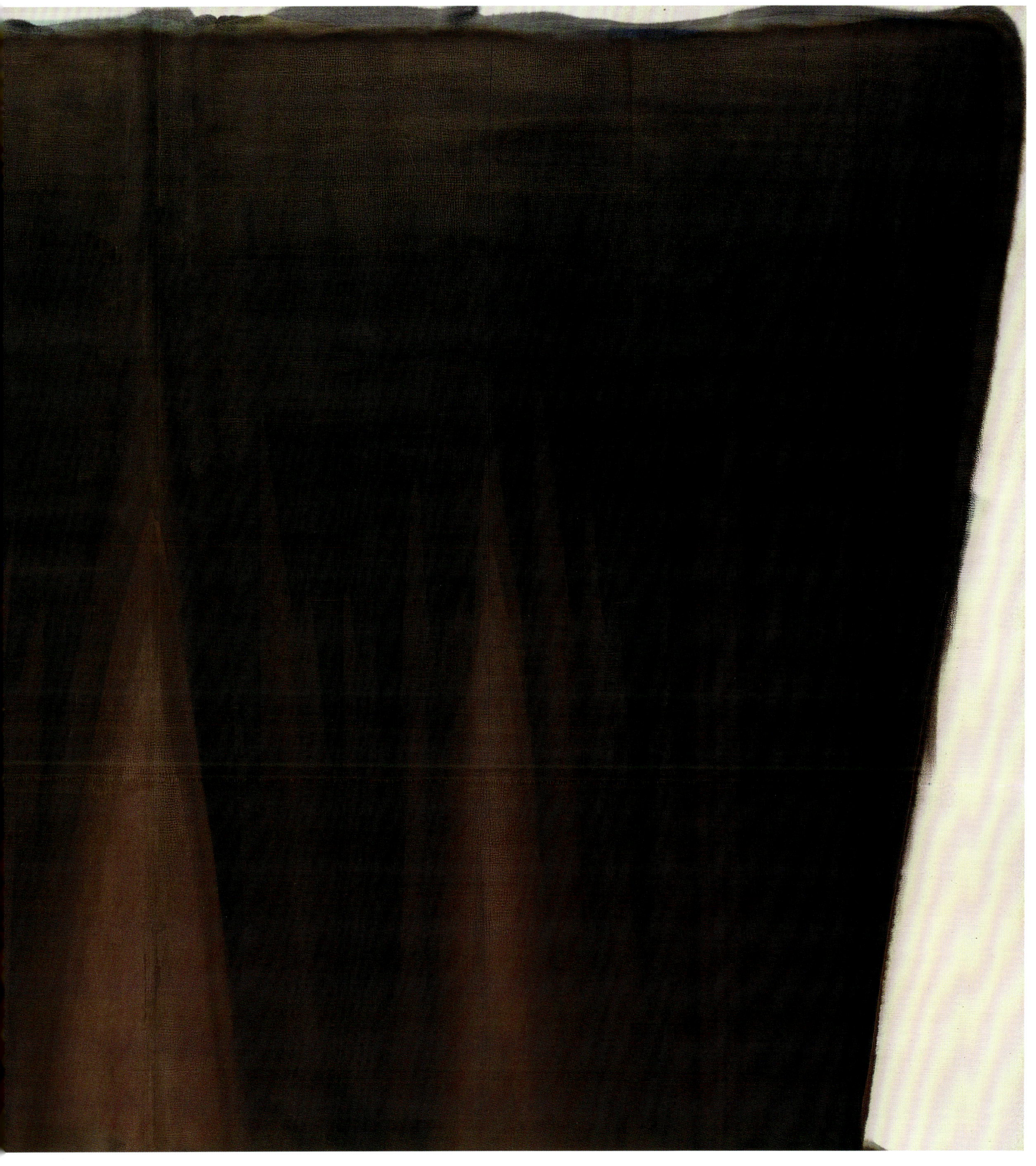

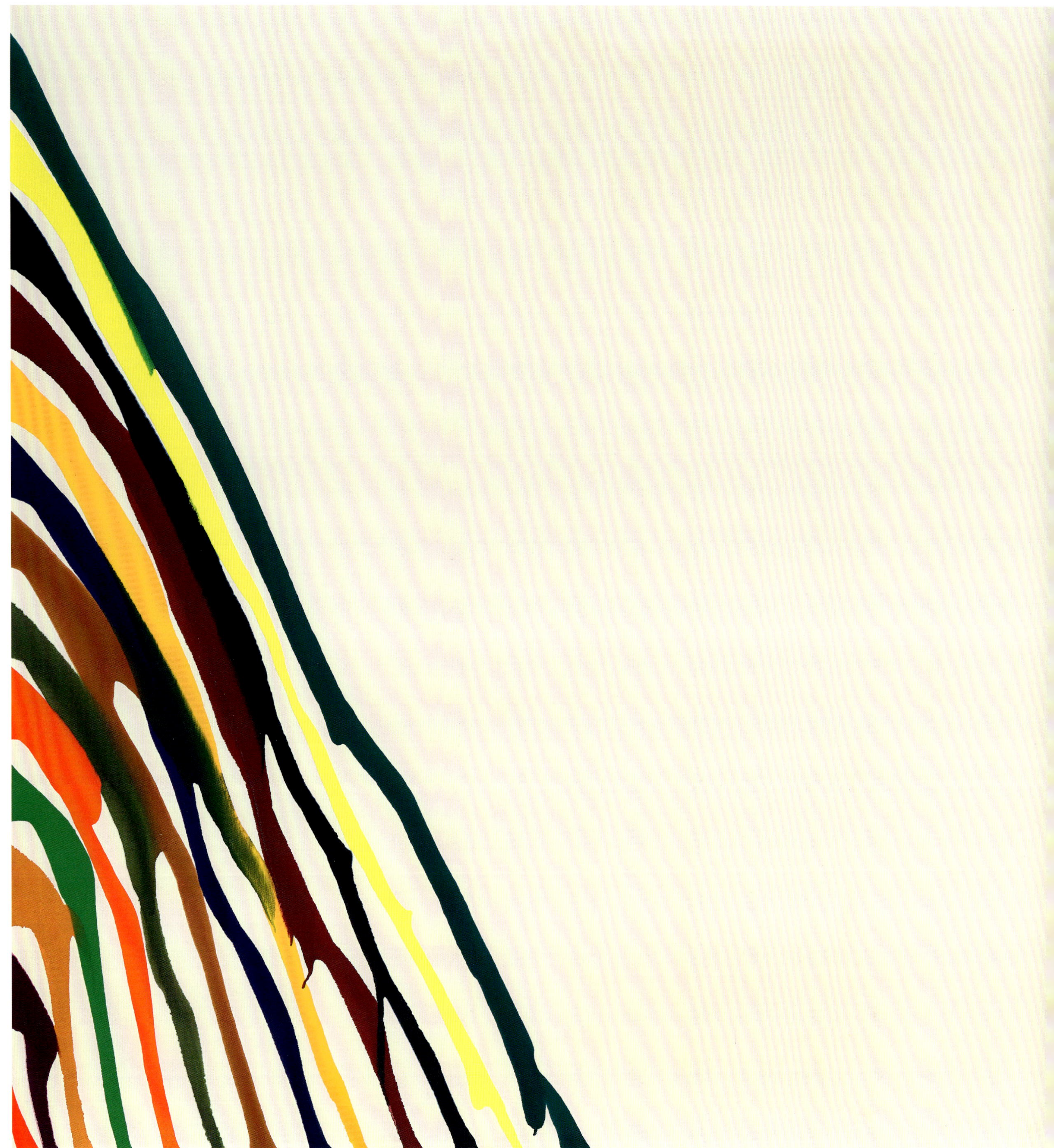

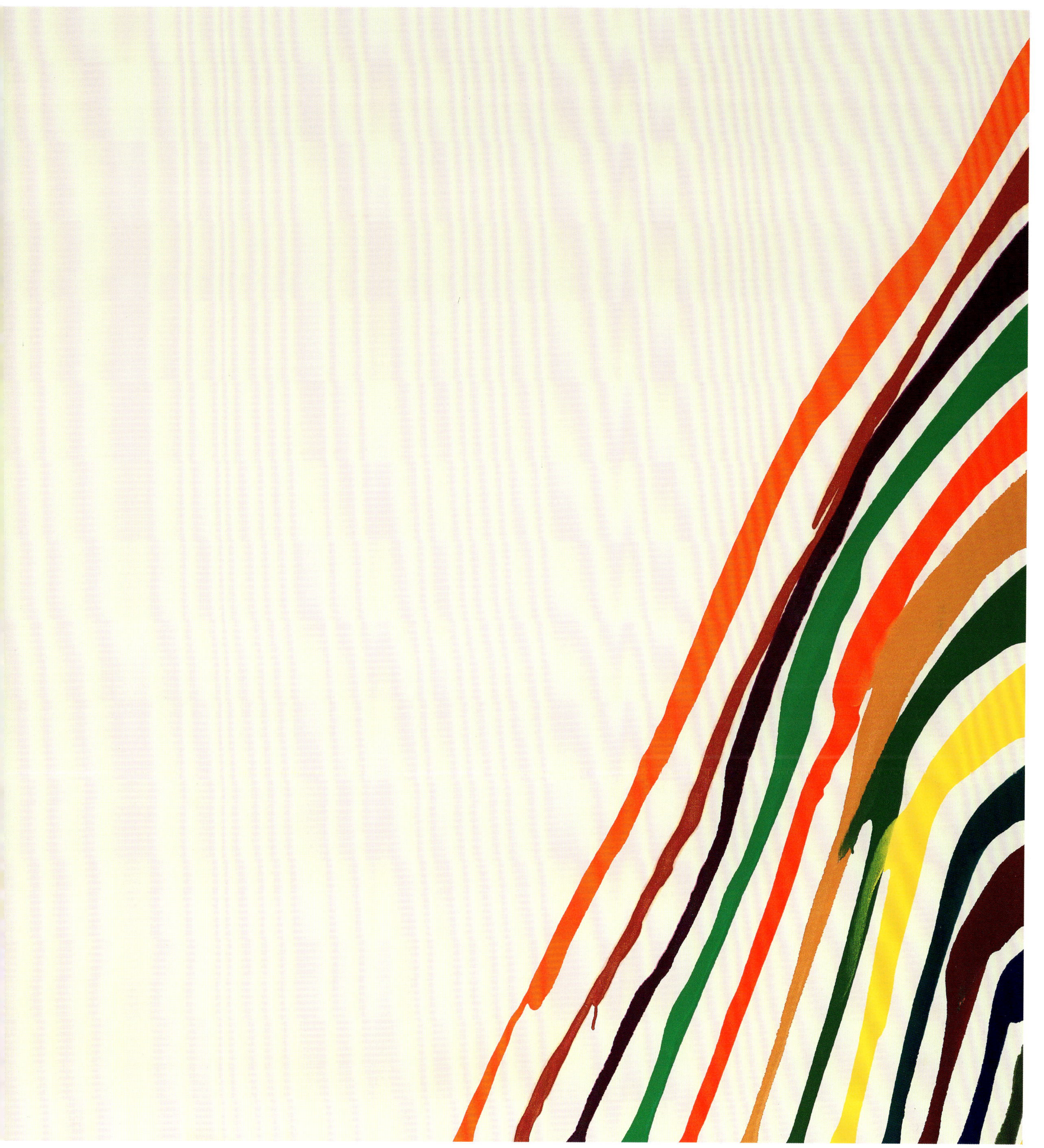

Al Loving
21 **Untitled, 1975**
Mixed media, 66 × 74 in. (167.6 × 188 cm)
Collection of Beth Rudin DeWoody

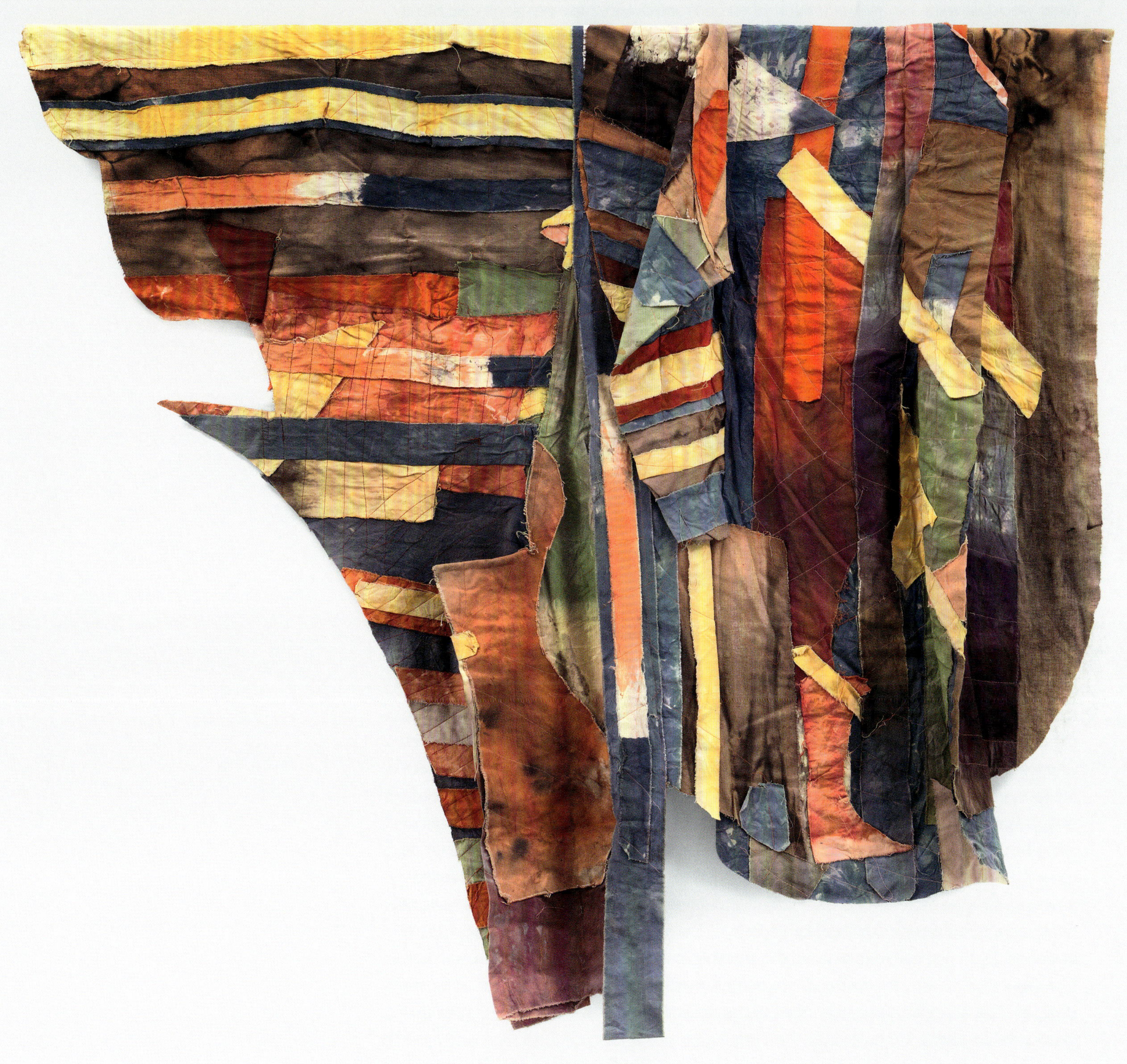

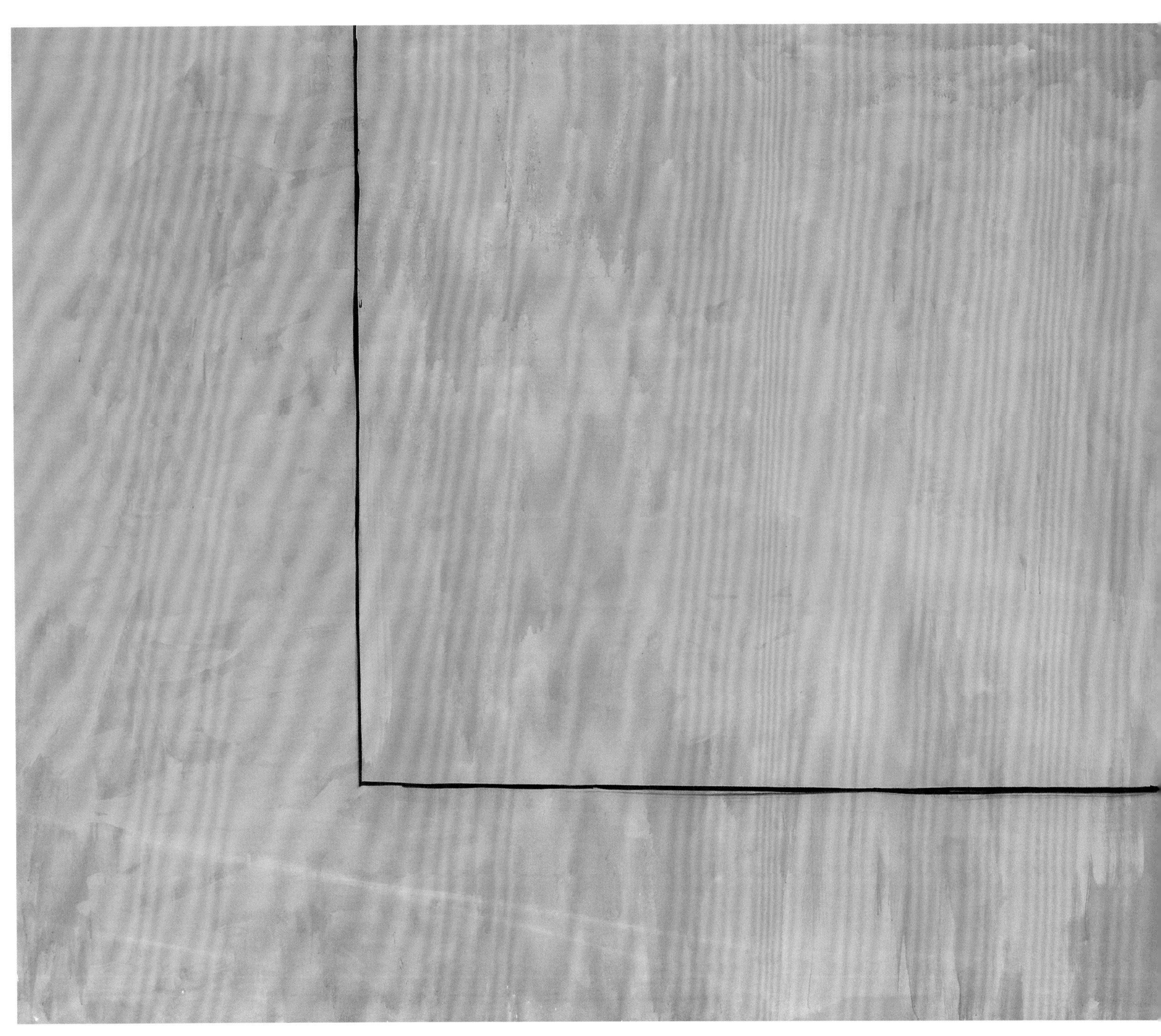

Robert Motherwell
22 **Open #149: In Ultramarine with Charcoal Line, 1970**
Acrylic and charcoal on canvas,
93 × 222 in. (236.2 × 563.9 cm)
Audrey and David Mirvish, Toronto

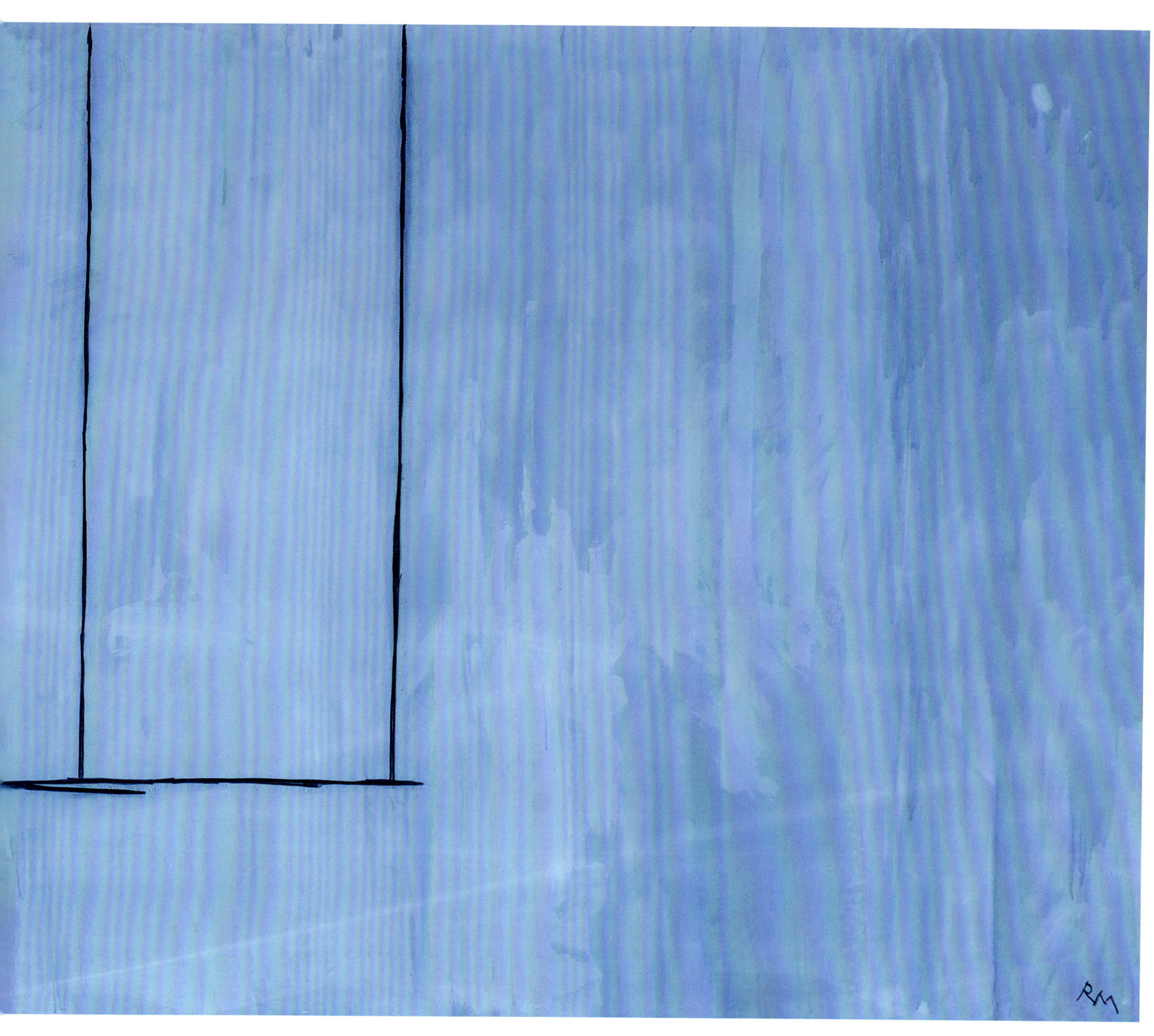
RM

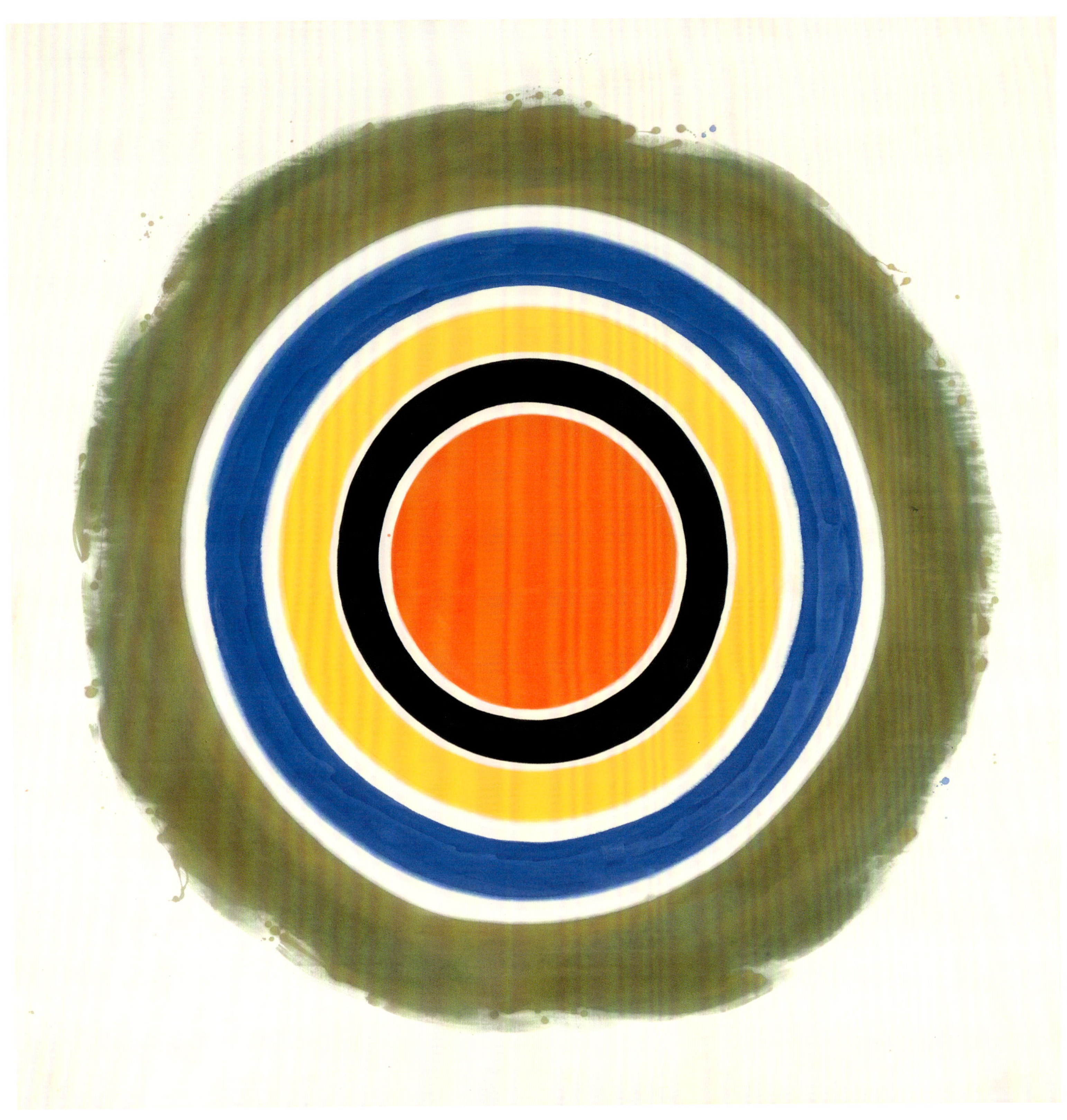

Kenneth Noland
23 **This, 1958–59**
Acrylic on canvas, 82 × 82 in. (208.3 × 208.3 cm)
Audrey and David Mirvish, Toronto

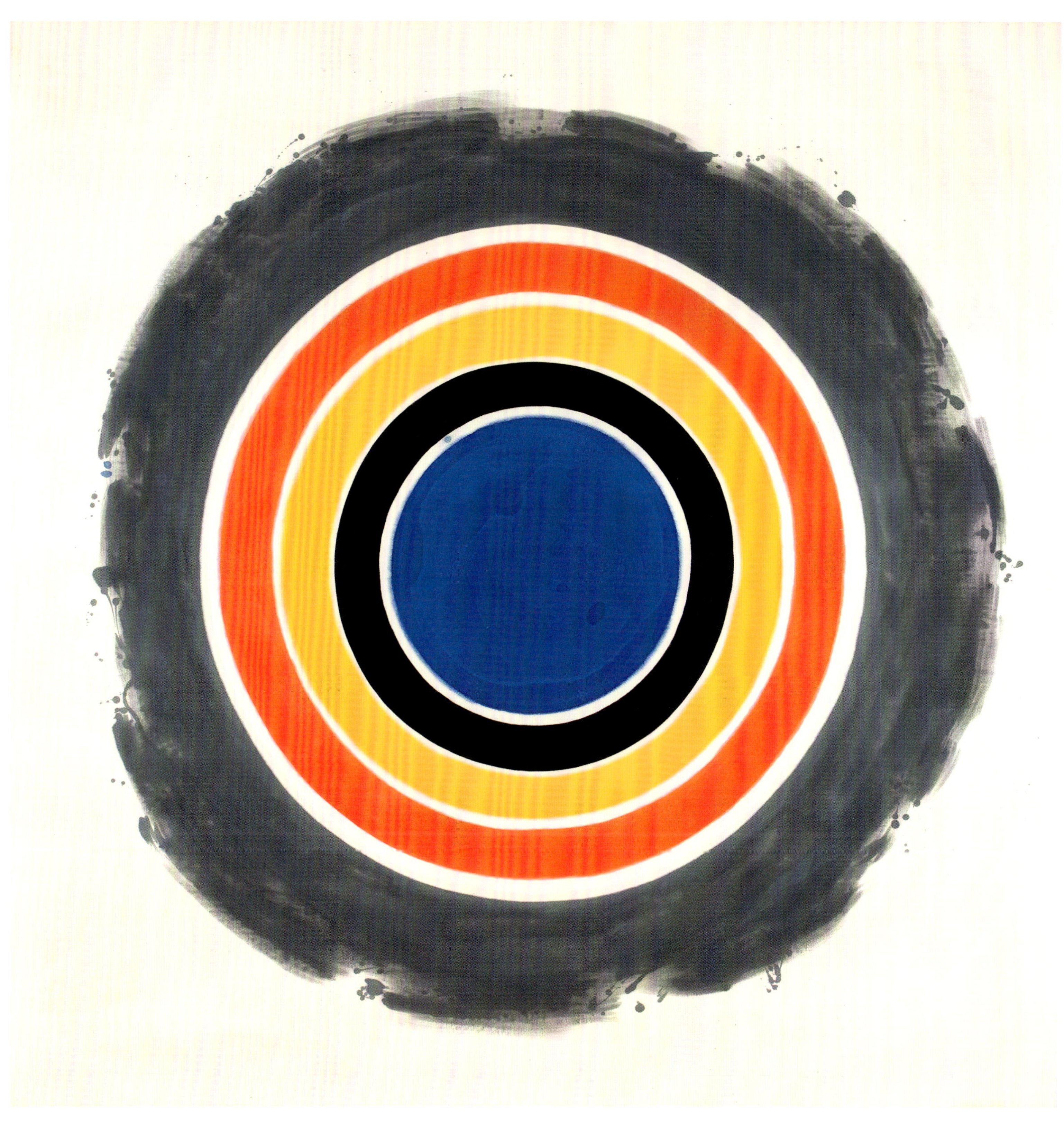

Kenneth Noland
24 **That, 1958–59**
Acrylic on canvas, 82 × 82 in. (208.3 × 208.3 cm)
Audrey and David Mirvish, Toronto

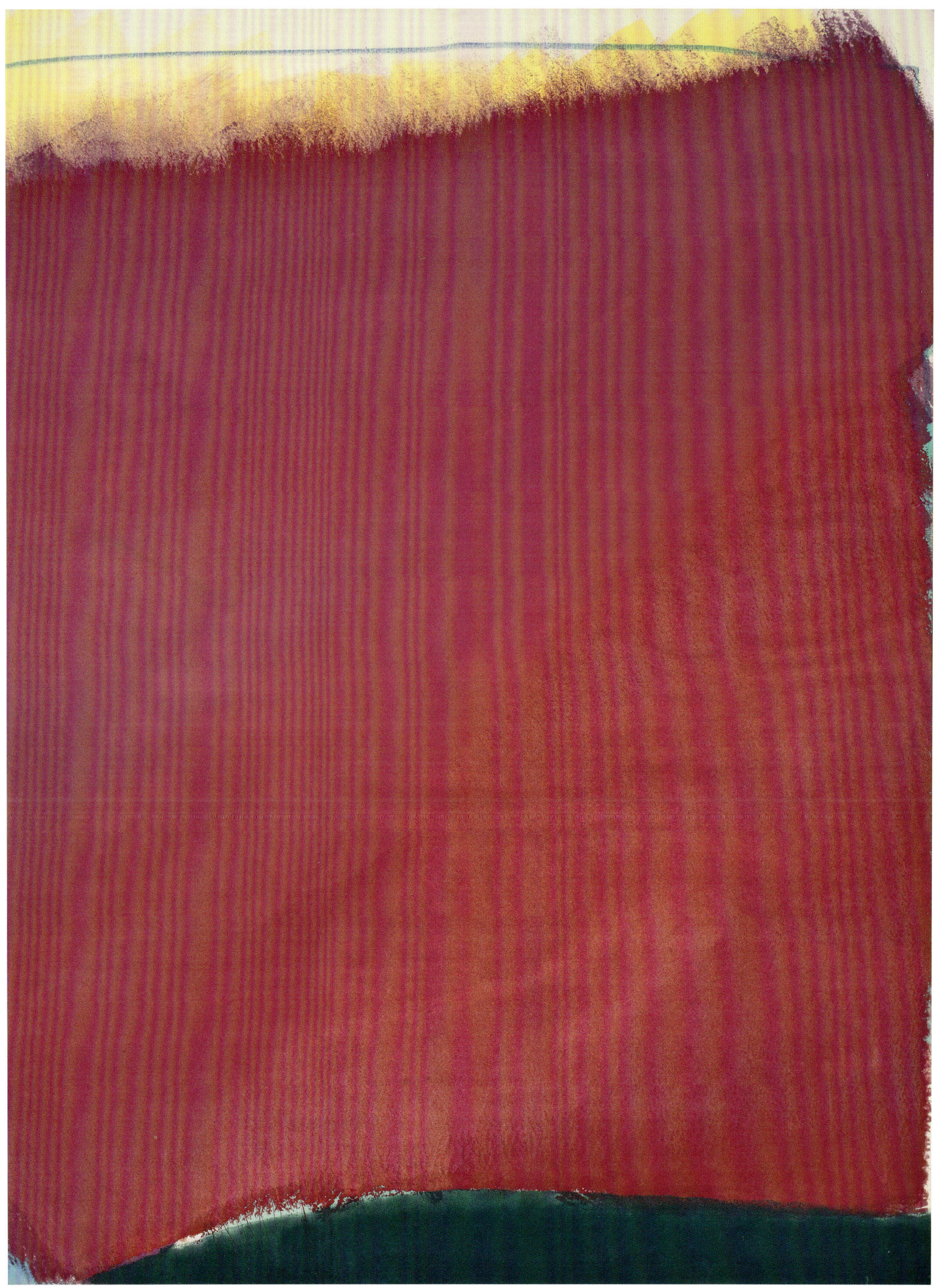

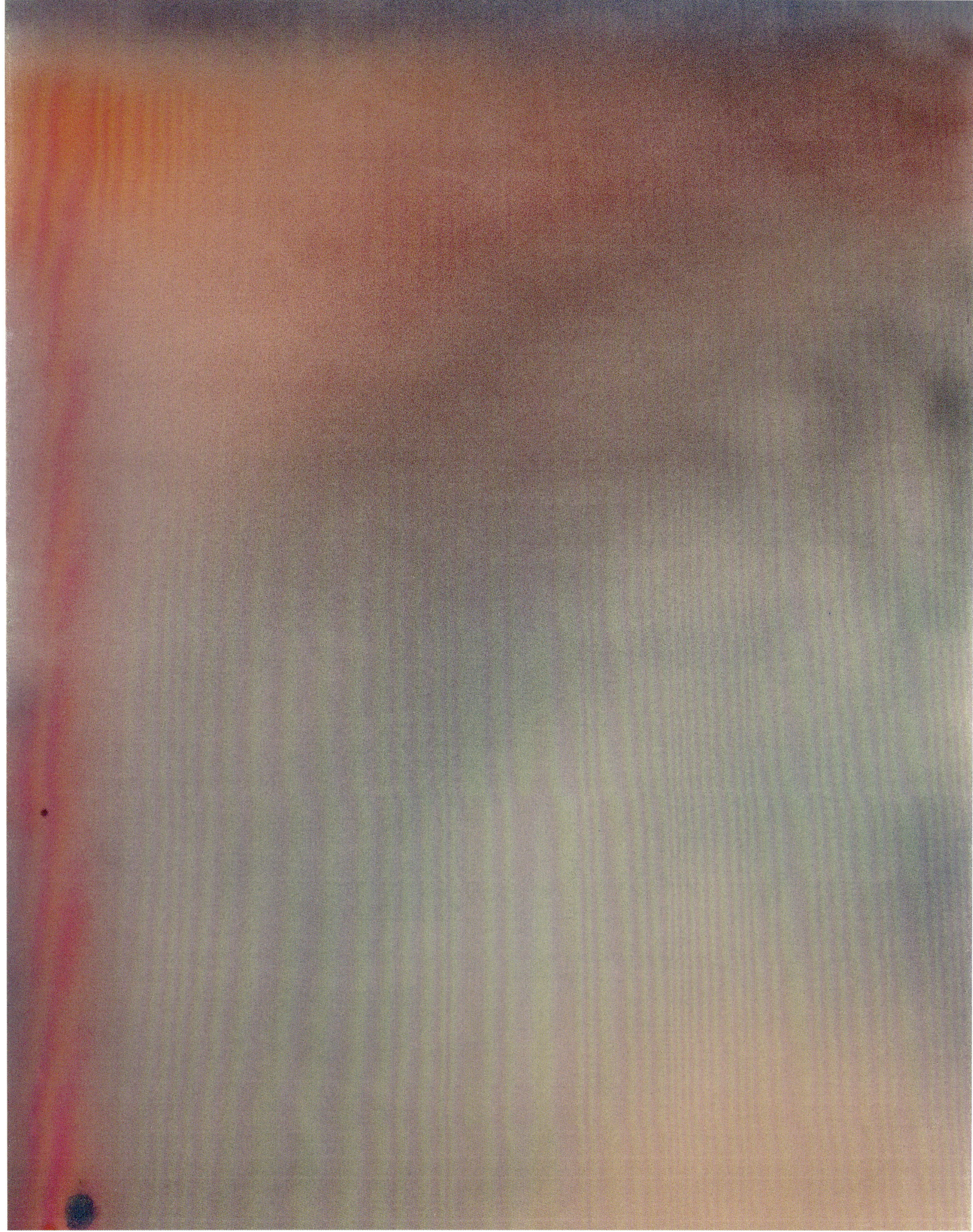

Jules Olitski
28 **Comprehensive Dream, 1965**
Waterbased acrylic and pastel on canvas,
112¾ × 92½ in. (286.4 × 235 cm)
Audrey and David Mirvish, Toronto

Jules Olitski
29 **Prince Patutsky Diary, 1965**
Waterbased acrylic and pastel on canvas,
92 × 85 in. (233.7 × 215.9 cm)
Private Collection

Jules Olitski
30 **Yellow Looshe, 1968**
Waterbased acrylic on canvas, 81 × 260 in. (205.7 × 660.4 cm)
Private Collection

Jules Olitski

31 **Eighth Loosha, 1970**

Waterbased acrylic on canvas, 115 × 68½ in. (292.1 × 174 cm)

Private Collection

It is harder to draw the line between Color Field painting and Minimalism, the other major art movement to emerge in the 1960s, as they stem from similar questioning regarding the conventions of art. Both used reductive abstract forms, explored unconventional art materials and processes to make unprecedented works, and embodied the artists' shared aspiration of creating an image that could be comprehended in a single glance. Donald Judd echoed the Color Field artists' sentiments regarding abandoning traditional relational compositions, noting that his work is "symmetrical because … I wanted to get rid of any compositional effects and the obvious way to do it is by symmetry."[67] One of the primary distinctions was the way Color Field painting and Minimalist three-dimensional works by Carl Andre, Judd, and Robert Morris, for instance, existed as objects. Color Field painting was clearly identifiable as "art" as it was generally installed on the wall in the way paintings had conventionally been displayed. Even though these paintings may challenge the viewer's concept of painting and intrude into the third-dimension as with Stella's shaped canvases, they are still experienced as paintings and address pictorial issues. The Minimalists, however, eliminated the convention of the pedestal from their work, and instead installed their structures directly on the floor in the same physical space as the viewer, thereby forcing a confrontation in which the viewer had to determine the nature of these objects.

Color Field was most closely associated with artists centered in New York and Washington, D.C., where Noland and Louis lived, taught, and spawned the art movement known as the Washington Color School. The Washington Color School is comprised of over thirty abstract artists including Gene Davis, Thomas Downing, Gilliam, Howard Mehring, Paul Reed, Alma Thomas, the sculptor Anne Truitt, and Rockne Krebs, who used the new technology of laser light as his medium. Walter Hopps relocated from Los Angeles to Washington, D.C. where he directed the Corcoran Gallery of Art (1967–72) and subsequently became the curator of 20th Century American Art at the Smithsonian's National Collection of Fine Arts (1972–79). He countered Greenberg's formalism by challenging artists to experiment. Other cities in the U.S. and Canada were also hotbeds of activity. Art schools such as Bennington College in Vermont drew Olitski and the British sculptor Anthony Caro as teachers, where they had fruitful interactions with Noland (who lived there), the sculptor David Smith, and Paul Feeley, the longtime director of the art department; Provincetown, Massachusetts, where Hans Hofmann had a studio as well as an art school and New York School artists summered; California, where it morphed into the Light and Space movement; and in Canada, where the annual summer Emma Lake Artists' Workshops at the University of Saskatchewan in Saskatoon drew artists such as Barnett Newman (1959), Noland (1963), Olitski (1964), John Cage (1965), and Stella (1967) as instructors, and where David Mirvish represented several of these artists in his eponymous gallery in Toronto (1963–78).

Greenberg was a one-man consensus-maker (or so it seemed), wearing multiple hats as critic and advisor to private collectors and art galleries. He also curated museum exhibitions, such as *Post-Painterly Abstraction* for Los Angeles County Museum of Art in 1964 (with James Elliot), taught and lectured, and was a constant presence in artists' studios.[68] Most of the artists featured here were friends with Greenberg and to some extent, their position in art history is tied to his reputation. Today, Greenberg is most closely associated with the Abstract Expressionists and the subsequent generation of Color Field artists including Frankenthaler, Louis, Noland, Olitski, and Poons. However, his validation of paintings by Black artists, especially Frank Bowling and Peter Bradley, is lesser known. Recent exhibitions and research on these and other Black artists are bringing greater attention to Greenberg's association with them.[69]

Bowling developed a figurative, Pop-like style as a student at London's Royal College of Art in the early 1960s. He moved to New York in 1966, where he broke loose with abstract paintings, overlaying stencils of maps of various coastlines as a comment on the slave trade and colonialism. Seduced by the physical properties of paint he eliminated the figurative elements altogether in 1972, a move Greenberg, who frequented Bowling's studio, encouraged.[70] In 1971, Bowling was included in the Whitney Museum of American Art Biennial in New York. The same year his text, "It's Not Enough to Say 'Black Is Beautiful'" (*ARTnews*, April 1971), was published after missteps made by several art museums in presenting exhibitions of work by Black artists prompted protests, and as a response to the censure Black abstract painters faced from the Black Arts Movement for relinquishing their responsibility to create empowering images for Black people.[71] Bowling noted how the then current "discussion surrounding painting and sculpture by blacks seems completely concerned with notions about Black Art, not with the works themselves or their delivery." He further contended that the more pertinent question was to ask, "What precisely is the nature of Black art?" As abstract art at that time was judged purely on its formal qualities, devoid of any outside references, including the artists' own life experiences and role as creator, how could abstract art by Black artists be assessed if it is labeled "Black art"? Using the abstract work of five of his peers as examples, Bowling offered a path towards discussing works by Black artists through their individual intent and innovations. In an interview from 2023, Bowling reminisced on the New York art scene of the 1960s and '70s: "there was Black and there was white, but the artists were striving for, aspiring to, a forward-looking view of American modernism."[72]

With an art education from the Detroit Society of Arts and Crafts and a brief stint at Yale School of Art, abstract artist Peter Bradley quickly became entrenched in the New York art scene. An associate director of the prestigious Perls Galleries (1968–75), his friendship with Greenberg and Noland helped him to secure representation at the prominent André Emmerich gallery in New York, which showed many of the leading Color Field artists. Bradley's paintings were also featured in the 1973 Biennial at the Whitney Museum of American Art. In 1971, Houston collector John de Menil invited Bradley to curate what is thought to be among the first racially integrated art exhibitions in the U.S., *The De Luxe Show*. Installed in the former DeLuxe movie theater in a predominantly Black neighborhood in Houston, Texas, Bradley exclusively selected abstract works by Walter Darby Bannard, Caro, Noland, Olitski, and Poons, as well as by artists of color, such as Ed Clark, Bradley, Gilliam, Robert Gordon, Virginia Jaramillo, Al Loving, and William T. Williams, among others. Noland and Gilliam helped Bradley install the exhibition, as did Greenberg. As art historian Mark Godfrey noted in the exhibition catalogue for *Soul of a Nation* (2017), the Black abstract artists in *The De Luxe Show*, not only constituted a community of colleagues, they represented a "generational group who shared a similar situation."[73] These artists "wanted their work to be part of a discussion of modernist art in America alongside their peers…" At the same time, they "insisted that a 'black sensibility' ran through their work."[74] Gilliam refuted the criticism by writers associated with the Black Arts Movement by arguing that "Figurative art doesn't represent blackness any more than a non-narrative media-oriented kind of painting, like what I do."[75]

Bradley's full title for the exhibition was *Hard Art at the De Luxe Show*. The common denominator of all these abstract works was that they were hard to look at, hard to understand, and hard to like. Bradley shared his expectations for the Hard Art in his group show, stating, "These works carry a particular clarity: a window into a new art. Their art is honest and wide open, not burdened with gestures and other cliches. This art should be like the new world we're all striving toward, free of obstruction."[76] Greenberg in his

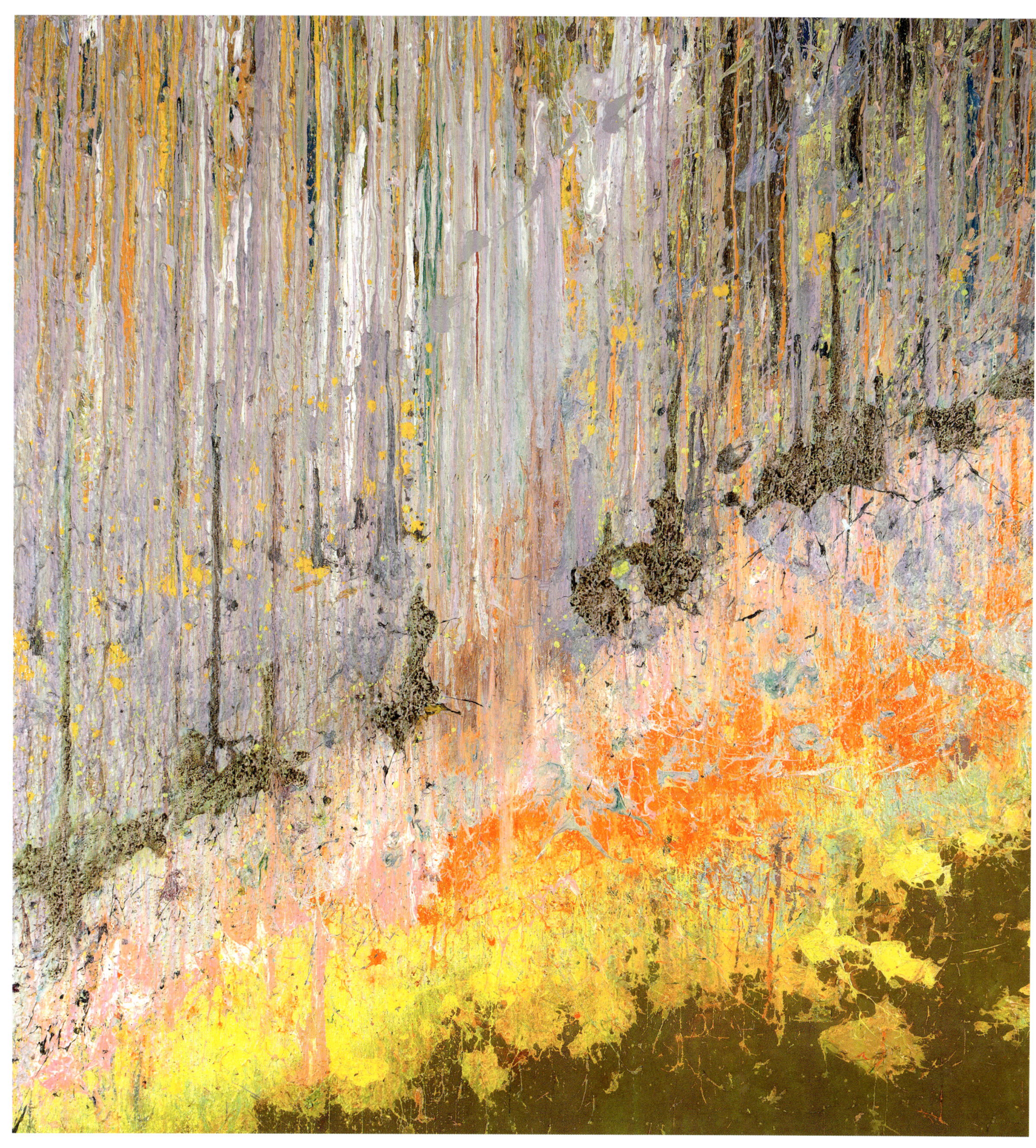

Lawrence Poons
32 **Big Purple, 1972**
Acrylic on canvas, 98 × 92 in. (248.9 × 233.7 cm)
Audrey and David Mirvish, Toronto

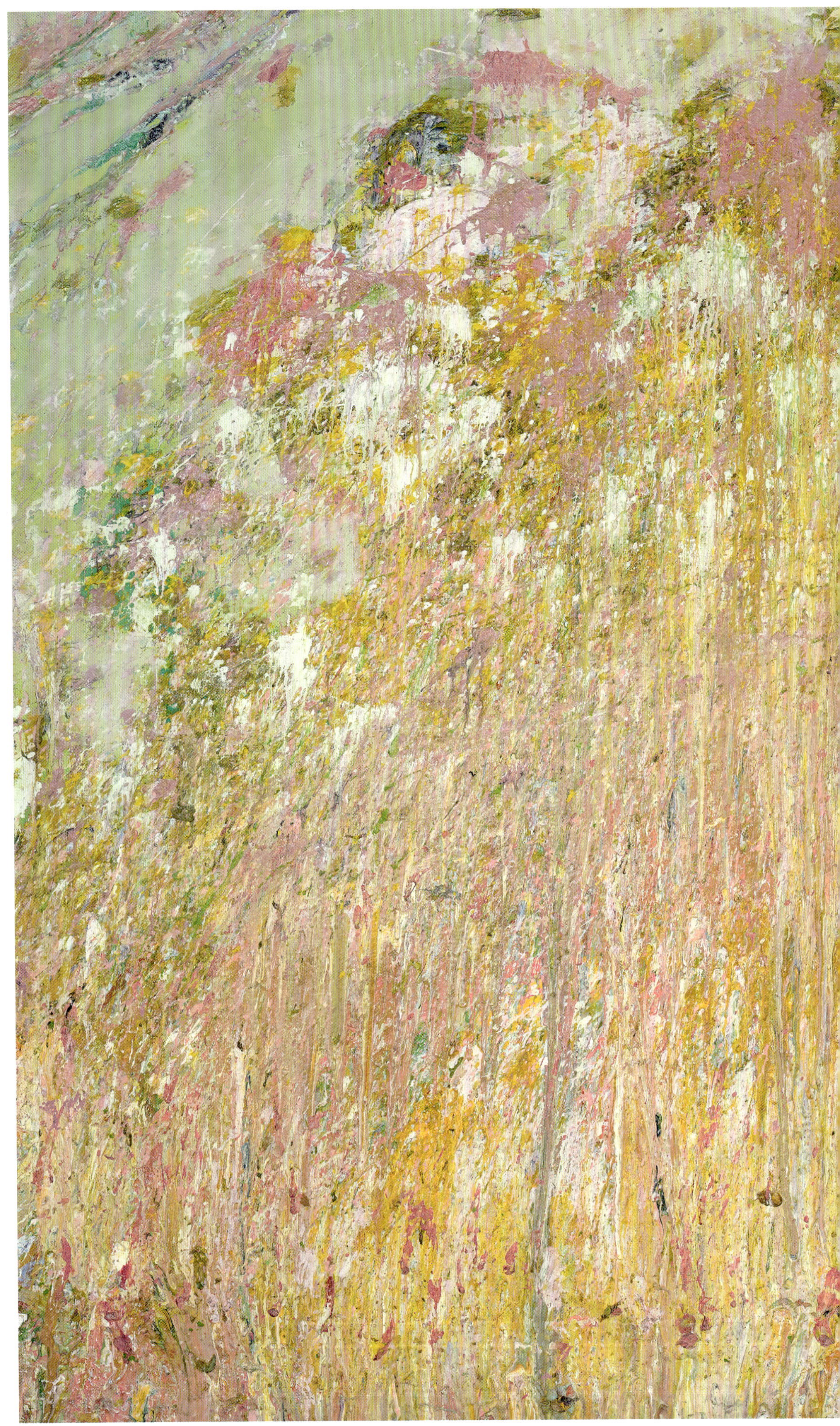

Lawrence Poons
33 **Rain Race, 1972**
Acrylic on canvas, 103½ × 155½ in.
(262.9 × 395 cm)
Audrey and David Mirvish, Toronto

FOLLOWING PAGES

Lawrence Poons
34 **"The Call," 1973**
Acrylic on canvas, 108½ × 192 in.
(275.6 × 487.7 cm)
Private Collection

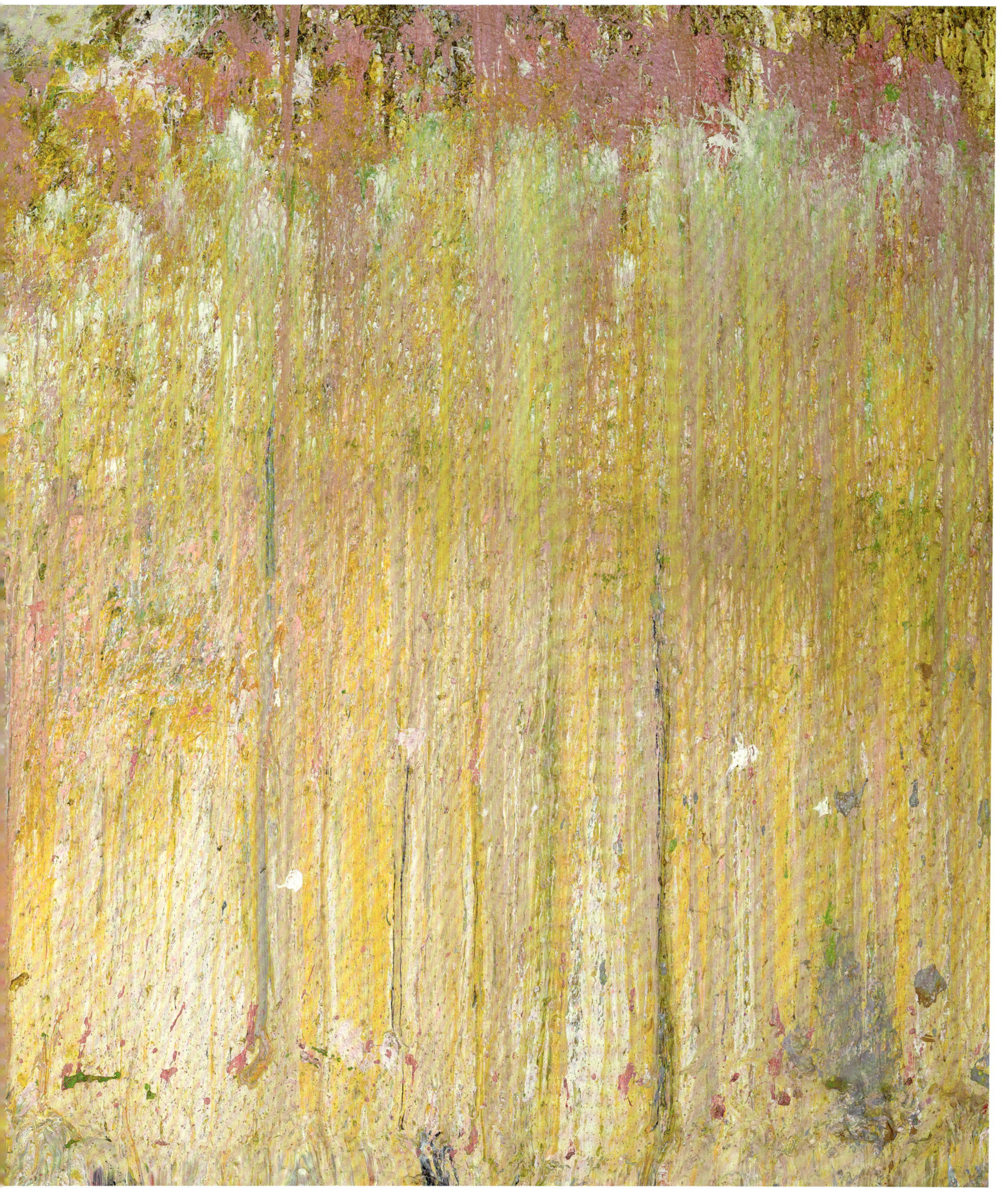

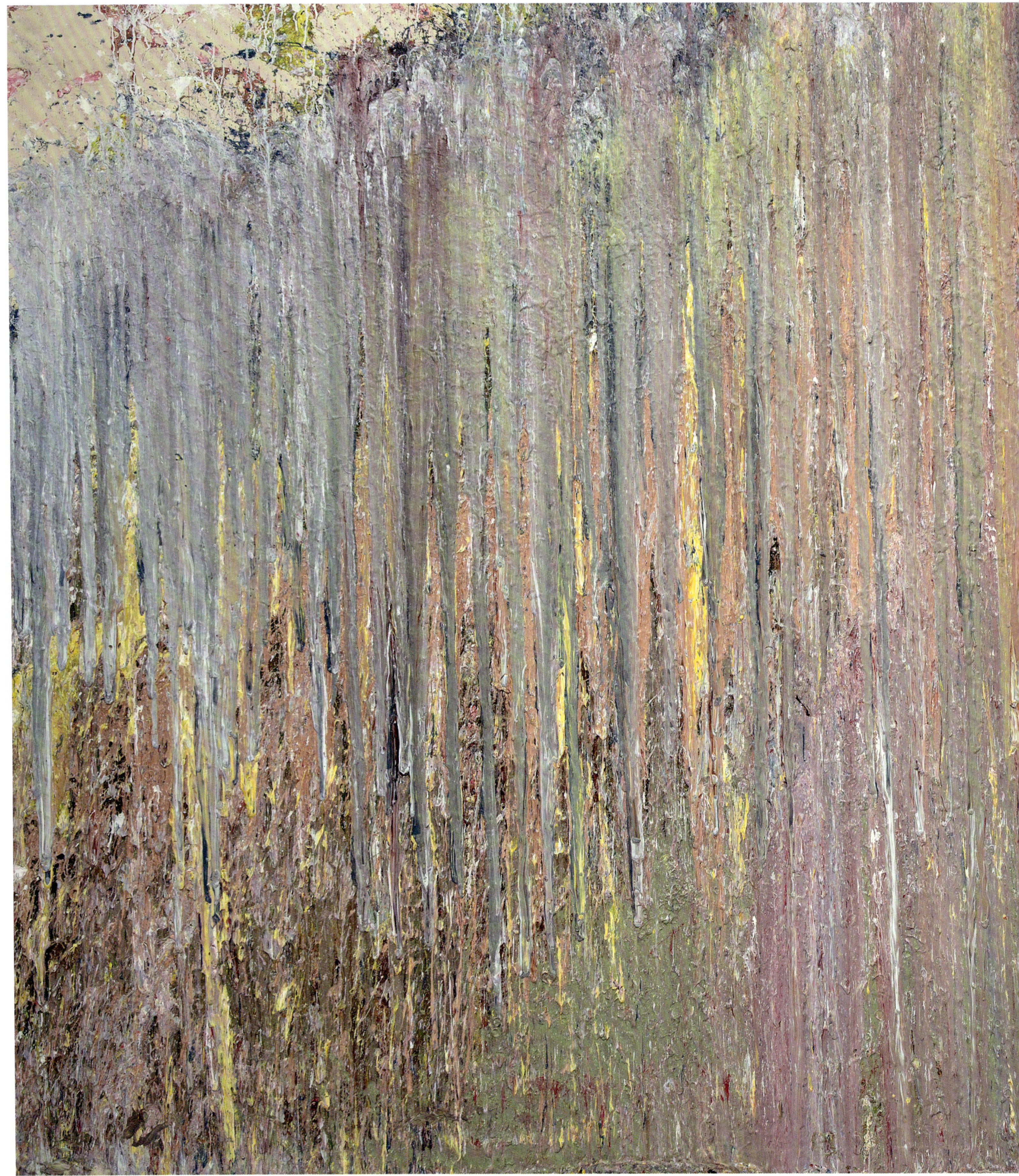

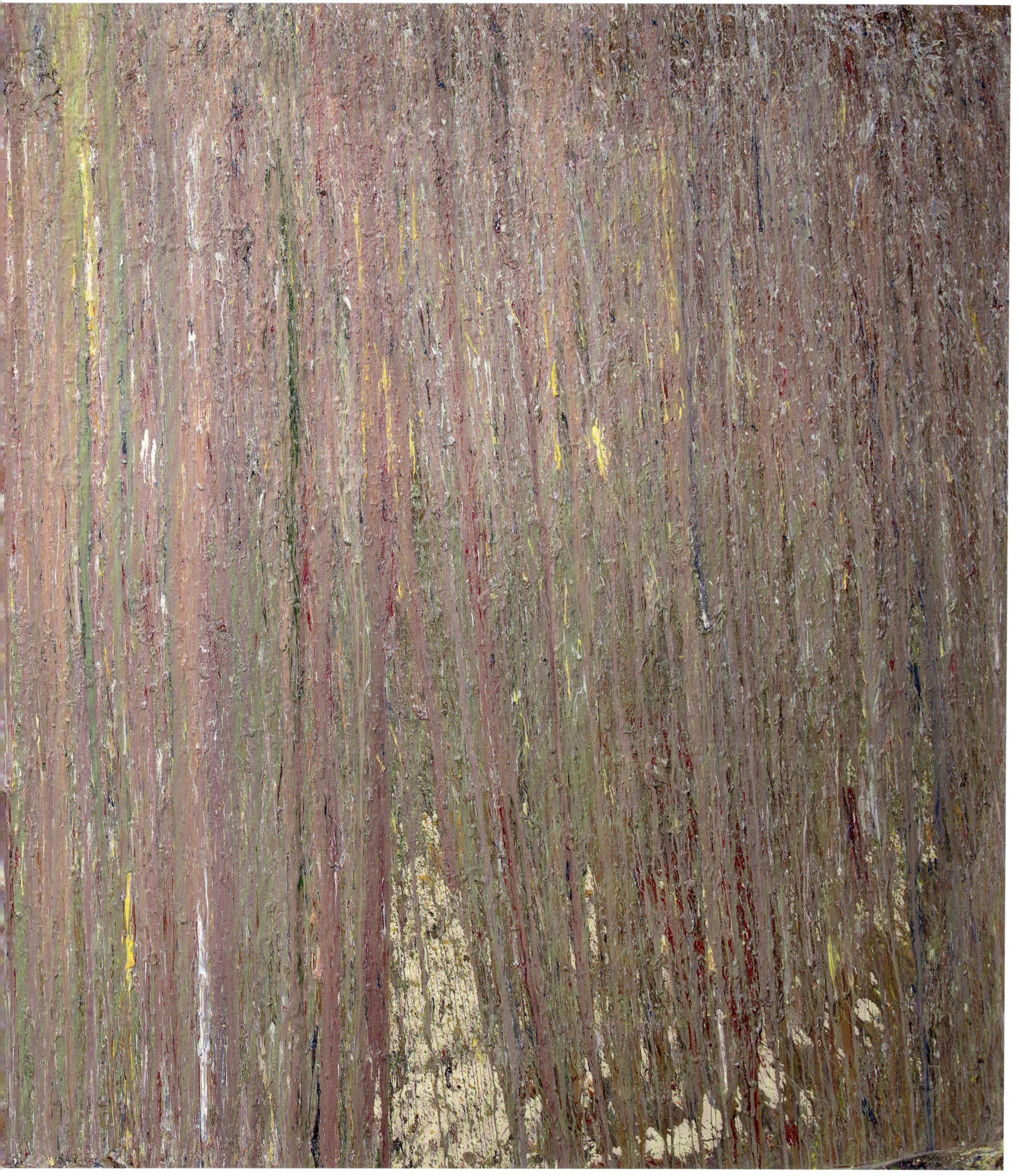

Lawrence Poons
35 **Lady Accessorie, 1976**
Acrylic on canvas, 115 × 47¼ in. (292.1 × 120 cm)
Private Collection

Lawrence Poons
36 **"To Clara from Robert," 1976**
Acrylic on canvas, 115¼ × 28 in. (292.7 × 71.1 cm)
Private Collection

Lawrence Poons
37 **The Morning Lies in the Afternoon Sun, 1976**
Acrylic on canvas, 114¼ × 48 in. (290.2 × 121.9 cm)
Private Collection

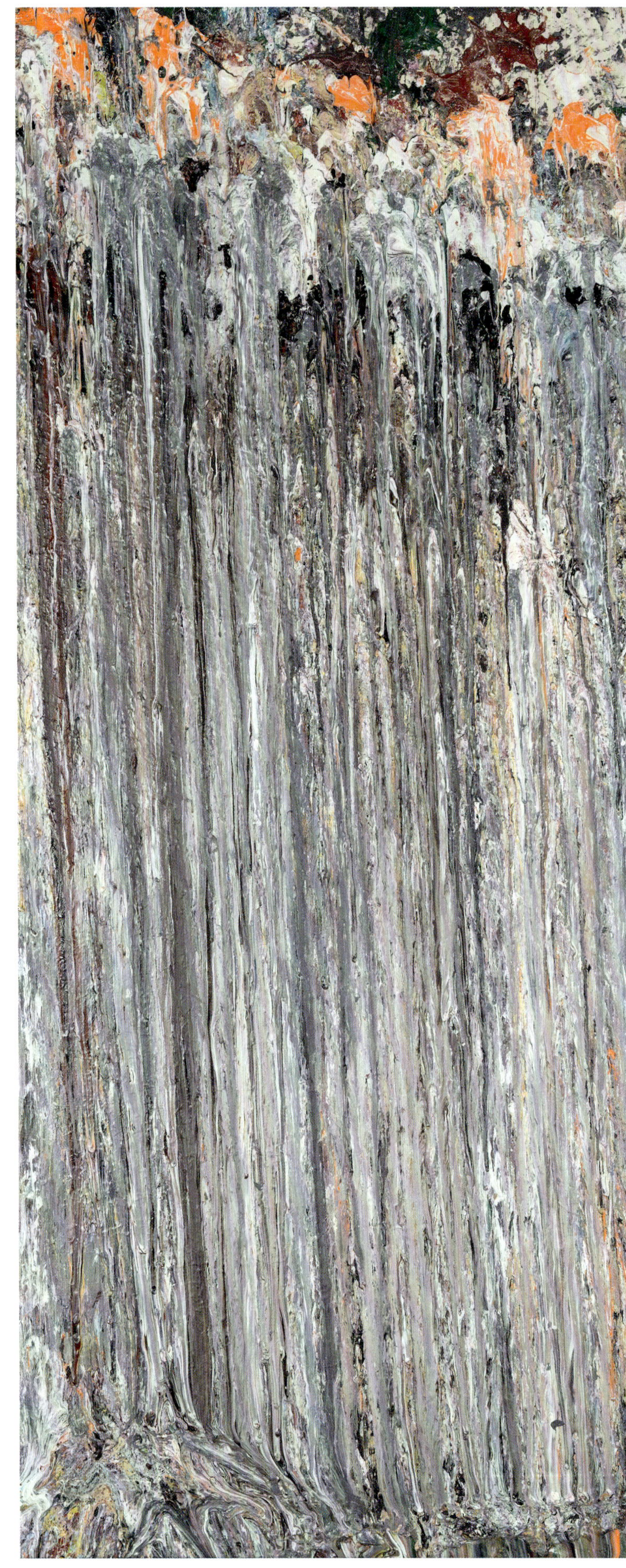

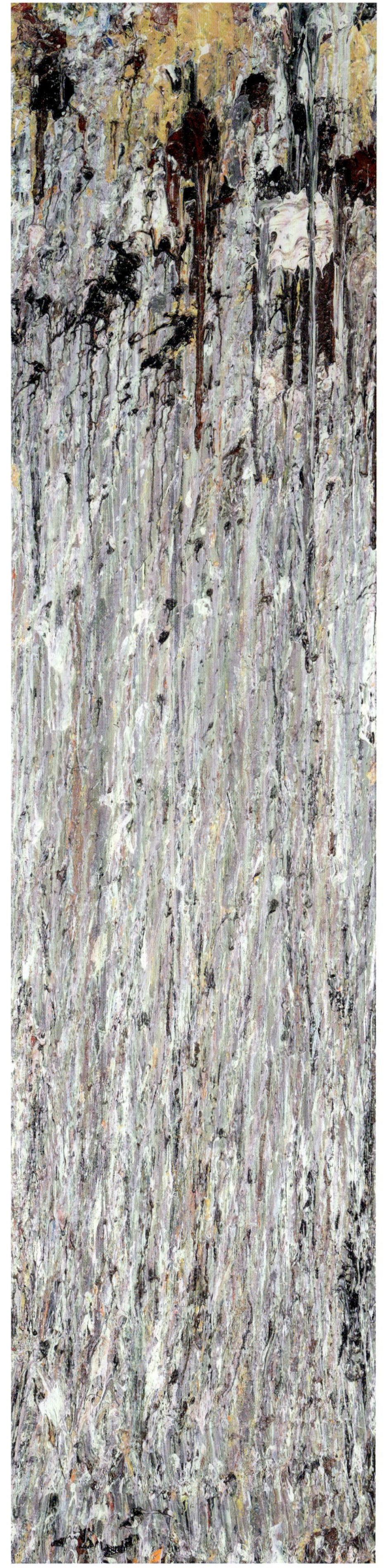

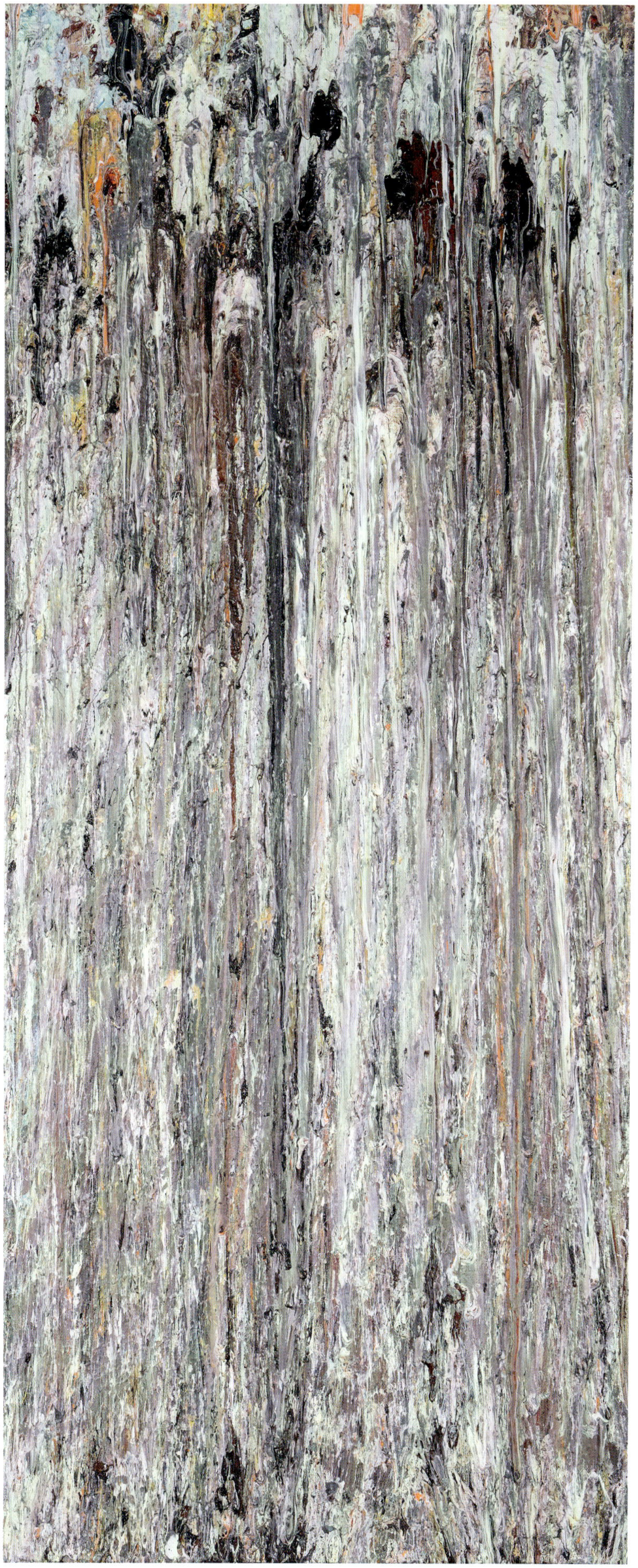

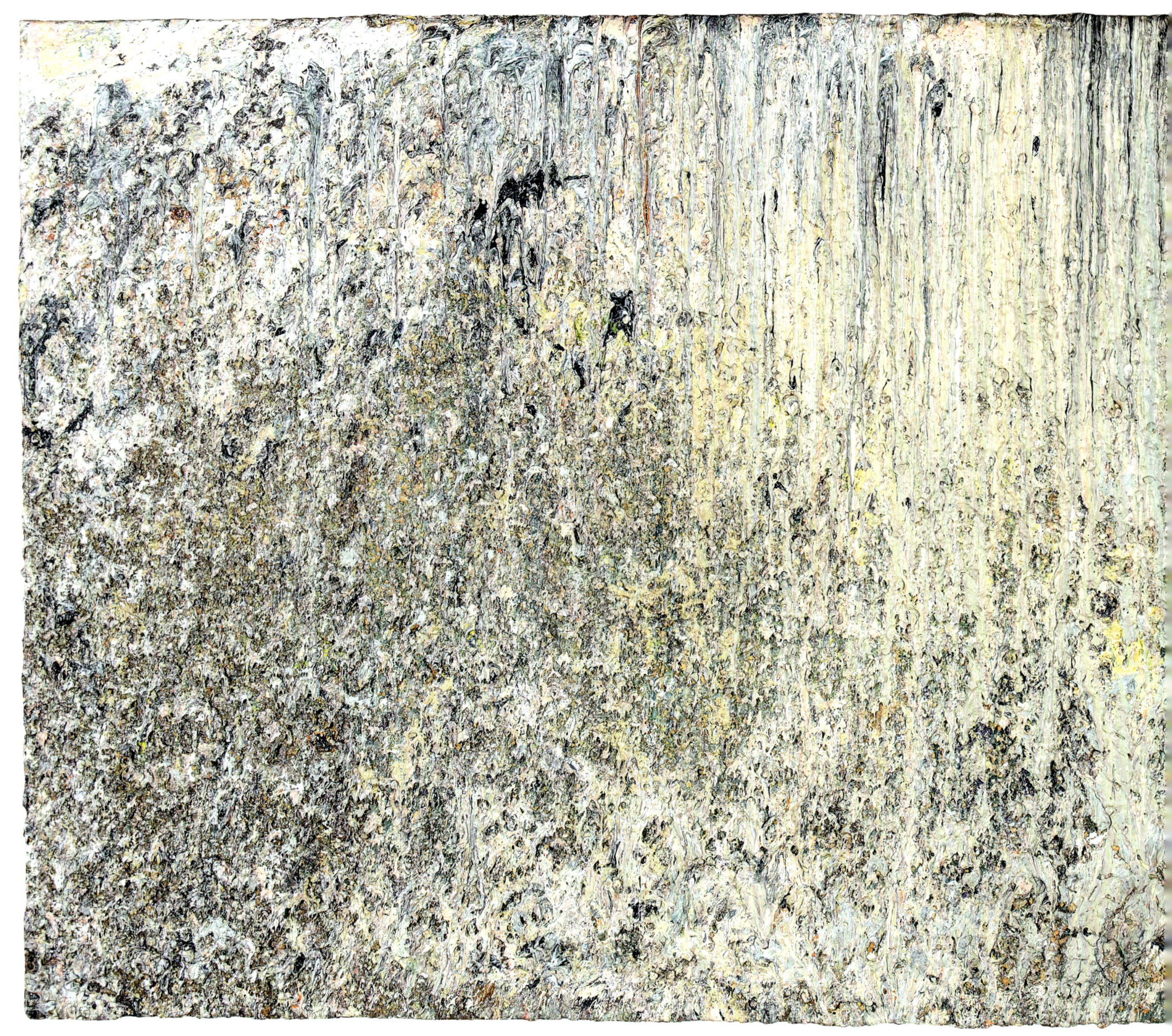

Lawrence Poons
38 **Pine Plains, 1983**
Acrylic on canvas, 91 × 217 in. (231.1 × 551.2 cm)
Private Collection

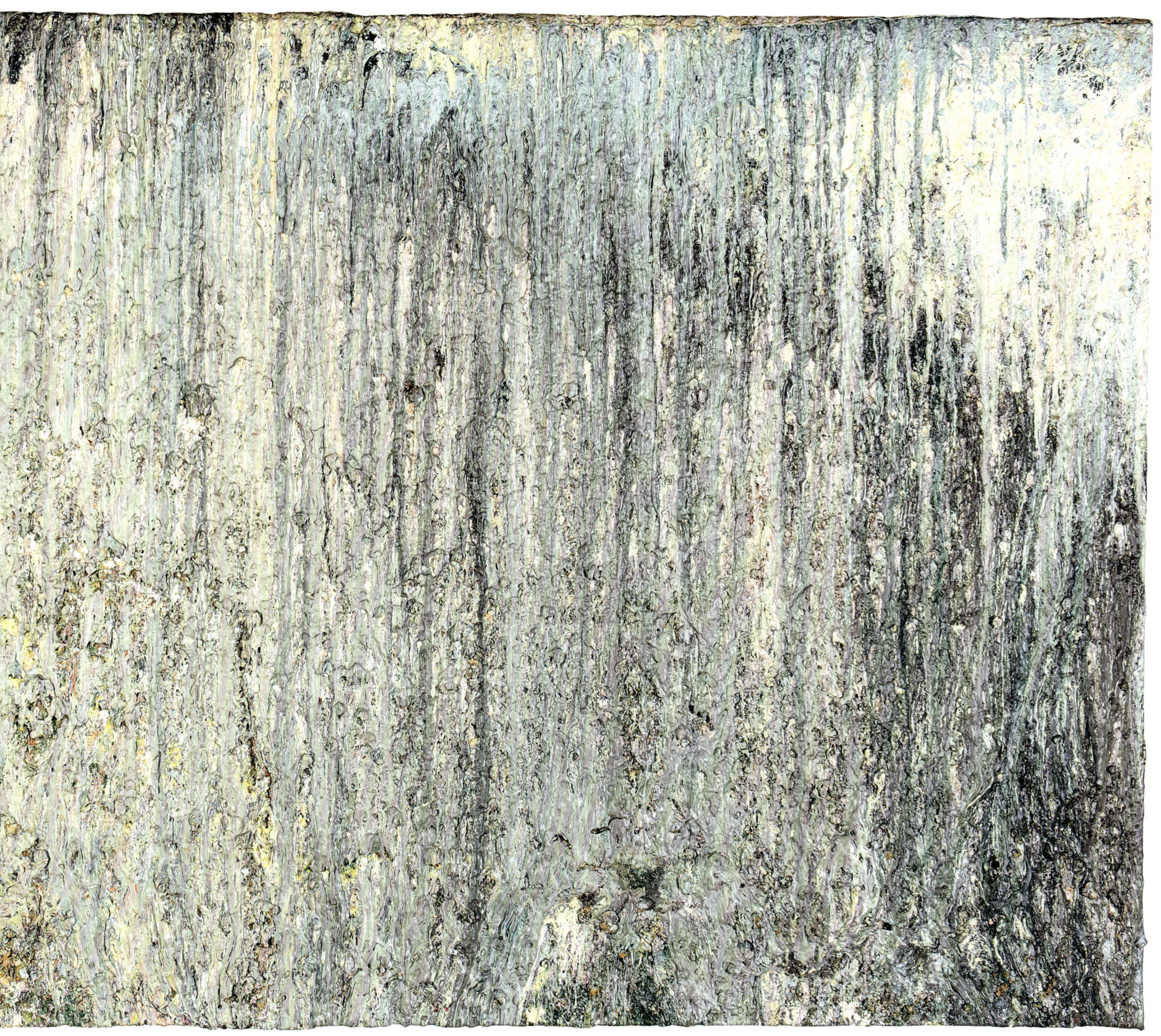

Lawrence Poons

39 **Regulus, 1985**

Acrylic on canvas, 90 × 103 in. (228.6 × 261.6 cm)

Private Collection

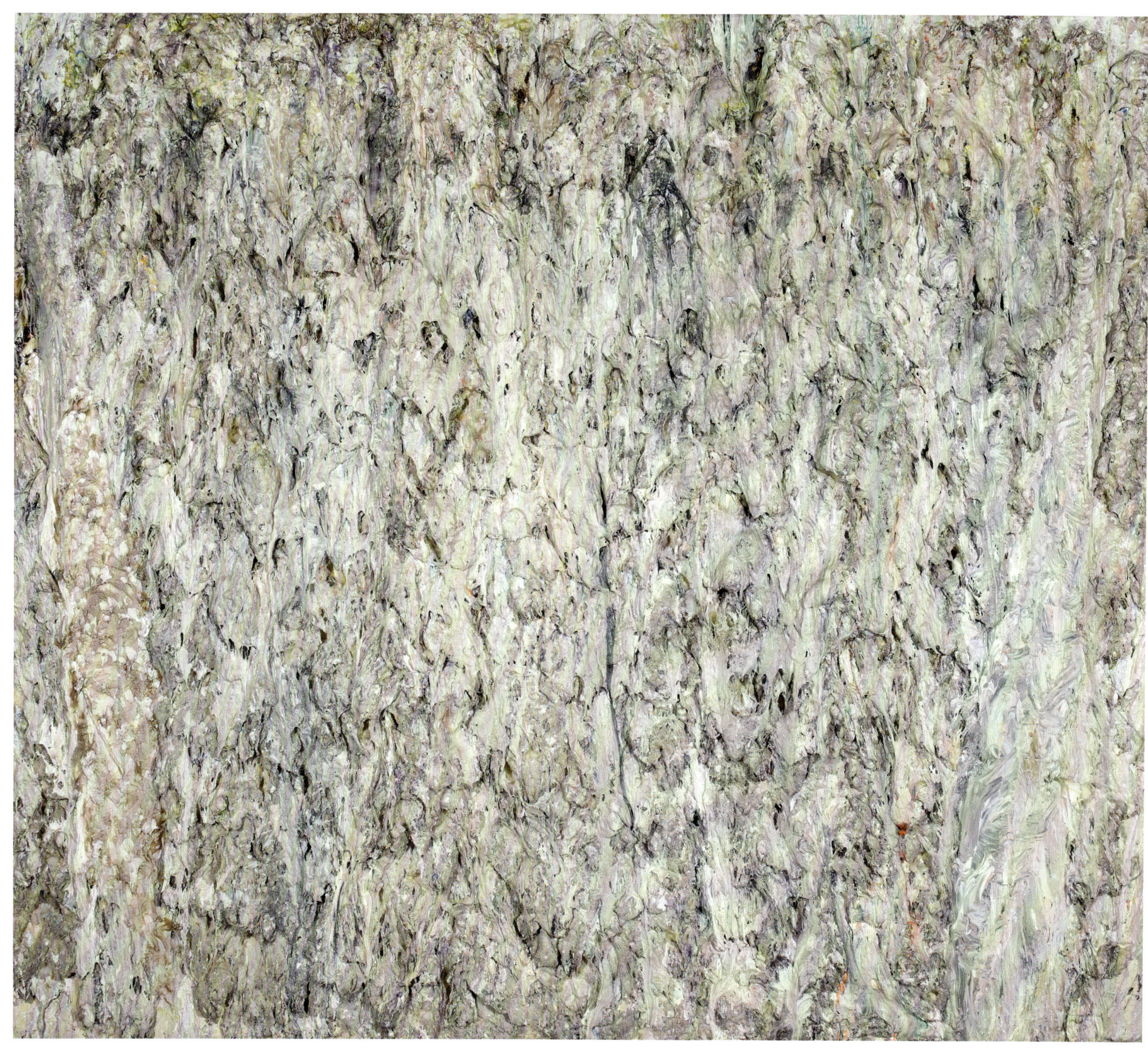

summation of this exhibition likewise used the term "hard" contemporary art to describe the works on view.[77] The response from the New York art world, however, was disappointing. The reality of the time, noted Bradley, was that "Anything that doesn't happen at the Modern Art Museum [sic] or some heady Madison Avenue gallery goes unnoticed, as far as the media's concerned."[78]

The catalogue for *The De Luxe Show* included an interview with Greenberg in which he expressed his enthusiastic support for the project, stating that "the Black artists included were there on the same basis of quality and ambition as the White ones. I can't praise the *De Luxe Show* enough on these scores. It sets a unique example, and one that I hope will be much imitated from now on."[79] Greenberg's influence seemed to reach its limits when it came to the careers of the Black artists he championed. Bowling, Bradley, Clark, Gilliam, Loving, and Thomas had all achieved significant art world status in the early 1970s. Although Greenberg's endorsement is one of the criterion used by curators and art historians to define the list of Color Field artists, none of the Black artists who were in *The De Luxe Show* were included in subsequent major Color Field museum exhibitions, with the exception of Gilliam, whose paintings were represented in the Color Field museum survey at the Smithsonian American Art Museum, Washington, D.C. in 2008, curated by Karen Wilkin.[80] In 2021, the Karma gallery in Los Angeles brought new attention to *The De Luxe Show*, when it staged an exhibition of the original integrated group of artists.[81]

Modern American art quickly spread throughout the globe in the 1960s and 1970s, especially at major international art festivals. Frankenthaler was featured in Documenta II in Kassel, Germany, and in the São Paulo Biennial in 1959. In 1964, Alan Solomon, Director of The Jewish Museum in New York, selected Louis, Noland, and Stella, as well as five other artists, to represent America at the Venice Biennale in two exhibitions. This introduction to an international audience validated the new American artists with both Noland and Rauschenberg as contenders for the coveted Golden Lion award (the award ultimately went to Rauschenberg, the first American so honored). As the United States Commissioner of the Eighth São Paulo Biennial in 1965, Hopps organized an exhibition that highlighted the affinities and differences between artists Barnett Newman, Donald Judd, Poons, Stella, and Los Angeles artists Larry Bell, Billy Al Bengston, and Robert Irwin. The 1968 Documenta IV international art exhibition was dominated by new American art, including large-scale Color Field paintings (Ron Davis, Louis, Noland, Olitski, Poons, and Stella), Minimal art and Pop art. In 1972, Gilliam became the first Black American to represent the U.S. at the Venice Biennale when Hopps included his work in a group exhibition he organized for the American Pavilion.

When We Talk about Space

According to Stella, Color Field's primary objective was to create real and convincing space. When we talk about space in American abstract painting, we usually refer to pictorial space. Many postwar artists reported experiencing an epiphany before Barnett Newman's paintings (fig. 28, p. 131). In the case of Poons, seeing Newman's exhibition at French & Company in 1959 instantly converted him from a career in music to devoting himself to painting. Dore Ashton, in a *New York Times* review, captured the jolt of seeing this survey exhibition organized by Greenberg: "Newman's largest paintings with their slender dividing lines unquestionably produce tension. It is the kind of tension projected by architecture. We experience a gracefully scaled ceiling and wall with pleasure. In the same way, it is an experience to encounter an overwhelming field of navy blue, stretching on and on, and giving different weights to its three major shapes, or, as the case may be, intervals … His idea—as revolutionary as it may be—speaks largely to the mind, frequently in the same terms, and deliberately discourages visual penetration." Ashton responded favorably to Greenberg's curatorial role in organizing the Newman survey, noting how he lent his "authority and impelling enthusiasm to the show."[82] Her observation regarding how Newman's paintings deliberately discourage visual penetration sounds more like Greenberg's assessment based on his favoring of flat picture planes, rather than the artist's actual intent. Newman created a new type of pictorial space. Instead of consisting of areas of color projecting and receding from the picture plane as in Hofmann's practice, Newman's space propelled outward in a lateral thrust. Stella so marveled at Newman's space and how the vertical intervals of his paintings (the "zips") seemed to stitch adjoining fields of color together, that he conceived his own Stripe paintings as consisting of a series of narrow bands conjoined or "zipped together" by pencil thin gaps of white, unpainted canvas.[83] In this way Stella captured the thrill of space accelerating outward as well as back to a central point.

Right from the beginning of his career Stella was preoccupied with incorporating space into his paintings without lapsing into perspective. He thinks of his space as in architectural terms. Even when working with flat canvases and minimal forms, he contended he was building space. He acknowledged the architectural associations in his work to William Rubin in 1970: "I enjoy and find it more fruitful to think about many organizational or spatial concepts in architectural terms, because when you think about them strictly in design terms, they become flat and very boring problems."[84] While other artists were working under the assumption that paintings were executed on a flat surface, Stella took the leap in the 1970s to challenge this convention by creating vital and exuberant paintings that literally and physically existed on multiple planes, and which incorporated the real space between and surrounding the shapes. "The assumption that the topography [of the painting] should be the flat surface of the canvas," remarked Stella "is the same thinking of the world as flat."[85]

The Abstract Expressionists established a precedent for large-scale paintings that the Color Field painters adopted. Examples of monumental paintings abounded during the Abstract Expressionists' formative period: the Mexican Muralists, José Clemente Orozco, Diego Rivera, and David Alfaro Siqueiros were hailed in New York; American artists competed to paint murals as part of the Work Progress Administration (WPA) during the Great Depression of the 1930s; and after World War II, restored travel to Europe made it possible for American artists to experience frescos decorating the walls of churches and cathedrals and monumental historical paintings in museums first hand. The large scale of the paintings by Abstract Expressionists, however, was deliberately proportioned to correspond to the viewer's body and calibrated to the architecture where it would ultimately be exhibited, such as low-ceilinged New York galleries and residences. Rothko placed considerable emphasis on the viewer's physical as well as perceptual participation in his paintings. He described his impetus for painting large in a symposium in 1951:

> I realize historically the function of painting large pictures is painting something very grandiose and pompous. The reason I paint them, however—I think it applies to other painters I know—is precisely because I want to be very intimate and human. To paint a small painting is to place yourself outside your experience, to look upon an experience as a stereopticon view or with a reducing glass … However you paint the larger picture, you are in it. It isn't something you command.[86]

To experience a classic Rothko abstraction, the viewer stands transfixed at the painting's center. The Color Field artists similarly used scale and, in many cases, symmetry, to

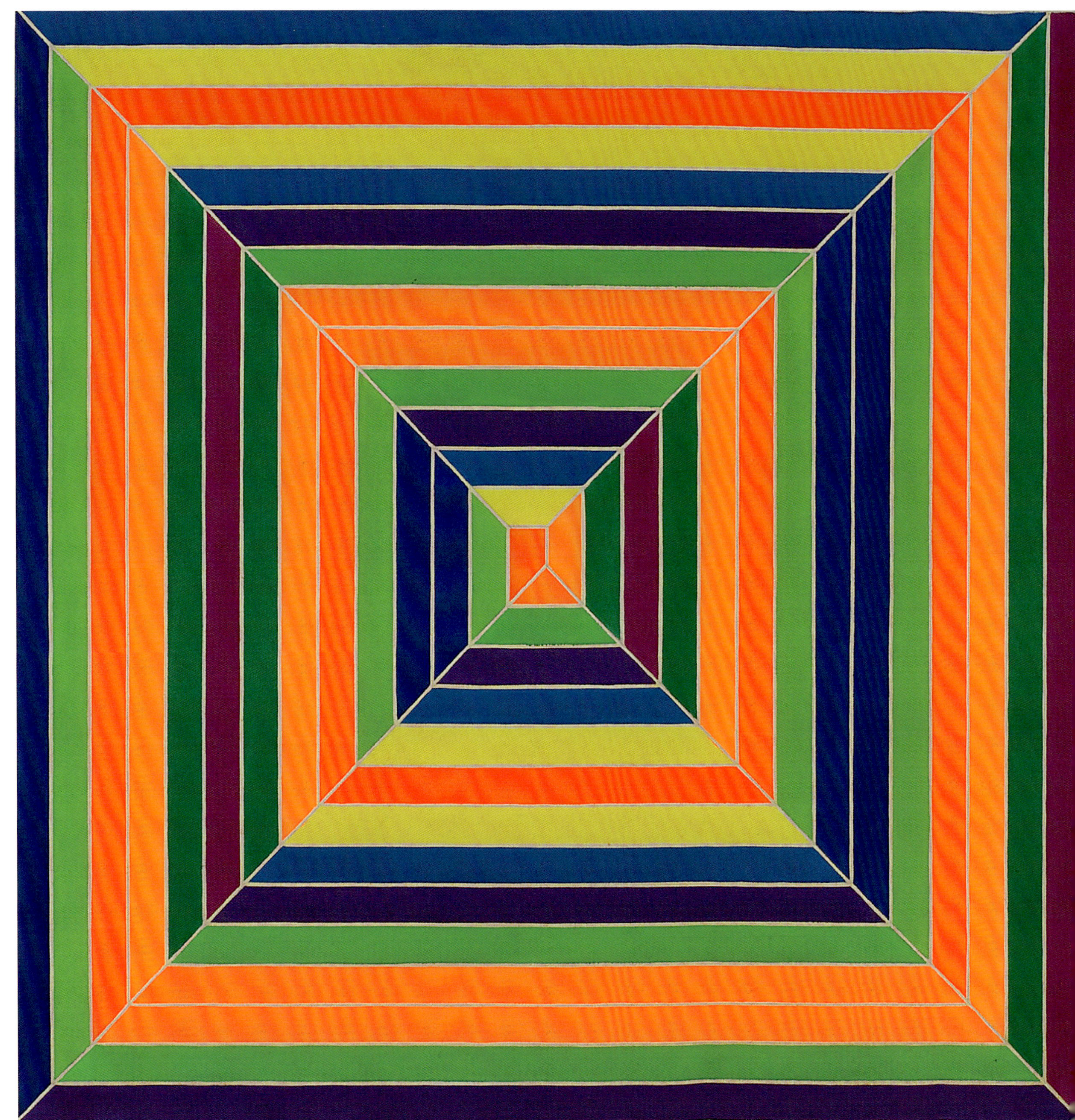

Frank Stella
40 **Fortín de las Flores, 1966**
Synthetic polymer paint on canvas, 77 × 154 in.
(195.6 × 391.2 cm)
NSU Art Museum Fort Lauderdale;
gift of Mr. and Mrs. Thomas Scofield

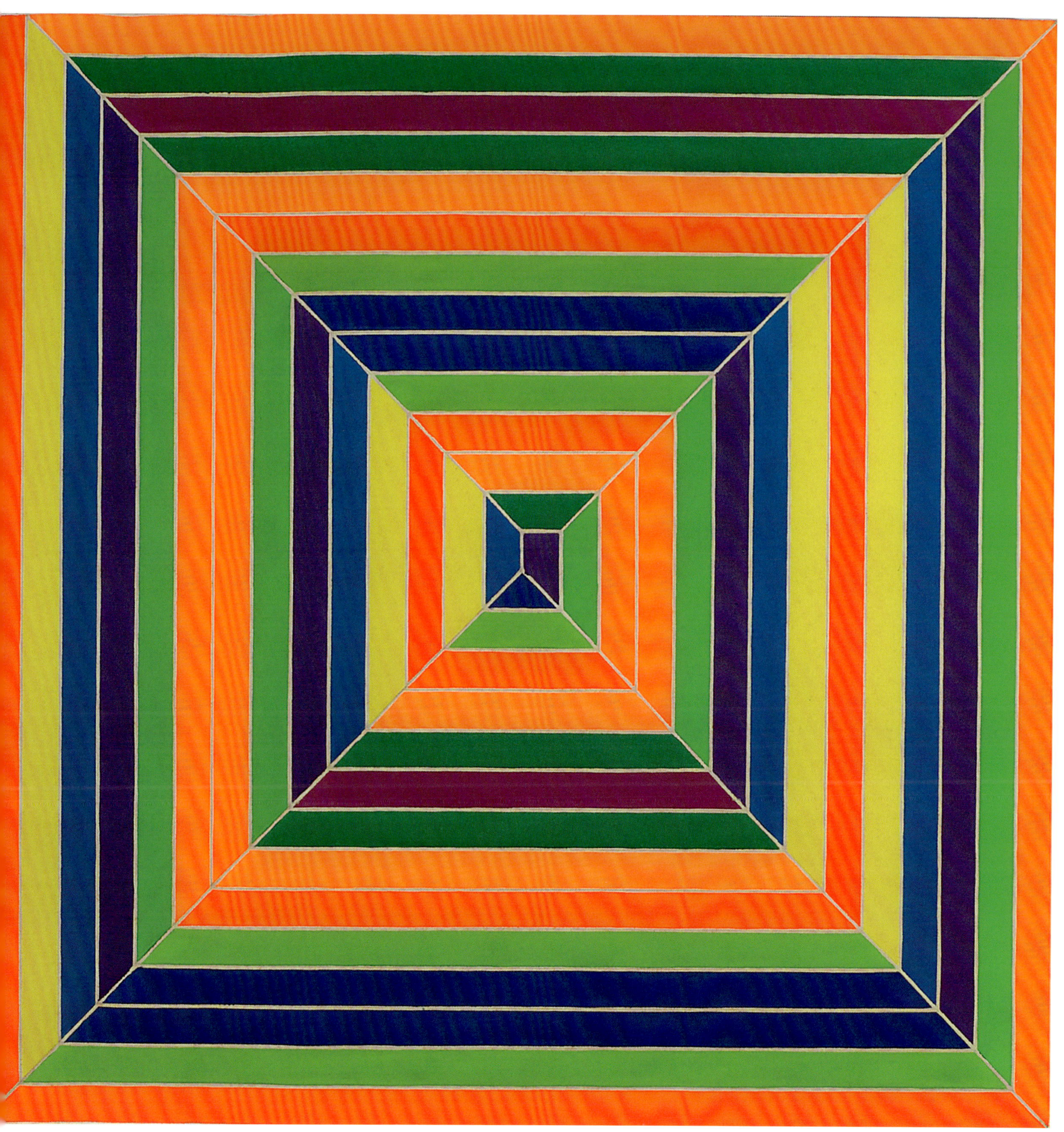

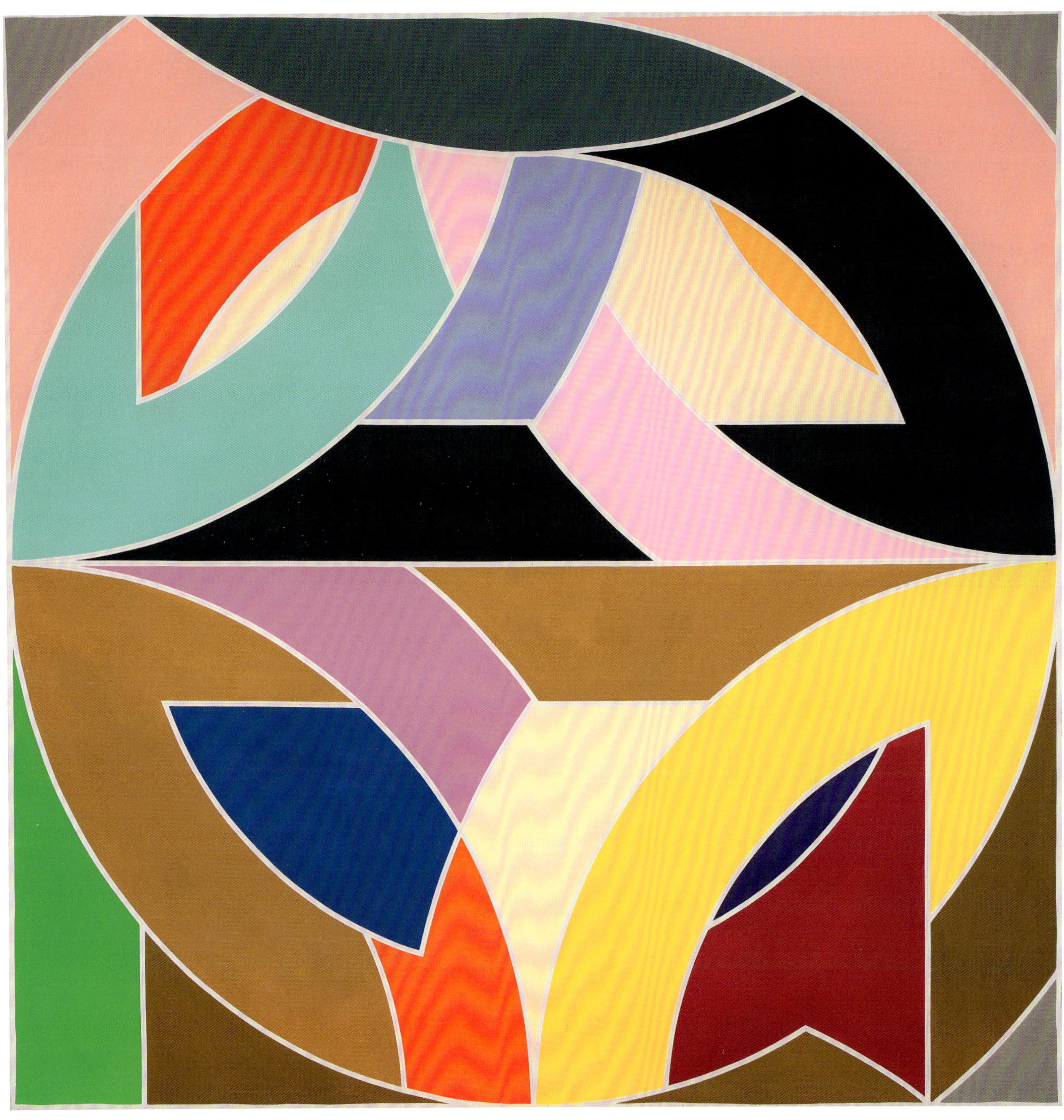

Frank Stella
41 **Waskwaiu II [Variations on a Circle], 1968**
Acrylic on canvas, 96 × 96 × 4 in. (243.8 × 243.8 × 10.2 cm)
Private Collection

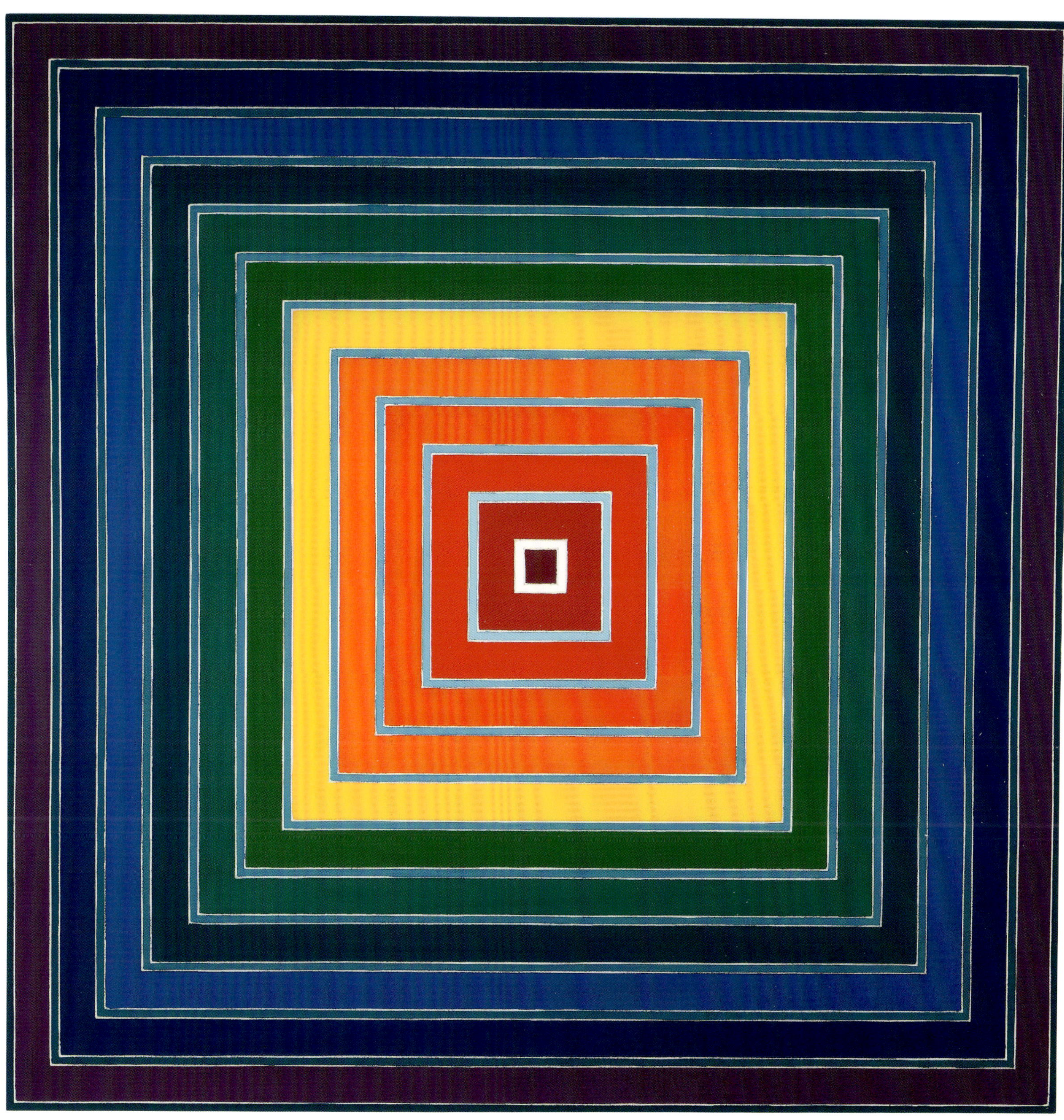

Frank Stella
42 **Sacramento No. 6, 1978**
Acrylic on canvas, 103¼ × 103¼ in. (262.3 × 262.3 cm)
S. Donald Sussman

Frank Stella
43 **Zolder—ONE ELEMENT, 1982**
Painted aluminum, 128 × 112 × 23 in.
(325.1 × 284.5 × 58.4 cm)
Private Collection

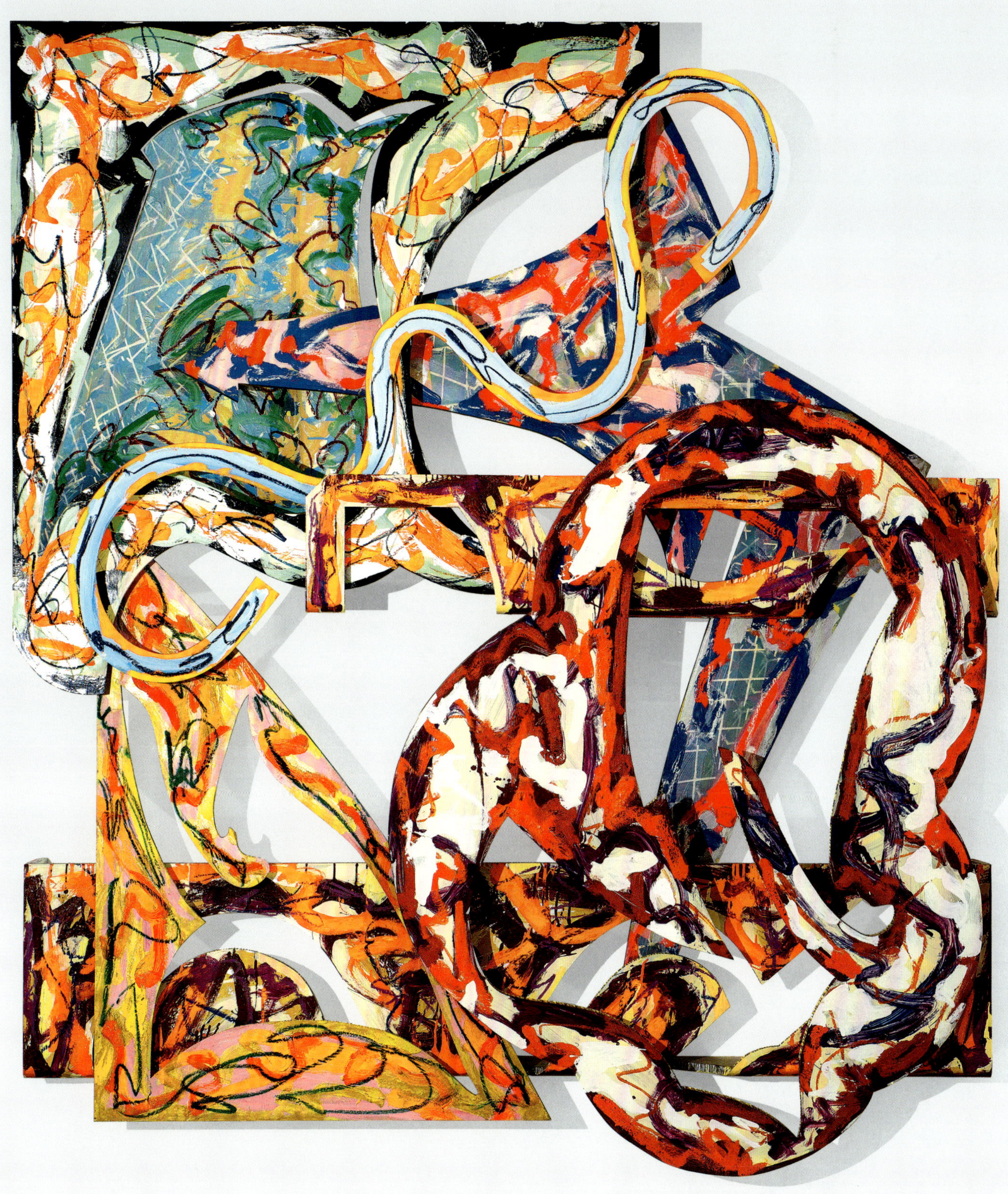

establish this direct correspondence to the human body so that they are absorbed into the painting's field. The symmetry and proportions of these paintings provide a sense of unity and wholeness.

All this talk about pictorial space was taking place during the period of the exploration of outer space. The vastness of the universe, the stargazing via NASA's awe-inspiring photographs and actual film footage of the lunar landings, and the first steps by humankind on the moon on July 20, 1969, impacted artists' psyches whether they were conscious of it or not.

Alma Thomas and Bradley were fascinated by the Space Age and captured the glories of the universe in their paintings. Thomas considered the moon landing to be one of humankind's greatest achievements. The staccato patterns of color in her paintings provide a glimpse into other galaxies and bursts of celestial energy.[87] For Bradley, outer space offers the romance of the spaceship, the moon landing, science fiction movies, and the possibility of extra-terrestrial life that might include a Black man that looks just like him.[88] Bradley conjured new worlds to explore with swirling pools of paint that coalesce on the canvas into rugged terrains, or by propelling pigment onto the picture's surface with a mechanical spray gun to create infinite galaxies.

The universe opens up different worlds and possibilities other than those experienced on Earth. The sky is one of the universals that unite all of humankind. It is the mysteries of creation itself and finding our place in the universe. It is about gravity-defying freedom. It is the "Glory of the World" that Stella discovered in Hofmann's paintings.

Experiment and Change

Classifying artists by styles and movements rarely takes into account that artists continue to live, work, and change their focus and methods beyond the time period of an art movement they were assigned. If the Color Field artists' goal was to reduce painting to its essence, which, as Greenberg proposed, was flatness, they would have ultimately wound up at a dead end with nowhere else to go.[89] Indeed, following this formalist logic, painting was declared dead in the 1970s. The formal analysis of these artists' work presumed that they were creating within the hermetically sealed realm of an art historical narrative that advanced linearly and was solely preoccupied with the properties of painting itself, when in fact these artists' encounters with art history were random, and their imagination was stimulated by triggers as wide-ranging as science, music, literature, popular culture, and even something as mundane as a yellow spiral beach hat.[90]

Greenberg, Michael Fried, and other formalist critics sought to establish a new criteria for assessing these artists' paintings based on how successful they were in achieving the elusive goal of pure painting, but the artists had their own ideas about what made their paintings work, which kept them experimenting and changing throughout their careers. Frankenthaler, for instance, never worked in a systematic way. Rather, she would often find herself circling back to earlier works in order to move ahead. Thinking back about her working process in later years, she remarked, "Arrive where you started—use your origins and what has happened since." When she wanted to head in a new direction she sometimes "psyched" herself back to *Mountains and Sea* and would usually come up with a work that had nothing to do with this painting.[91]

Frankenthaler also had established her own criteria by which she could instantly discern the impact of her paintings that was conditioned by her art education. In many ways, the questions Frankenthaler always asked when analyzing work by other artists and her own were the questions Paul Feeley, her mentor at Bennington College, impressed on her to consider: "What made them work? What was 'light' in a painting? What did that cadmium red [dot on a horizon in a Corot] painting do to the rest of the picture? Would it work without it? Were there other reds in it? If it were in another spot, would it work as well? Similar questions were asked about the placement of a pipe in a 1910 Georges Braque or the yellow square in a Piet Mondrian."[92]

The "rightness" in Frankenthaler's paintings conformed to the high standards of acknowledged masterpieces, and in this sense were a continuity with the past. In contrast, Morris Louis admonished his students to "avoid painting anything that had been done before. Go to museums if you must," he told them, "but destroy any work of your own that is vaguely reminiscent of the past."[93] Similarly, Olitski took great pains to unlearn his art education, and even tried painting blindfolded to free himself from his training.[94] He aspired to produce the appearance of pigment suspended in space in his paintings, but none of his experiments achieved this effect until he turned to the unconventional use of the air gun. Where this apparatus provided Olitski a way to mist his paintings, Bradley saw it as a means to pour as much pigment onto his painting as fast as possible.

Stella, whose life-work seems to have taken the most dramatic twists and turns of all the Color Field artists, sees a coherent logic in his work in retrospect, such as his grappling with the problem of how to make a painting that was all figure and no ground, which has been a preoccupation since his earliest notched and shaped canvases of the 1960s to his current paintings that occupy real space. His changing thoughts about perception also influenced the course his paintings followed. Seeking to create an image that the viewer could absorb in a flash, Stella opted for arrangements of single simple geometric forms early on (pl. 40, pp. 92–93 and pl. 42, p. 95). He later came to the realization that the mind could actually take in more visual complexity at once than he originally assumed, which led him to create the elaborate compositions of multiple shapes, such as *Organdie* (1997; fig. 15, p. 118), that have characterized his paintings since the 1990s.[95] It might seem impossible to reconcile the chaotic drift in his paintings of the 1990s with the rational geometry of his canvases of the 1960s. Stella, in fact, devised two contrasting systems of organization to stabilize each type of painting; he bridled the fluctuating spatial occurrences in works such as the Mitered Mazes (pl. 40, pp. 92–93) and Concentric Squares (pl. 42, p. 95) of the 1960s and 1970s by containing them within the simple geometry of the square, whereas he unified the complex arrangements in the abstractions of the 1990s into a single image by keeping the perceptual space at a consistent, measurable distance from the viewer. He summed up the shift in pictorial organization as: complicated space bound within a simple geometric form, or a maximum of complicated shapes counterbalanced by essential and constant pictorial space. Both methods produced works that can be perceived within a single glance.[96] "Fussiness" remains a criteria by which Stella judges his work.[97]

Stella's continued experimentation through the 1990s and 2000s reveals his deep involvement and fascination with organic growth forms, from the spiriling Mitered Mazes of the 1960s to the 3D images of bifurcating smoke rings of more recent work (fig. 15, p. 118). His engagement with Chaos theory and infinitely complex fractal mathematical shapes in the late 1980s reinforced his early intuitive response to the rhythmic patterns found in nature and mathematical principles that govern the universe. Far from divorcing his paintings from life as the Formalist critics had contended, Stella's work is fully immersed in the glories of the world.

Experiments in perception also led some of the artists to explore peripheral vision. Olitski's experiments resulted in canvases such as *Yellow Looshe* (1968; pl. 30, pp. 72–73), which is over six feet high and more than twenty-one feet wide. Without a defined center, Olitski sets the viewer's eye adrift in a nebulous space until it hits more defined shapes at the painting's lower left that redirects the gaze back into the painting.

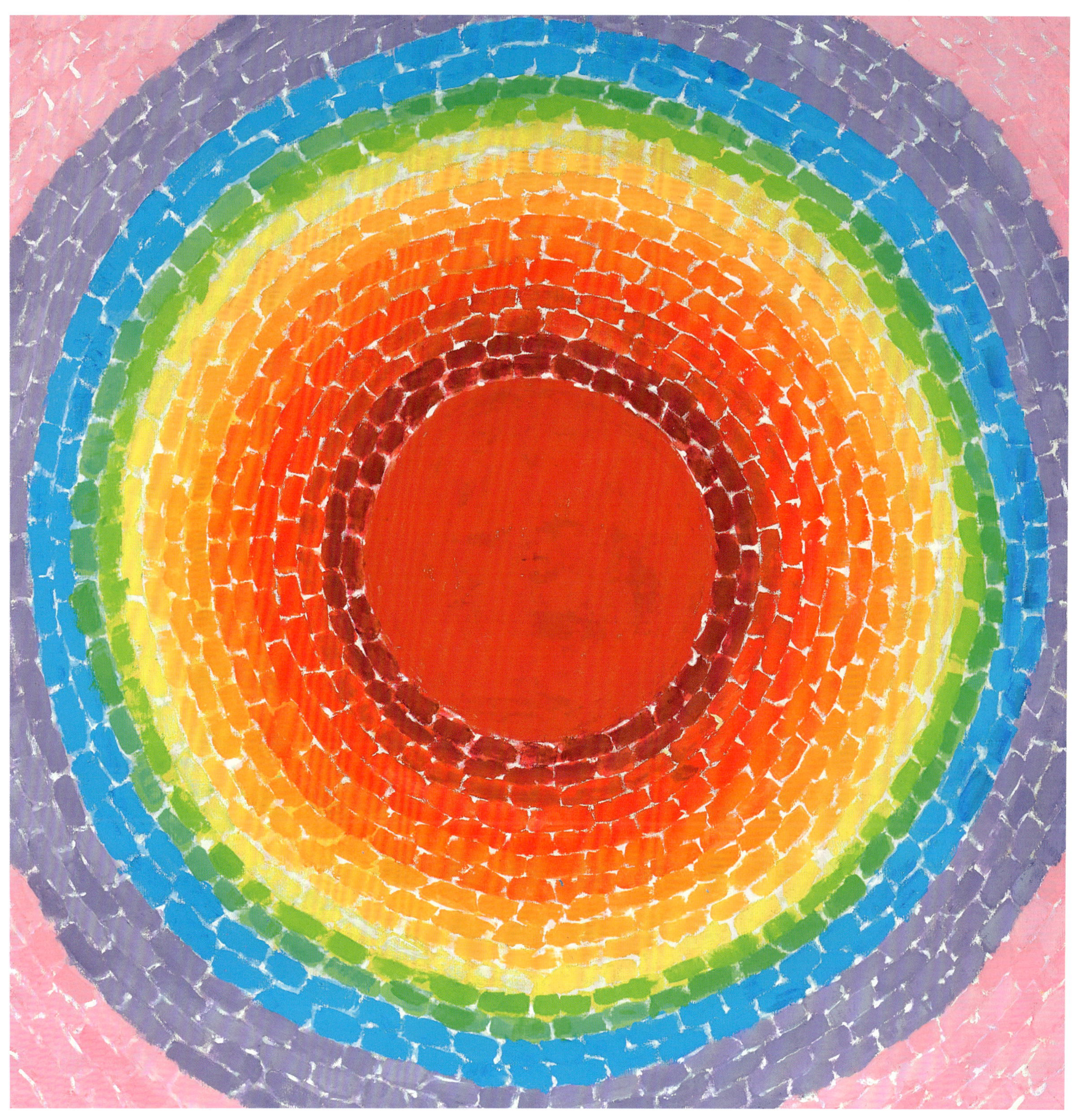

Alma Thomas
44 **A Fantastic Sunset, 1970**
Acrylic on canvas, 48 × 48 in. (121.9 × 121.9 cm)
Anonymous

Noland painted narrow canvases scored with parallel bands of color that stretched to 30-feet wide. Likewise, Stella tested the limits of human peripheral vision in his monumental elliptical Race Track paintings of 1973, *Deauville* and *Agua Caliente* (each measuring 10 × 45 feet). Focusing at the painting's center, the oblong extremities just barely enter the viewer's field. As with all of his paintings, Stella expects viewers to glance at them from a single spot, where their central vision is sharpest. Nevertheless, viewers grasp that Stella's Race Track paintings and Noland's extralong Stripe paintings appear basically the same no matter where they position themselves to view them. These artists' interest in the mechanics of seeing was distinct from the Op art paintings of Victor Vaserely and Bridget Riley, which were dependent on optical illusions.

Serendipity, chance, and opportunity also drove experimentation. When Hopps invited Gilliam to work in spaces thirty-by-sixty feet for his exhibition at the Corcoran Art Gallery in 1969, Gilliam responded by making his first Drape paintings (pl. 11, p. 39) and tacking twenty-five-yard sections of canvas to the wall rather than stretching individual paintings on wooden supports. Al Loving's visit to an exhibition of American quilts at the Whitney Museum in 1971 and a solo exhibition of Black collagist and art activist Romare Bearden at the Museum of Modern Art the same year prompted him to make paintings from scraps of painted or dyed fabrics he sewed together to form multi-layered, patchwork paintings (pl. 21, p. 59).[98] Poons' paintings took a startling turn in 1971 after Greenberg drew his attention to the residual drips and splatters of paint he spotted in his studio. Poons immediately saw potential in these haphazard paint spills, and began throwing full pails of paint onto rolls of unstretched canvas covering the walls surrounding him as he worked. Unlike his early minimal Dot and Ellipse paintings that were worked out in advance within the painting's rectangular format, these free-form paintings, known as Throw paintings, were cut out of the entire canvas roll after it was painted. Poons would mark off sections of the canvas with masking tape to crop individual paintings.[99] He cut *Lady Accessoire*, *"To Clara from Robert,"* and *The Morning Lies in the Afternoon Sun* (pls. 35–37, pp. 84–85) from the same painted roll of canvas in 1976. Although his early Dot paintings and the Throws look dissimilar, the overall unified image remains a constant.

Color Field painting was made possible in part by the new commercially produced fast-drying synthetic paints called Magna in the late 1940s. Developed by Leonard Bocour and Sam Golden, Magna had a high concentration of color that maintained its intensity even when thinned by turpentine. In the late 1950s, Bocour and Golden marketed the paint to artists by giving them samples to try out. The artists in turn would report back their satisfaction with the medium. When soaked into the raw canvas, the pigment and turpentine would separate, resulting in the ghosting effect that is particularly evident on the unpainted surfaces. The next generation of fast-drying water-based acrylic paint, which became available in the mid-1950s, especially appealed to the Color Field artists as it could be thinned with water or acrylic medium to a stain without losing its intensity. Mixing the paint with acrylic medium produced a glossy or matte finish, which the artists exploited to create novel light and textural effects. Both Magna and water-based acrylics could be applied in thin layers. As Wilkin notes, "The transparent, glowing layers of Louis' Veils … could only have been achieved because he used Magna … while Olitski's nuanced sprays of the 1960s (pls. 28–30, pp. 70–73) similarly depended upon the physical characteristics of acrylic at the time he made them."[100] The same could be said about the velvety rich wine and plumb shapes in Frankenthaler's *Wine Dark* (1965; pl. 8, p. 33).

Stella experimented with a variety of industrial paints, including house paints, epoxy enamel, and metallic paints and "daylight fluorescent" which he began using in the 1960s (pl. 40, pp. 92–93). Developed between the 1930s and 1950s, fluorescent paints were primarily used by the American military during World War II to paint aircrafts and produce fabrics for troops to "ensure visibility and safety,"[101] as well as by graphic designers to grab consumers' attention. Even Donald Desky's successful bullseye Tide logo was updated in 1959 with contrasting rings of fluorescent yellow and orange that signal to the consumer that this brand of detergent would get their wash brighter than bright.

Fluorescent paints' intense visibility made it an ideal medium for Stella who aimed not only to direct the viewers' sight to his paintings but heighten their consciousness of the process of seeing, while their garish colors challenged conventions of taste in art. Other artists similarly chose colors that ran counter to the tasteful decorum of traditional painting. Bowling, for instance, opted to use fluorescent, metallic and pearlescent spray paints as they were favored by graffiti artists (pl. 1, p. 17).[102]

Greenberg's opinions and evaluations of artists' work also evolved over time. In an interview from 1966, he clarified that it was not just a "so-called formal problem," it was "a question of feeling." Further stating that Newman, Rothko, and Still, and subsequently Louis, Noland, Olitski, and Bush "startled" him with their color in a way other painters did not.[103] In this sense, one could imagine that Greenberg's analysis started from his attempts at trying to understand for himself why these artists' paintings had such a profound impact on him. In 1978, he published a postscript to his 1960 essay regarding the "rationale" of Modernist art, in which he corrected what he perceived as an error in the reception of his discourse, "one of interpretation and not of fact."[104] Greenberg remarked that in his original essay he had tried to "account in part for how most of the very best art of the last hundred-odd years came about," but he was not "implying that that's how it *had* to come about, much less that that's how the best art still has to come about."[105] In 1998, art historian Karen Wilkin succinctly summed up Greenberg's writings as "descriptive" rather than "prescriptive."[106] Whether the artists accepted or rejected Greenberg's description of the ultimate thrust of modern painting towards its elemental characteristic of flatness, his writings and critiques furnished them with ideas and ideals to pursue or argue against. Greenberg, himself disparaged how much of his early writing "contributed to the mystification that passes as art criticism," adding, ultimately, good abstract painting is "about life; it's about experience."[107] *Gloriamundi!*

It is hard today to fathom how compelling modern art's overriding ideals of progress, innovation, and originality were to postwar American artists; or how a single critic could be so authoritative and persuasive that he could shape the parameters by which these artists worked and their paintings were judged. These artists' breakthroughs took place at a time when the art historical significance of an artist was based on lineage; in order to be historically relevant, an artist had to inspire future artists as well as further the achievement of artists who preceded them. Greenberg elevated Frankenthaler to this status when he identified her stain paintings as the essential link between Pollock and Louis and Noland. Color Field as a classification of a type of painting was imperfect and limited the appreciation of the scope of each artist's intentions and accomplishments. Although painted decades ago, these paintings exist in the present. What do they say to today's audience? Based on visitor response to the exhibition, *Glory of the World*, these "one-shot paintings" stopped viewers in their tracks and immersed them in their immense swaths of color. Viewers seemed compelled to test their own vision: as they responded to the pictorial space these abstract shapes opened up on the flat picture plane. Today's audience still finds these abstract paintings to be "hard paintings," as they continue to contest preconceived notions about art.

For a new generation of artists, most significantly Eric N. Mack (b. 1987), Color Field continues to hold out the promise of the future of painting. Mack considers himself "essentially a formalist."[108] Growing up in Maryland, near Washington, D.C., he frequented its museums, especially the National Gallery of Art, where he was not only exposed to its exceptional collection of Abstract Expressionist and Color Field paintings, but experienced Frankenthaler's *Mountains and Sea*, the painting credited for launching Color Field.[109] He encountered Gilliam's paintings at a crucial juncture when he was learning the rules of abstraction as a student at an art magnet high school. Mack admired Gilliam's "relentless dedication to paint, the soaked canvas and his connection to Frankenthaler; the way he can really attack the architecture and impose his own kind of language…"[110] A few years after this encounter he saw a Morris Louis exhibition "that began to spur similar questions."[111] Mack's interest in abstraction was further informed as an undergraduate at Cooper Union in New York, where he had professors who identified as second generation Abstract Expressionists, and during graduate school at Yale School of Art (MFA, 2012), where visiting artist Shinique Smith introduced him to using found and personal textiles, and by his exposure to influential revisionist studies and exhibitions, notably art historian Kellie Jones' exhibition *Energy/Experimentation: Black Artists and Abstraction 1964–1980* (Studio Museum in Harlem, 2006). These new studies focused on how the formal experiments by many Black abstract artists reflected and addressed social and political subjects as well as raised questions regarding aesthetic judgement; a subject Mack addressed in an interview reprinted in this book (see Appendix p. 160). Color Field painting offered Mack endless possibilities, such as in his homage to Hofmann, *Tessuti Raponi (Ciao Milano)*, comprised of individual textiles stitched together to form a single pulsating picture plane (fig. 34, p. 138). As he stated, "It's all [about] the degree of questions that maneuver and problem solve with a kind of wit and resourcefulness that eludes traditional means of value."[112] It still boils down to the two dilemmas artists face: What to paint, and how to paint it.

[1] Larry Poons in Conversation with Karen Wilkin/ Episode Six: Ambition (video). Produced in conjunction with the exhibition *Color as Field: American Painting 1950-1975*, American Federation of Arts, 2007.
[2] "Jackson Pollock: Is he the greatest painter in the United States," *Life*, August 8, 1949, pp. 42–45. Photographs by Arnold Newman.
[3] "Irascible Group of Advanced Artists Led Fight Against Show," *Life*, January 15, 1951, pp. 34–38. Photograph by Nina Leen.
[4] Michael Seuphor, "Paris–New York 1951," *Art d'aujourd'hui*, 1951. English translation by Francine du Plessix and Florence Weinstein, in *Modern Artists in America*, eds. Robert Motherwell and Ad Reinhardt (New York: Wittenborn Schultz, 1951), p. 118–22. According to the editors of *Modern Artists in America*, Seuphor "is perhaps the first European to deal in his article … sympathetically and understandably with the history and present status of American avant-garde art…," p. 118.
[5] Ibid.
[6] "'Artists' Sessions at Studio 35," ed. Robert Goodnough, in *Modern Artists in America*, pp. 8–22.
[7] In Ibid., p. 20.
[8] Ibid.
[9] *Defining Modern Art: Selected Writings by Alfred Barr*, eds. Irving Sandler and Amy Newman (New York: Harry N. Abrams, 1986), p. 41.
[10] Frank Stella in conversation with the author, 2017.
[11] Frank Stella, "Bombs Away: Hans Hofmann at 2000," in Bonnie Clearwater, *Frank Stella at Two Thousand: Changing the Rules* (North Miami, FL: Museum of Contemporary Art North Miami, 1999), p. 106. See Appendix pp. 158–60.
[12] The focus of this book is on American painting between the early 1950s to 1983. The development of painting in Europe during the same period followed a different course shaped by the conditions artists faced after World War II, as well as the dynamic of various artists' collectives, cohorts, and academies of art. While the logical conclusion of Greenberg, Michael Fried and other American formalists' theories would toll the death of painting, the medium revived with new vigor by the late 1970s in America with Neo-Expressionism. American artists such as David Salle and Julian Schnabel, countered the modernist tenet of progress, and concluded that there was no difference whether they painted figures or abstractions, it was all painting. The novelty of this new direction in painting that arose in Europe as well as in the United States, received major global attention in blockbuster exhibitions in Europe, including the 1981 exhibition that assumed various titles at each venue—*Westkunst* in Cologne, *Zeitgeist* in West Berlin, and *A New Spirit of Painting* at the Royal Academy, London. A collision between Minimal art and Neo-Expressionism transpired at the major international art exhibition Documenta 7, Kassel, Germany, 1982.
[13] Harold Rosenberg, "The American action painters," *ARTnews*, December 1952, p. 23.

[14] Clement Greenberg, "American-Type Painting" (1955, 1958); reprinted in Clement Greenberg, *Art and Culture: Critical Essays* (Boston, MA: Beacon, 1961, 1965), p. 209.
[15] Ibid., p. 225.
[16] Prior to painting *Mountains and Sea*, Frankenthaler was influenced by the way de Kooning created enclosed spaces with his lines, which he filled in with paint. The remnants of these looping lines or "keyhole views" as Frankenthaler called them, are still present in *Mountains and Sea*, especially in the upper region. These became less pronounced in subsequent paintings as the thinned pigment itself spread out to define each shape's contours.
[17] In *The New York Tapes: Alan Solomon's Interviews for Television, 1965-66*, ed. Matthew Simms (New York–Washington, D.C.: Circle and Archives of American Art, 2022), pp. 388–89.
[18] In Ibid., p. 304.
[19] Ibid., pp. 304–05.
[20] Ibid., p. 305.
[21] *Oral history interview with Kenneth Noland, 1987 July 1-16*, by Avis Berman, transcript, Archives of American Art, Smithsonian Institution, Washington, D.C. (aaa.si.edu).
[22] Clement Greenberg, "Louis and Noland," *Art International*, May 1960. See Appendix pp. 151–54.
[23] William Rubin, "Younger American Painters," *Art International,* January 1960. See Appendix pp. 147–51.
[24] In *The New York Tapes*, p. 367.
[25] Karen Wilkin in conversation with the author, September 2023.
[26] Greenberg was describing Louis' paintings in this quote but it applied to Frankenthaler's technique as well. See Appendix pp. 152–53.
[27] In James Truitt, "Art—Arid D.C. Harbors Touted 'New' Painters!" *Washington Post*, December 1961, p. A.20.
[28] Frankenthaler in conversation with the author, 2002, quoted in Bonnie Clearwater, *Frankenthaler: Paintings on Paper* (North Miami, FL: Museum of Contemporary Art North Miami, 2003), p. 9.
[29] Ibid., p. 11.
[30] Frank Stella, "The Pratt Lecture," presented at Pratt Institute, New York, Winter 1960. Reprinted in Brenda Richardson, *Frank Stella: The Black Paintings* (Baltimore, MD: Baltimore Museum of Art, 1976), p. 78.
[31] Irving Sandler noted that "Painterly Painting" was the artists' preferred neutral term as opposed to "Abstract Expressionism" and "Action Painting," which most artists rejected. See Irving Sandler, *American Art of the 1960s* (New York: Harper & Row, 1988), p. 17.
[32] Barnett Newman, "What about Isolationist Art?," in *Barnett Newman: Selected Writings and Interviews*, ed. John P. O'Neill (Berkeley–Los Angeles, CA: University of California Press, 1992), p. 23. Newman wrote this article in 1943 but never published it.
[33] Larry Poons in *The New York Tapes*, p. 409.
[34] Carl Little, "Jack Bush's Stripes and Solids," *Hyperallergic* (March 2, 2019), hyperallergic.com
[35] Conversation with the author, 1999.
[36] In *The New York Tapes*, p. 375.
[37] Mary Gabriel, *Ninth Street Women* (New York: Little Brown, 2017) and Prudence Pfeiffer, *The Slip* (New York: Harper Collins, 2023).
[38] *Modern Artists in America*, p. 124.
[39] In "Appendix A, 'The Western Round Table on Modern Art, San Francisco, 1949', in *West Coast Duchamp*, ed. Bonnie Clearwater (Miami Beach: Grassfield, 1991), p. 111.
[40] Ibid., p. 108.
[41] Ibid., pp. 106–07.
[42] In "A Conversation with Sam Gilliam," with Hans Ulrich Obrist, *Sam Gilliam: Existed, Existing* (New York: Pace, 2020), p. 53.
[43] Ibid.
[44] Ibid.
[45] In "Questions to Stella and Judd," Interview by Bruce Glasser, ed. Lucy R. Lippard, *Minimal Art: A Critical Anthology,* ed. Gregory Battcock (New York: E.P. Dutton, 1968), p. 148.
[46] In *The New York Tapes*, p. 290.
[47] Noland used the term "one-shot painting" to describe the appeal of Frankenthaler's *Mountains and Sea.* He remarked, that it was "a phrase we'd [sic]used [at] that particular time … We were very interested in the idea of … making a picture quickly, put everything down [at] once, and without it being modified or re-worked and letting it stand … first off." In *The New York Tapes*, p. 304.
[48] In "Questions to Stella and Judd," p. 150.
[49] Ibid.
[50] Greenberg, "Modernist Painting," *Art & Literature*, Spring 1983, p. 87. Reprinted in *Ethics Contemporary*, ed. Richard Kostelanetz (Buffalo, NY: Prometheus Books, 1978 [rev. ed. 1988]), p. 196: Greenberg noted how the singular self-defining condition of painting is its flatness, as it "was the only condition that painting shared with no other art."
[51] The elimination of the conventions of illusory pictorial space (perspective and light-and-dark modeling) by Abstract Expressionists such as Rothko was based on modern scientific and psychological studies, rather than a desire to reinforce the flatness of the picture plane as Greenberg proposed. In Rothko's treatise on his philosophy of art, written in the 1940s (unpublished until 2004 as *The Artist's Reality: Philosophies of Art*, ed. with introduction by Christopher Rothko, New Haven: Yale University Press, pp. 59–61), he described two modes of space intuition: the tactile type and the visual or illusory type. In tactile space, the viewer has the sense of an actual physical and tangible sensation of recession and advancement. It is a space that is known by touch, even when only sensed by the eye. Illusory space (created by perspective and light-to-dark modeling), in contrast, is systematic. Rothko dismissed perspective on the grounds that modern psychology proved that this is not the way the human eye perceives space. Moreover, as science had proven that air is an actual substance, with a pressure of fifteen pounds per square inch, he began conceiving his pictures as "a plate of jelly" in which "a series of objects are impressed at various depths" (Ibid., p. 56). For Rothko, choosing between illusory and tactile space was a philosophical rather than a formal issue. He agreed with art historian Bernard Berenson, that tactile space appeals to the primal impulse in humans who in infancy learn about the world through touch. Rothko used color to structure tactile shapes that seem to have real dimension, density and weight, without resorting to perspective. For a full analysis of Rothko's philosophy of pictorial space, see Bonnie Clearwater, *The Rothko Book* (London: Tate, 2006), pp. 74–78. See Clearwater, "Mark Rothko:

The Training of a Future Artist," *The Seduction of Light: Ammi Phillips/Mark Rothko* (New York: American Folk Art Museum, 2008), pp. 15–18, for Rothko's research on tactile space.

[52] Conversation with the author, 2002.

[53] In *Painters Painting,* documentary film, 1972.

[54] In "Questions to Stella and Judd," p. 158.

[55] Stella confirmed this rephrasing in 1999 when I proposed it in the text for the exhibition catalogue (See Clearwater, *Frank Stella at Two Thousand*, p. 27). Additionally, in 1991 he wrote "What the best art does, consciously or otherwise is to never lose its connection to the immediate, everyday, ever-present perceptions" (Stella, "Grimm's Ecstasy," in Clearwater, *Frank Stella at Two Thousand*, p. 68).

[56] See Bonnie Clearwater, *Roy Lichtenstein: Inside/Outside* (North Miami, FL: Museum of Contemporary Art North Miami, 2001) for a discussion on the teachings of Hoyt Sherman at Ohio State University.

[57] György Kepes, *Language of Vision*, with introduction essays by S. Giedion and S.I. Hayakawa, first published, 1944 (Chicago: Paul Theobald, 1967). Kepes acknowledged the influence of the Berlin-based Gestalt psychologists on his theories.

[58] Albers left Black Mountain College in 1950 to chair the department of design at Yale University, New Haven, Connecticut (through 1958), where, following the Bauhaus model he integrated the curriculum to include all the arts under the common purpose of design. Hungarian-born Kepes was an acolyte of the Hungarian photographer László Moholy-Nagy, who taught at the Dessau Bauhaus. Kepes brought the teachings of the Bauhaus to Chicago, where he directed the new Institute of Design (1937-43), popularly known as the New Bauhaus. He subsequently founded the interdisciplinary research laboratory, the Center for Advanced Visual Studies, at Massachusetts Institute of Technology (MIT), Cambridge, Massachusetts, in 1968 where he served until 1972. For an in-depth study on Kepes and the influence of the Bauhaus in America, see John R. Brakinger, *György Kepes: Undreaming the Bauhaus* (Cambridge, MA: The MIT Press, 2019).

[59] Kepes, *Language of Vision*, introductory essay, p. 7.

[60] Ibid., p. 60.

[61] Charles Biederman, *Art as the Evolution of Visual Knowledge* (Red Wing, MN: Charles Biederman, 1948), p. 7. American abstract artist Charles Biederman was a leading figure in the postwar international Constructivist art movement of geometric art that was concurrent with Color Field. He wrote *Art as the Evolution of Visual Knowledge* during World War II as a treatise on art history in terms of the evolution of "visual thinking." His influential theories made significant inroads in America, Canada, and Europe. Biederman contended that art history is essentially "a process of scientific development...in which ever greater insight has been gained into the natural laws of the world and how best to utilize them for making a useful art," in ibid., p. X. Biederman wrote his book as a reaction to the role propaganda had played during the Nazi regime. He warned, the propagandist "knows that few realize the possibilities of using language in such a way as not only to misrepresent the facts, but also to lead us altogether into a world of fiction" (p. 7). He advocated for the creation of art works that would encourage an empirical understanding of the physical laws of the world. Noting that we exist in the four dimensions measured by height, width, depth, and time, he created constructions that emphasize this reality with three-dimensional forms rather than the illusory pictorial space of painting on a flat surface. Viewers experience these constructions in real time, as these three-dimensional works require them to move position in order to view them from various directions. The Constructivists' three-dimensional shapes cast real shadows that change depending on lighting conditions, thereby raising awareness to the fourth dimension of time.

[62] In Barbara Rose, "Rebel With A Cause: The 1950s and 1960s," in *Larry Poons* (New York–London: Abeville Press, 2023), p. 25.

[63] Lichtenstein thought primarily in formal abstract terms. He selected cartoon imagery for his Pop paintings based on whether he could do "something aesthetic with it" (see Interview with John Jones, Archives of American Art, Smithsonian Institution, Washington, D.C., October 5, 1965, transcript, p. 7). Once the cartoon image was selected, he drew it on the canvas, "then it became a process of painting in traditional ways but not with traditional means," (in Interview with John Jones, p. 4). Lichtenstein considered his paintings simultaneously figurative and abstract, acknowledging that the "formal statement" in his work would become "clearer in time" (See G. R. Swenson, "What is Pop Art? Answers from 8 painters, Part I," *ARTnews*, November 1963, p. 63).

[64] Oral history interview with Kenneth Noland.

[65] In Interview with John Jones, p. 8.

[66] Clement Greenberg, "Avant-Garde and Kitsch," in *Art and Culture*, pp. 3-21.

[67] In "Questions to Stella and Judd," p. 150.

[68] *Post-Painterly Abstraction* traveled to the Walker Art Center, Minneapolis, and the Art Gallery of Toronto (now known as the Art Gallery of Toronto). In 1966, Greenberg estimated that he visited Washington, D.C. every six months in the late 1950s and early 1960s, in *The New York Tapes*, p. 369.

[69] In multiple interviews and correspondence, Peter Bradley and Frank Bowling noted that Greenberg was one of the few American critics to support the work of Black artists. Bowling, for instance, recalled in an interview in 2018, that Greenberg was ultimately the person who convinced him to pursue his passion (Zachary Small, "Historical Memory Haunts Frank Bowling's New Paintings," *Hyperallergic*, October 1, 2018). His correspondence with the critic is preserved at the Tate in London, while Greenberg's with Bowling are housed at the Archives of American Art, Smithsonian Institution, in Clement Greenberg papers (Box 1, Folder 81). Bradley noted that "the only one[s] who said I had great talent was [sic] Kenneth Noland and Clement Greenberg ("Peter Bradley: A Life in Paint," Getty Trust Oral History Project, African American Art History Initiative, Getty Research Institute, Interview conducted by Adrianna Campbell and Shanna Farrell, 2019, p. 36).

[70] Greenberg encouraged Bowling to "think" the way he was thinking in his critical writing but to get it into his work rather than his writings, in "Frank Bowling with Alex Bacon," *The Brooklyn Rail*, July/August 2023.

[71] See *Soul of a Nation: Art in the Age of Black Power* (London: Tate, 2017), pp. 80-87, 106, for an

overview of the controversies concerning exhibitions organized by museums, including *Harlem on My Mind* (Metropolitan Museum of Art, New York, 1969) and *Contemporary Black Artists in America* (Whitney Museum of American Art, 1971), among others in the United Sates and the responses by the Black Emergency Cultural Coalition (BECC) to these exhibitions. See Ibid p. 84, for a synopsis of abstract exhibitions organized by Black artists, including *X to the 4th Power* (Studio Museum in Harlem, 1969), organized by William T. Williams, *5 + 1*, curated by Frank Bowling (State University of New York, Stony Brook, and Princeton University, 1969), and *The De Luxe Show*, curated by Peter Bradley (Houston: DeLuxe Theater, 1971). See Mark Godfrey, "Notes on Black Abstraction," in *Soul of a Nation*, p. 148, regarding criticism of Black abstract painters by writers associated with the Black Arts Movement.

[72] "Frank Bowling with Alex Bacon."

[73] Godfrey, "Notes On Black Abstraction," p. 165.

[74] Ibid.

[75] In Oliver Basciano, "Sam Gilliam Obituary," *The Guardian*, June 30, 2022.

[76] In "The Deluxe Show: Art Goes to the People," *Southwest Art Gallery Magazine*, September 1972, p. 14. See Bridget R. Cooks, "Revisiting the Deluxe Show: Black, White and 'Hard Art in Houston, 1971," *Gulf Coast,* vol. 26, Winter/Spring 2013, p. 246.

[77] In "De Luxe Interview with Clement Greenberg," with Simone Bradley, *The De Luxe Show*, Houston, Texas, 1971, exh. cat., p. 65.

[78] In "Conversation with Peter Bradley, Curator of The Deluxe Show," Simone Bradley, *The De Luxe Show*, p. 70.

[79] In "De Luxe Interview with Clement Greenberg," p. 65.

[80] The exhibition, *Color as Field: American Painting 1950-1975*, curated by Karen Wilkin for the American Federation of Arts, was the first full-scale examination of Color Field. This traveling exhibition opened at the Smithsonian American Art Museum in 2008, and was accompanied by a catalogue with essays by Wilkin and Carl Belz. The exhibition *The Shape of Color* (Art Gallery of Ontario, 2005), which explored Color Field from 1950 to 2005, also included Gilliam's work.

[81] Karma, New York, and Parker Gallery, Los Angeles, restaged Peter Bradley's pioneering exhibition, *The De Luxe Show* at their galleries in 2021, and published an accompanying catalogue with text by Amber Jamilla Musser and Bridget R. Cooks.

[82] Dore Ashton, "Art: A Change of Style; Newman Shows Paintings at French & Co. in First Exhibition Here Since 1951," *The New York Times*, March 12, 1959, p. 28.

[83] In a conversation with the author in 1999, Stella noted that he conceived each of the bands of his Stripe paintings as "one individual gesture that connects together with the other bands."

[84] In William S. Rubin, *Frank Stella* (New York: The Museum of Modern Art, 1970), p. 15.

[85] Conversation with the author, 1999.

[86] In "A symposium on How to combine Architecture, Painting and Sculpture," *Interiors*, 110, no. 10 (May 1951), p. 108.

[87] Thomas in *Alma W. Thomas: A Retrospective of the Paintings* (Fort Wayne: Museum of Art, 1998), p. 106.

[88] Dieter Buchhart, "Living Color," in *Peter Bradley: Ruling Light 1970s*, ed. Dieter Buchhart (New York: Karma, 2023), p. 11.

[89] Greenberg, "Modernist Painting," p. 87.

[90] In the 1980s, Stella discovered a sun hat in Rio de Janeiro that introduced not only a new image into his work but furthered his investigations into a concept of a truly inhabitable pictorial space (his "kids" bought it for him from a souvenir shop). The hat was a flat piece of foam rubber with cut radial curves fanning out from its center. He was drawn to the spatial properties of this headgear, which could be transformed from two dimensions to a fully-volumetric dome, when pulled over one's head. As Stella remarked, "the transformation of the beach hat is truly amazing. Using it without any particular effort or skill, one can create from a bland planar object complex spaces with complex surfaces" (Frank Stella, "Grimm's Ecstasy," in Clearwater, *Frank Stella at Two Thousand*, p. 62, ills. p. 18).

[91] In Clearwater, *Frankenthaler: Paintings on Paper*, p. 9.

[92] In Ibid., p. 12, p. 34, n. 12. Bracketed text denotes Frankenthaler's edit to the original quote published in John Elderfield, *Helen Frankenthaler* (New York: Abrams, 1989), p. 4.

[93] John Elderfield, *Morris Louis* (New York: Museum of Modern Art, 1987), p. 19.

[94] Kenneth Moffett, *Jules Olitski* (Boston: Museum of Fine Art, 1973), p. 34.

[95] Stella, "Grimm's Ecstay," in Clearwater, *Frank Stella at Two Thousand*, p. 66: "All of the recent developments in visual arts indicate that our minds do and want to embrace many objects and many situations at the same time."

[96] Conversation with the author, 2000.

[97] In *The New York Tapes,* p. 440. Stella used the word "fussy" to describe his early compositions (predating his breakout Black Stripe paintings, 1958–60).

[98] Godfrey, "Notes on Black Abstraction," *Soul of a Nation*, p. 148.

[99] Karen Wilkin, "A Controlled Moment of Light," in *Larry Poons*, p. 91.

[100] Ibid.

[101] DayGlo Color Corp, "History of Daylight Fluorescent Pigments," dayglo.com

[102] "Mapping a Life in Paint: An Interview with Frank Bowling," by Carolina Harris, Alexxa Gotthardt and Cristina Chan, July 2023.

[103] In *The New York Tapes*, p. 378.

[104] Clement Greenberg, Postscript to "Modernist Painting," in *Ethics Contemporary*, p. 201. Greenberg further noted that the quotation marks around "pure" and "purity" should have alerted the reader that he used these terms as a "useful illusion" and that it was erroneous to deduce from his writings that he used "flatness" as a criteria of aesthetic judgement.

[105] Ibid.

[106] Karen Wilkin, "The real Greenberg," *The New Criterion*, June 1998.

[107] In *The New York Tapes*, p. 381.

[108] In *Lux et Veritas: Pushing a White Wall*, ed. Bonnie Clearwater (Milan: Skira, 2023), p. 136.

[109] Ibid., p. 157.

[110] Ibid., p. 152.

[111] Ibid.

[112] Ibid,. p. 158.

The following color plates document the exhibition *Glory of the World: Color Field Painting (Early 1950s to 1983)*. The descriptions of each artist's works follow the layout of the exhibition. Multiple works by an artist are listed in the first entry for each artist.

Hans Hofmann
b. 1880, Weissenburg in Bayern, Germany; d. 1966, New York

Hans Hofmann's paintings marked the high bar that many of the Color Field artists aimed to achieve. The German-born artist emigrated to the United States in 1932. Having studied art in Paris from 1904 to 1914, when modern art itself was still new, Hofmann brought the excitement of the avant-garde to a new generation of artists in New York who were seeking to find their own artistic paths that would equal or surpass their European counterparts. In 1933 he opened his art school in New York, where he taught his methods for translating the sensation of three-dimensionality onto the two dimensions of the flat picture plane. He referred to this method as "push-and-pull" to describe the perceptual shifts in colored planes as they project forward and recede back into space. He instructed students how to counteract the movement of these shapes so that the overall composition was anchored to the flat picture plane.

Hofmann's paintings, such as *Gloriamundi* (1963; fig. 2), which range from expressionistic abstraction to geometric abstractions consisting of bold slabs of color, such as his late painting *Iris* (1964–65; pl. 15, p. 45), demonstrate the principles of push-and-pull. His influence on the American Abstract Expressionists and the Color Field artists was succinctly expressed by Frank Stella in 1999:

> We revere Hofmann ... for proving that the straightforward manipulation of pigment can create exalted art. Simply put, Hofmann's ability to handle paint, to fuse the action of painting and drawing into a single, immediate gesture carried colored pigment into the viewer's presence with the force of a bomb.[1]

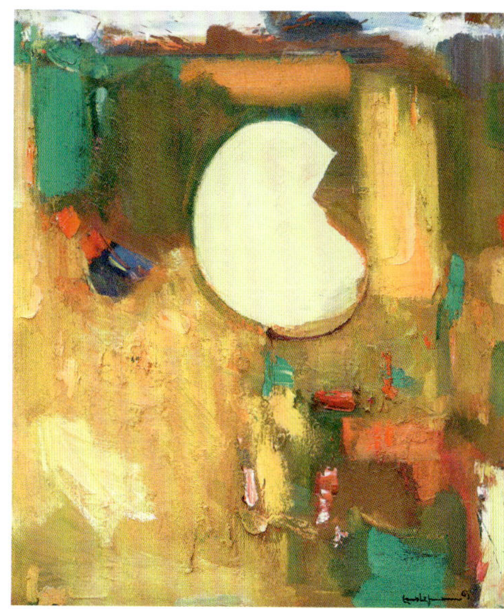

Fig. 2 Hans Hofmann
Gloriamundi, 1963
Oil on canvas
60⅛ × 52 in. (152.7 × 132 cm)
University of California, Berkeley Art Museum and Pacific Film Archive, gift of Hans Hofmann with permission of the Renate, Hans & Maria Hofmann Trust

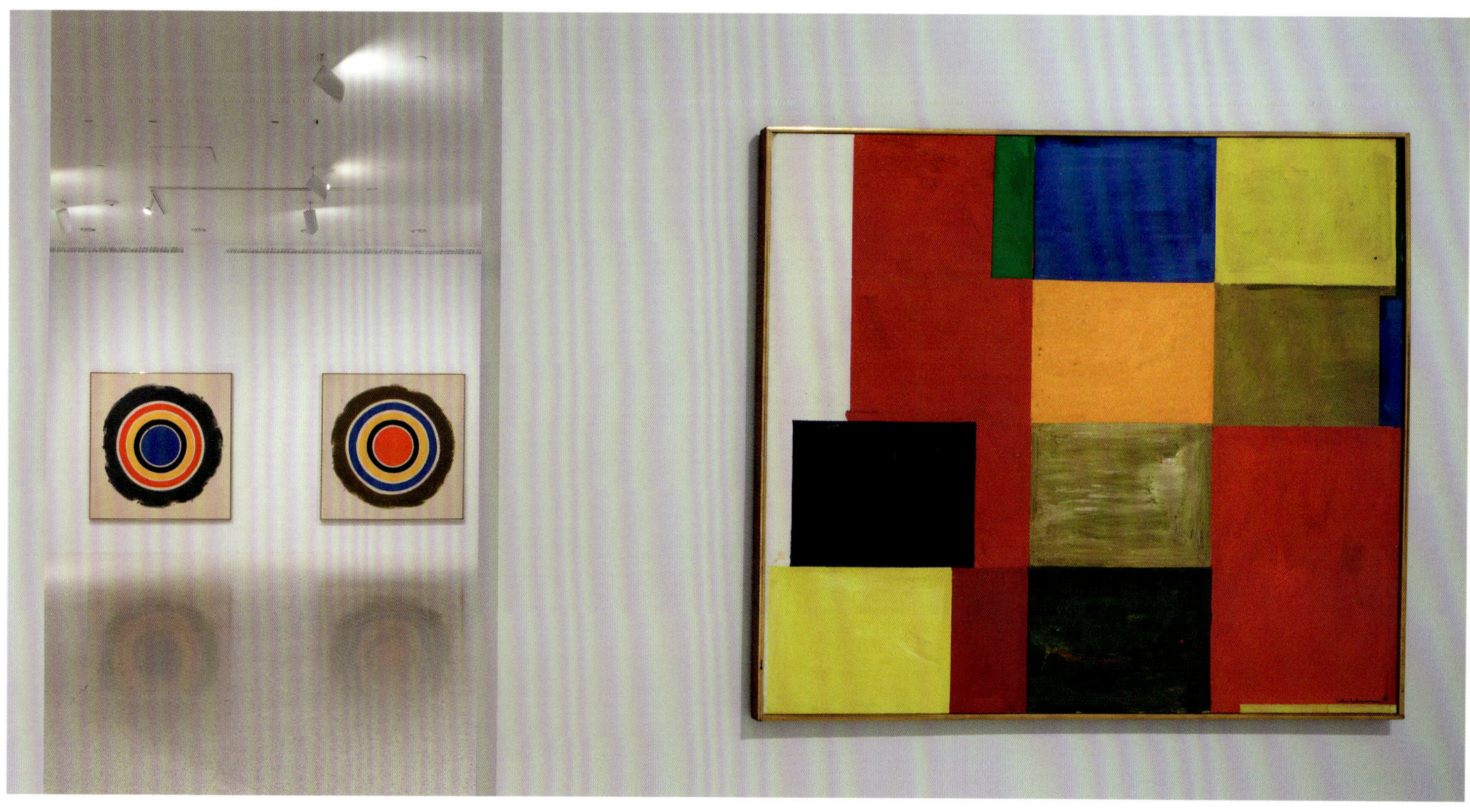

Fig. 1 Left to right:
Kenneth Noland, *That*, 1958–59
Kenneth Noland, *This*, 1958–59
Hans Hofmann, *Iris*, 1964–65

Adolph Gottlieb
b. 1903, New York; d. 1974, New York

Adolph Gottlieb was among the founding artists of Abstract Expressionism. One of the problems with classifying artists by art movements is that it rarely takes into account that they continue to live, work, and change their focus and methods beyond the time period of the art movement they helped to define. Gottlieb was especially close to Mark Rothko in their formative years. Both abandoned expressionistic figurative painting in the late 1930s in favor of creating abstract symbols to convey the universality of ancient myths. Gottlieb's solution was to divide his compositions into several rectangular compartments in which he inserted personal symbols. The grids of these paintings, known as Pictographs, suggest building blocks of ancient edifices incised with hieroglyphics.

By the early 1950s Rothko had achieved his classic painting of shimmering blocks of color unified into a single iconic image, while Gottlieb began his Imaginary Landscape series, comprised of horizontal canvases divided into two registers enlivened by vivid rudimentary shapes such as glowing orbs suggestive of the regenerative power of nature. The Imaginary Landscapes established Gottlieb as a forerunner of Color Field. His subsequent Burst series begun in 1957, consisting of vertical compositions of elemental forms unified in a single, immediate image, coincided with the formative stage of Louis, Noland, and Stella's search for a new direction in abstract painting. Both generations of American abstract artists shared a similar relation to the history of art. As Gottlieb stated in 1950, "If we depart from tradition, it is with our of knowledge, not innocence."[2]

Gottlieb's late painting, *Green Turbulence* (1968; pl. 14, pp. 42–43), further distills the symbolic forms that remained a constant throughout his career on a monumental scale that are akin to the Color Field artists' immersive paintings. Although he divided his painting into two distinct registers, he held the entire image in check through the generation of energy fields that simultaneously repel and attract each form rather than through the conventional means of composing a painting by balancing its parts within the structure of the rectangular support. Even the small yellow orb that looks like it is trying to escape the painting itself is immobilized by the gravitational pull of the green mass in the bottom register. Although the image appears frozen in place, each element simmers with an inner light within a vast white field that gives this painting its breath and life. The blue orb is even encircled by a slight aura emanating from a substratum of magenta paint.

Fig. 3 Left to right:
Frank Stella, *Zolder—ONE ELEMENT*, 1982
Al Loving, *Untitled*, 1975
Adolph Gottlieb, *Green Turbulence*, 1968

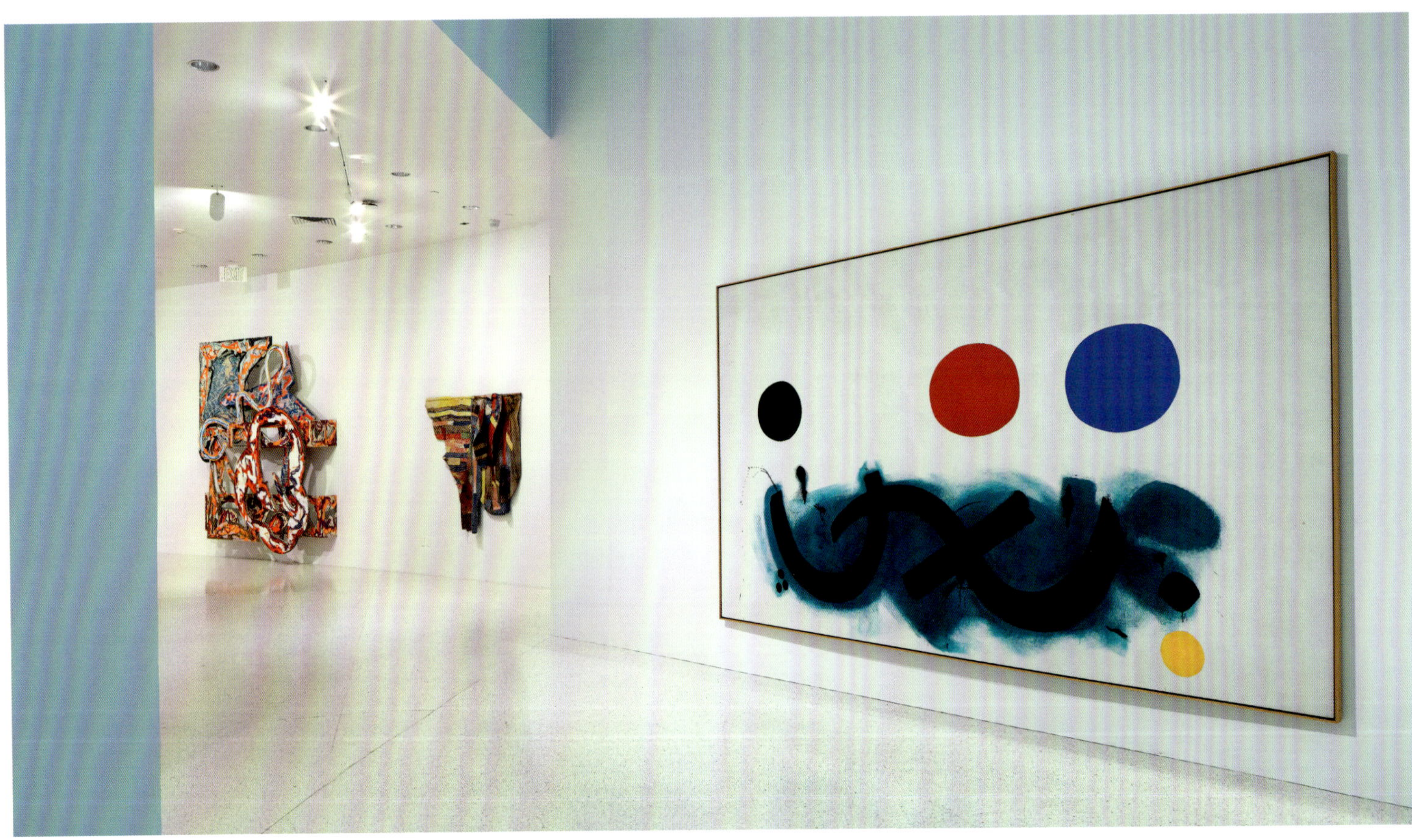

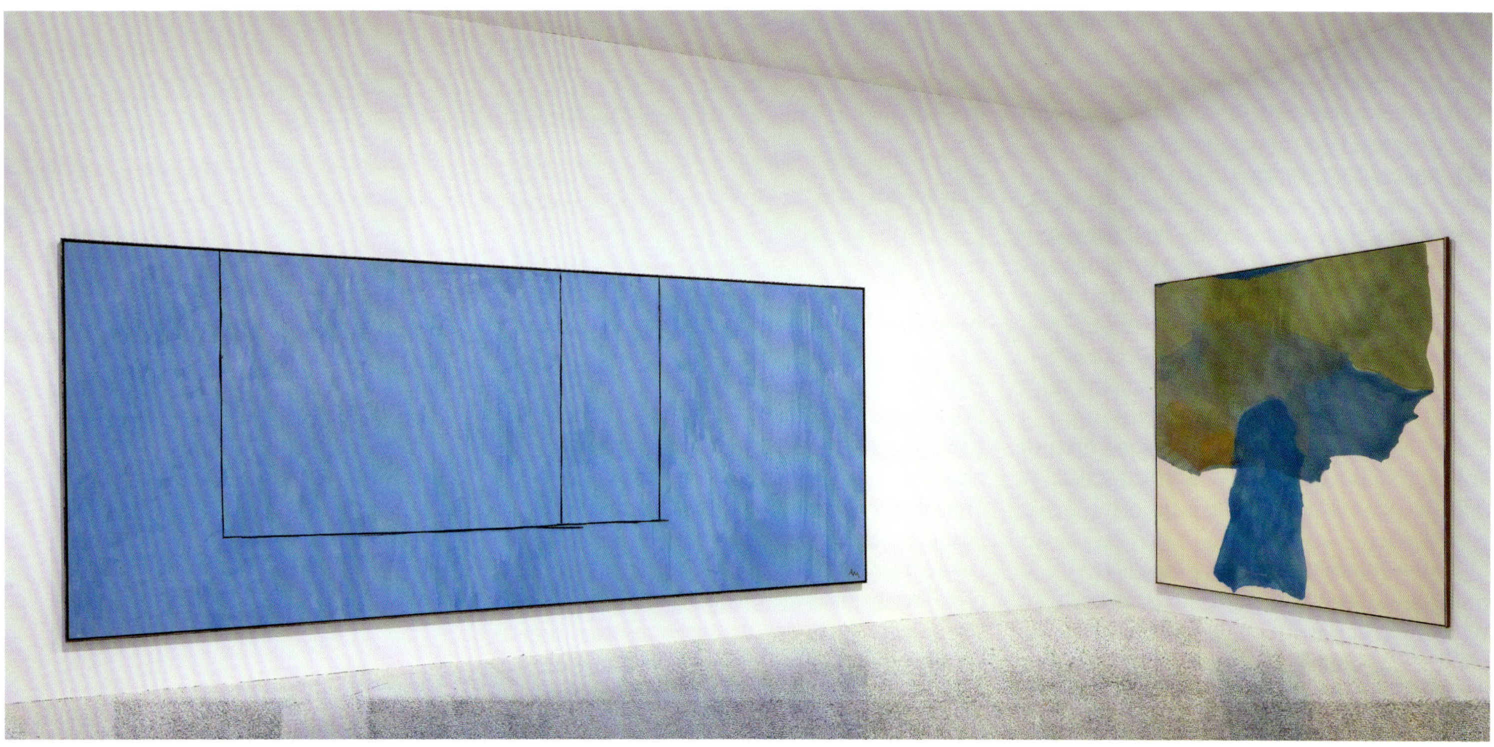

Fig. 4 Left to right:
Robert Motherwell, *Open #149: In Ultramarine with Charcoal Line*, 1970
Helen Frankenthaler, *Signal*, 1969

Helen Frankenthaler
b. 1928, New York; d. 2011, Darien, CT

Few artists ever make it into art history. Even fewer actually influence the direction of art. Helen Frankenthaler is recognized among the trailblazers of modern painting. With her large-scale painting *Mountains and Sea* (1952; fig. 5), Frankenthaler innovated the soak-stain painting technique by applying greatly diluted paint onto raw canvas. This painting was widely acknowledged as an important link between the poured paintings of Jackson Pollock (fig. 6) and Color Field painting. The velvety rich *Wine Dark* (1965; pl. 8, p. 33) and *Signal* (1969; pl. 9, p. 35) exemplify how Frankenthaler expanded Pollock's fluid lines into broad areas of color that flow into each other and interlock with the unpainted canvas to form a unified picture plane. Frankenthaler would often start a new painting by first addressing the negative space of the unprimed canvas, which in turn shaped the stained areas. This resulted in paintings in which the white, unpainted areas are equal in value to the painted shapes. Consequently, the blank canvas is read as active positive space rather than negative space or background.

Frankenthaler met Greenberg in 1950 when she organized an alumni exhibition in New York for her Alma Mater, Bennington College, Vermont. By the time the two met, her opinions and artistic vision were fully formed thanks to

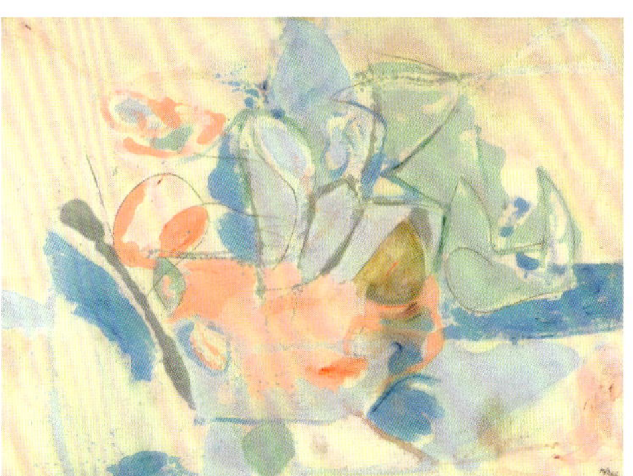

Fig. 5 Helen Frankenthaler
Mountains and Sea, 1952
Oil and charcoal on canvas
86⅝ × 117⅝ in. (220 × 298.8 cm)
Collection Helen Frankenthaler Foundation, New York, on extended loan to the National Gallery of Art, Washington, D.C.

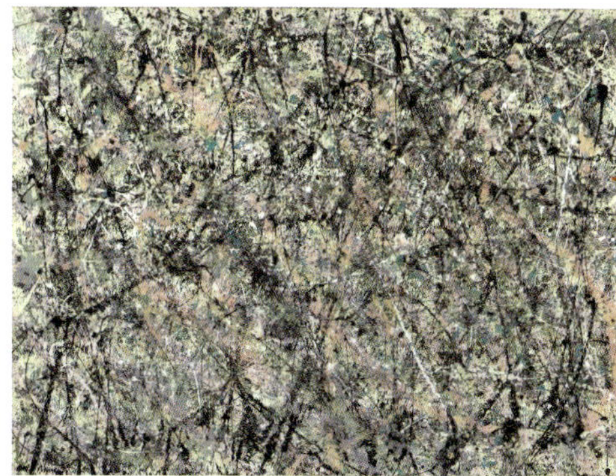

Fig. 6 Jackson Pollock
Number 1, 1950 (Lavender Mist), 1950
Oil, enamel, and aluminum on canvas
87 × 118 in. (221 × 299.7 cm)
National Gallery of Art, Ailsa Mellon Bruce Fund

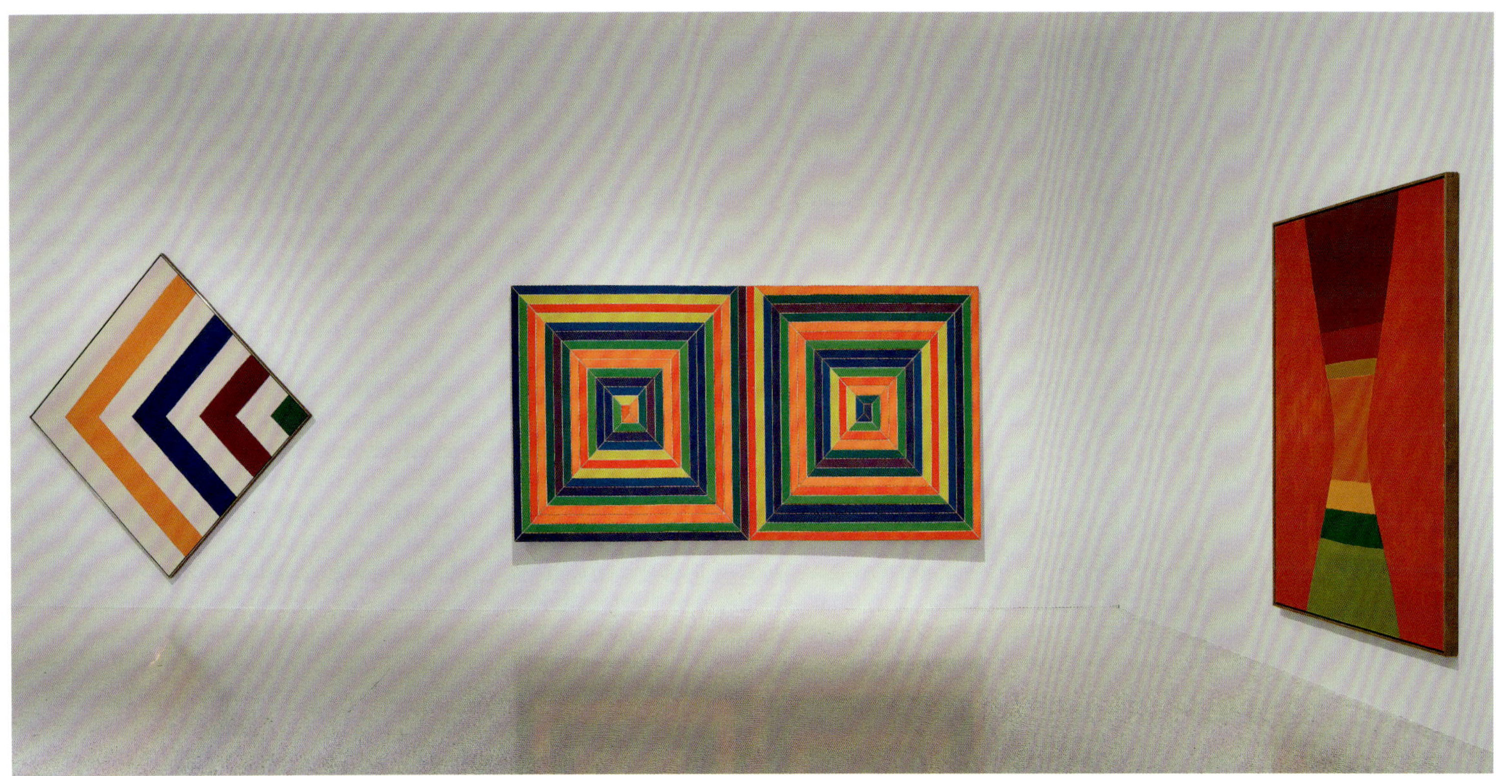

Fig. 11 Left to right:
Kenneth Noland, *Carriage*, 1964
Frank Stella, *Fortín de las Flores*, 1966
Jack Bush, *Pinched Orange*, 1964

art."[5] Although the image is recognizable at a single glance, these paintings continuously seem to radiate outward and contract inward the longer the viewer gazes at them.

Concentric patterns were used by both Noland and Jasper Johns at the same time to different ends. William Rubin made this distinction in his 1960 article "Younger American Painters." After describing the uncanny effect of Johns' target paintings, in which he made his subjects "identical with the pictorial field" itself, he makes it clear that Noland's central motif is not a target, rather "They should be called simply concentric circle compositions."[6] Artists are keenly aware that the viewer does not perceive a figurative image and an abstract one the same way. As Rubin pointed out, Johns confronts the viewer with a familiar object. Presented without context, Johns' target becomes surreal and enigmatic (see Appendix pp. 147–51).[7]

Although Noland's concentric circle paintings are abstract, the geometric shape is a knowable archetype. Its origins in Noland's work occur as rough and ragged circular bursts in paintings of the early 1950s. By the late 1950s, his stain-painted concentric patterns, such as in *This* and *That* (1958–59; pls. 23 and 24, pp. 64–65), share the generative power of Gottlieb's Bursts series that predates these paintings. Noland was not just painting a geometric pattern, rather the centrifugal force of the whipping outer band splattered with sputtering paint droplets in *This* and *That* creates the effect that it is fueling the power at its core, akin to the formation of the eye of a hurricane or the compression of atomic power.

These two paintings were originally paired in a single giant vertical painting (14-by-7 feet) titled *This and That*. In 1961, he installed this initial vertical state with one concentric circle stacked over the other in his solo exhibition in the New Gallery at Bennington College, Vermont. (The barn-like construction of the gallery had a wall tall enough to accommodate the upright *This and That*; fig. 10.) One of the installation photographs shows the painting towering over the artist standing beside it. This arrangement created the visual sensation of two orbs propelling away from or towards each other. In 1963, Noland dissected the work into two 82-inch square canvases that were in proportion to the viewer. These two separate, symmetrical paintings (one titled *This* and the other *That*) have their own focal point that commands the viewer's attention. The more confined space of the square compresses the energy of each concentric circle as it spins outward and inward.[8]

While color is the dominant force in Noland's paintings, his color sense is more intuitive than that of Josef Albers, whose theory sought to describe the way the placement and position of colors influence how the eye perceives them. It also differs from Hofmann's technique of push-and-pull to create the illusion of space, depth, and movement with abstract shapes.

Noland selected the chevron motif for another open-ended series. Chevrons also offered a range of possibilities to mine. Although abstract, this ancient V-shaped pattern was ubiquitous during Noland's day as a ranking insignia in the military and in commercial logos, most famously as the red, white, and blue emblem for the Standard Oil Company and Chevron (the company's trademark name in the western part of the United States), and in directional signs. Like concentric circles, the chevron could be absorbed in a single glance, however, by rotating the canvas in such paintings as *Carriage* (1964; pl. 25, p. 67) to form a diamond shape, Noland complicated the directional thrust of the pattern. Logically, the eye would follow in the direction the arrows point, which in this painting is to the left, but the small green lozenge at the right grabs the viewer's attention. Although viewers might assume they are looking at three complete V-shapes and a fragment of a cropped green one, the unpainted canvas forms four more.

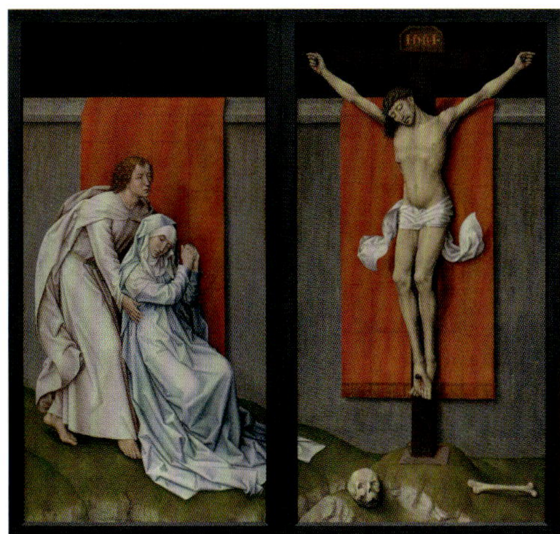

Fig. 12 Rogier van der Weyden
The Crucifixion, with the Virgin and Saint John the Evangelist Mourning, c. 1460
Oil on panel
Left panel: 70 × 35⅜ in. (177.8 × 89.9 cm); right panel: 70⅛ × 35⅝ in. (178.1 × 90.5 cm)
Philadelphia Museum of Art, John G. Johnson Collection, 1917

Frank Stella
b. 1936, Malden, MA; lives and works in New York

An initial spark for Frank Stella's artistic aspirations was the experience of seeing Rogier van der Weyden's early Netherlandish painted panels *The Crucifixion, with the Virgin and Saint John the Evangelist Mourning* (c. 1460) at the Philadelphia Museum of Art while he was a student at Princeton University (fig. 12). Although presumed to be two panels from a triptych devotional piece, Stella experienced it as a diptych as it was commonly known at the time. This work's startling impact gave him a goal to achieve. This revelation charted a new way of understanding Stella's art, in that it favored his ambition to create compelling abstract paintings that could attain the visual potency of van der Weyden's Crucifixion over any quest for pure painting as the overriding impetus that has driven his career-long experimentations.

Stella may seem out of place among the Color Field artists, as his reductive early Stripe paintings are often classified as minimalist or hard-edge painting. To some extent, it was Stella's friendship with this cohort of Color Field artists and their shared aspirations that placed him within their orbit. (Greenberg included Stella in the seminal exhibition *Post-Painterly Painting* in 1964.) Like other Color Field painters, Stella opted for an allover composition that filled the pictorial field. In paintings such as *Fortín de las Flores* (1966; pl. 40, pp. 92–93), from his Mitered Mazes series (in this case, it is a Double Mitered Maze), bands twist and turn in a regimented pattern until the entire surface of the painting is filled. The effect is similar to Pollock's drip paintings, albeit executed with neatly painted straight bands Stella applied with a house-painting brush instead of in fluid loops. Stella conceived his stripes as narrow, self-contained color fields "zipped" together on a single plane. The blurry edges caused by the bleed of the pigment and the pencil-thin gaps of white canvas exposed between the bands breathe life into an otherwise uniform emblem. These gaps were key to keeping his stripes from looking like mechanically drawn and hard-edged paintings.

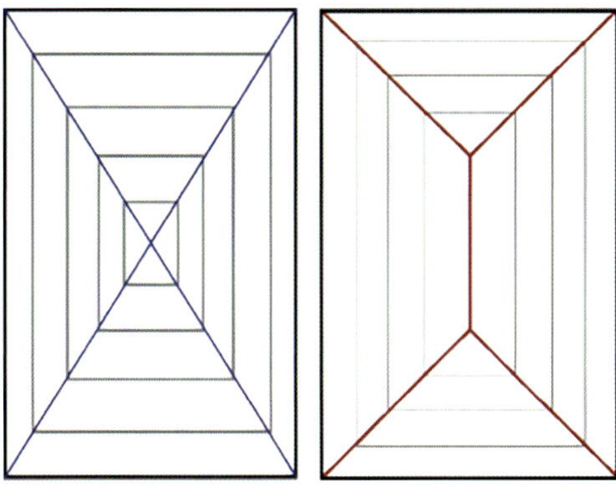

Fig. 13 Two mathematical models for shape constancy. For a rectangle, the algorithmically generated form is highlighted in blue for the Size Constancy hypothesis (left) and in red for the Medial Axis hypothesis (right)
Jackson, Gabrielle (2018). *Seeing what is not seen. Phenomenology and the Cognitive Sciences*. 17.

Rather than staining the canvas, the paint in Stella's paintings stays on the surface, which he sized with a vinyl-soluble glue. He found the way that paint sat atop the canvas appealing as it emphasized the two-dimensional surface of the picture plane. While his peers were experimenting with the newly available artist-grade acrylic paints, which maintained their pigment intensity even when diluted, Stella preferred industrial paints with their higher content of white and harder surface quality. Consequently, his palette appears more muted than other Color Field paintings. Although pencil lines are clearly visible in his paintings, they were there to guide his hand as he applied paint, not as rules to produce hard-edged bands.[9]

Unlike Hofmann, who used color theory to create the pulsating movement of flat planes in his paintings, Stella's color selections are based on predetermined schemes, such as the combinations of primary and secondary colors in *Fortín de las Flores*. In this and other works, Stella used fluorescent paints, a medium that is intended to make objects more visible, thereby leaving no question that this painting was meant not only to be looked at but also to give the viewer a jolt with just a single glance. The Mitered Maze paintings create the illusion of movement and speed, with the bands spiraling outwards and back to the centers of each half. Stella prescribes a quick look at his paintings, as a lingering glance tends to break down the unity of the image. With prolonged observation, viewers may begin to notice how the sharp angles of the mitered edges form rippling diagonals that cause shapes to recede into a vortex, or pop out like an aerial view of a pyramid. Stella discourages this reading as he himself does not see this phenomenon in operation in his paintings.[10]

Fortín de la Flores and other Double Mitered Maze paintings deliver the visual punch of the two conjoined van der Weyden paintings. The Double Mitered Maze paintings look like distillations of the Van der Weyden "diptych," with their division into two equal parts (each with their own focal points), the flattened pictorial space, broad areas of color, and the central V-shape that echoes the upward thrust of Christ's arms. They almost function as visual diagrams of the van der Weyden painting, sharing a dynamic quality akin to the illustration of Gestalt psychology's Principle of Invariance in which "simple geometrical objects are recognized independent of rotation, translation, and scale."[11] (fig. 13)

Stella began his Protractor series in the late 1960s, using the semi-circular shape of protractors (a common drafting tool) to create interlacing bands of color. Although the Protractor series introduces curved shapes that seem to be a departure from the narrow, rectilinear forms of his previous paintings, it is consistent with his thoughts about creating dynamic pictorial space and patterns. This impulse can be traced to a report he wrote at Princeton University comparing Pollock's drip paintings and the interlacing ornamental motifs in early medieval Celtic illuminated manuscripts such as the Book of Kells (c. 800; fig. 14).[12] A visit to Iran, in 1963, where he was mesmerized by elaborate Islamic ornamentation, was another spark for this series. Like Pollock, the Irish Medieval monks, and Islamic artists, Stella produced an elaborate labyrinth of curving lines that create dramatic field shifts. The mysterious labyrinth in *Waskwaiu II* (1968; pl. 41, p. 94), as well as in his Mitered Maze and Double Mitered Maze paintings, appeals to a basic human instinct. The arcs quickly move the sweeps of color around the painting, taking the viewer's eye along the same route. Stella complicated the pictorial space by representing the interlacing curves as though they were transparent colored planes like real plastic drafting tools, an effect created by the alteration that occurs when viewing the color of one segment as it intersects with another.[13] When looking at overlapping forms as in this painting, the viewer tends to assume that the shapes are transparent and therefore exist spatially on two different planes. The viewer mentally shifts the position of the forms so that they constantly alternate between being on or underneath the intersecting shapes. This complicated spatial effect encourages the viewer to focus on the individual segments rather than to comprehend the arc of each semi-circle as a whole. The edges of the square canvas in this series create a tension with the bold arching patterns. Introducing curves into his geometric compositions changed everything, as they created the illusion of pictorial space, which Stella struggled to limit. The Protractor series' dynamic curves played an increasingly important role in Stella's thinking of pictorial space, leading to his three-dimensional paintings such as *Zolder—ONE ELEMENT* (1982; pl. 43, p. 97), which moves the viewer's eye through a circuitous path, but this time, the ride takes place in real space—instead of inert negative space, air fills the voids; instead of illusionistic space, the distance between the "frozen gestures" (cut from industrial honeycomb aluminum) is measurable and the shadows are real. These constructed paintings can be viewed from the sides and the rear as well as from the front.

Stella, like Noland, works in series.[14] Where Noland's various series are open-ended, Stella's are finite as he typically calculates the potential permutations of the arrangement of forms and color combinations in drawings and models before he embarks on a series. In the mid-1970s, Stella reprised the Concentric Square series that he began in 1962. The availability of newly manufactured oversized canvas was one of the impetuses for addressing these paintings anew. The initial Concentric Squares measure an average of six feet square. Scaled to the human body, the viewer can comfortably stand at the painting's center to take the image in at a single glance, whereas the architecturally-scaled later versions (measuring upwards to over 11-feet square) dwarf the viewer who is forced to stand further at a distance to perceive the painting as a whole. In paintings such as *Sacramento No. 6* (1978, pl. 42, p. 95), Stella followed the color spectrum order he used for the bands in the earlier Concentric Squares, however the significantly larger format allowed for the addition of more stripes and a wider range of the color spectrum. While the colored bands are broader, the gaps exposing the white canvas between them are narrowed by the addition of supplemental thinner pale colored stripes. Consequently, the individual bands appear to blend when viewed from a distance. In this painting, Stella painted the smallest white band at the center with white paint instead of leaving it unpainted like the others. This added highlight separates the red square and the first red band which would otherwise merge in the viewer's eye when observed from a distance. The entire painting radiates with the visual jolt of van der Weyden's fifteenth-century masterpiece that inspired Stella during his student years.

Jack Bush
b. 1909, Toronto, Canada; d. 1977, Toronto, Canada

Canada had its own abstract art movement, Painters Eleven, founded in 1954, of which Jack Bush was a member. Influenced by the paintings of Matisse and Frankenthaler, Bush

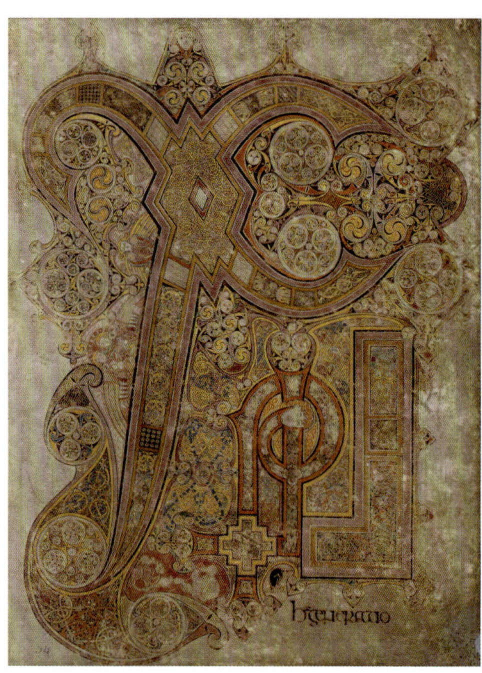

Fig. 14 The Book of Kells, c. 800 A.D.
340 folios, pigments on vellum
Courtesy The Board of Trinity College

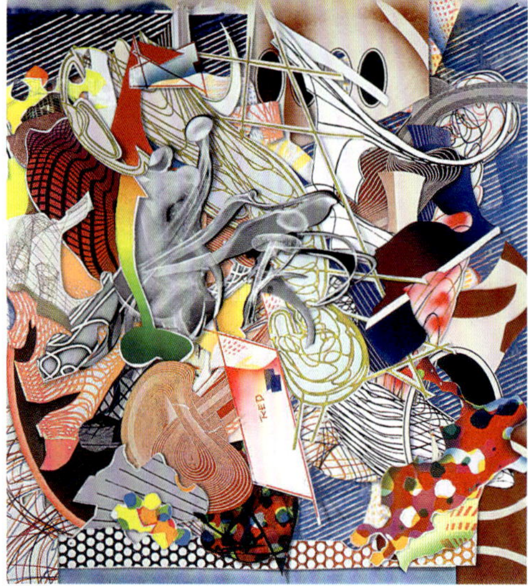

Fig. 15 Frank Stella
Organdie, 1997
Acrylic on canvas
80 × 59 × 40 in. (203.2 × 149.9 × 101.6 cm)
Private Collection, New York

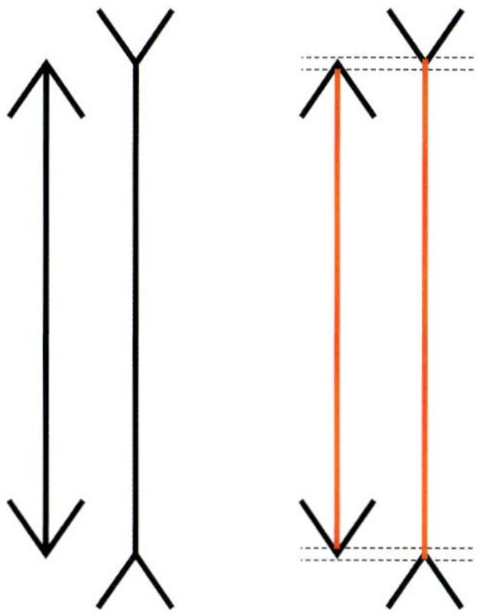

Fig. 16 Example to Illustrate Müller-Lyer illusion in which the vertical lines have the same length

gravitated to the artists associated with Color Field and was mentored by Greenberg, whom he first met in 1957 when the critic made studio visits in Toronto. Greenberg included Bush in the *Post-Painterly Abstraction* exhibition in 1964. Like many of the other Color Field artists, Bush had high ambitions for his painting, stating, "What I'd like to do is hit Matisse's ball out of the park."[15] Bush's paintings seem especially aligned with the playful spirit of Matisse's late paper cut-out collages (begun in the 1940s), where bold colorful shapes are surrounded by equally active negative space. Bush's unique color palette appears to be calibrated to one or two shades off of Matisse's. Bush used a paint brush to apply his thinned-down paints to stretched raw canvas, rarely leaving any part of the surface unpainted. Despite using the stain technique, his paintings are spectacles of intense color.

Bush's compositions exhibit a playful awkwardness, with shapes slightly off kilter or off center, which is counterbalanced by his use of colors of equal intensity or by anchoring the shapes to the painting's edge. *Pinched Orange* (1964; pl. 5, p. 25) plays with the viewer's perception of space by tricking the eye with diagonal lines leading to a vanishing point that disappears mid-way, thereby locking the shapes into their full-frontal architectonic position. The central shape itself was based on a shop-window mannequin attired in a sashed dress.[16] *Pinched Orange*, *Red Column #2* (1963; pl. 4, p. 23), and *January Reds* (1966; pl. 6, pp. 26–27) are suggestive of illustrations of the principles of Gestalt psychology that were popular in the postwar era among artists and in advertising, which Bush, a graphic designer, likely would have known. The Gestalt principle of figure/ground reversal in *Pinched Orange* creates the visual tension one experiences in the ambiguous vase-face illusion, in which the viewer shifts between seeing either the central form or the surrounding area as dominant. It was also an effect Matisse mastered in his paper cut-outs. Likewise, the column in *Red Column #2*, with its inverted capital and base isolated against a blue field, suggests the Gestalt principle of closure that effects the viewer's ability to judge the length of the central shape (fig. 16). Although the title identifies this jaunty flat shape as a column, Bush liberated it from its function as an architectural support. In fact, if the viewer focuses on the diagonals of the column's base and capital, the flat shape seems to transform into a narrow passage that leads out of the dark blue room and towards a luminous red portal. In the case of *January Reds*, Bush used what is known as the "similarity in color contrast" by painting the central shape in three shades of red so close in value that the spectrum of hues only reveals itself over prolonged viewing. Bush's bold, jazzy shapes and saturated hues not only give Matisse some competition, but keep viewers on their toes, as well, by heightening their awareness as to how they make sense of the world through organizing visual cues.

Fig. 17 Left to right:
Jack Bush, *Pinched Orange*, 1964
Jack Bush, *January Reds*, 1966

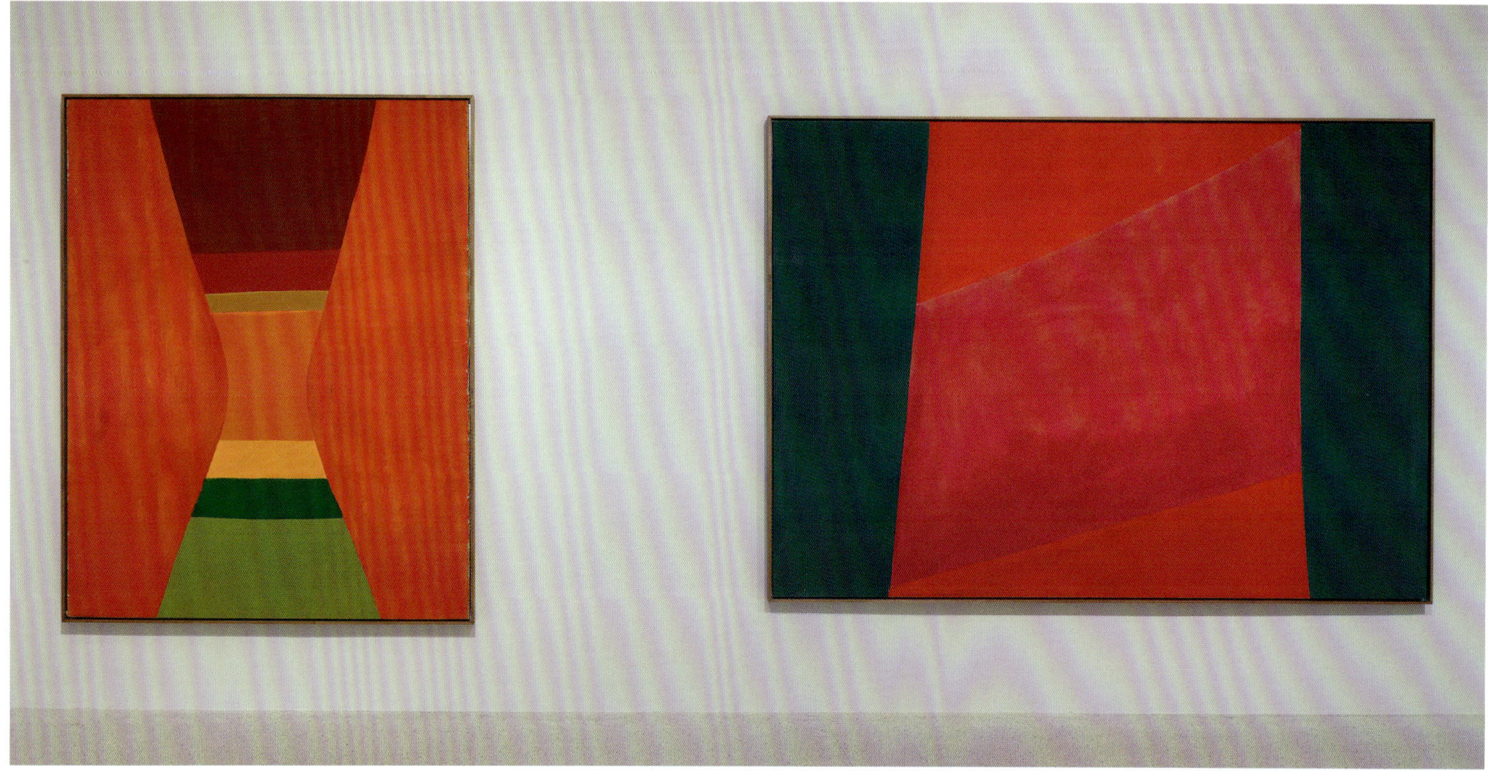

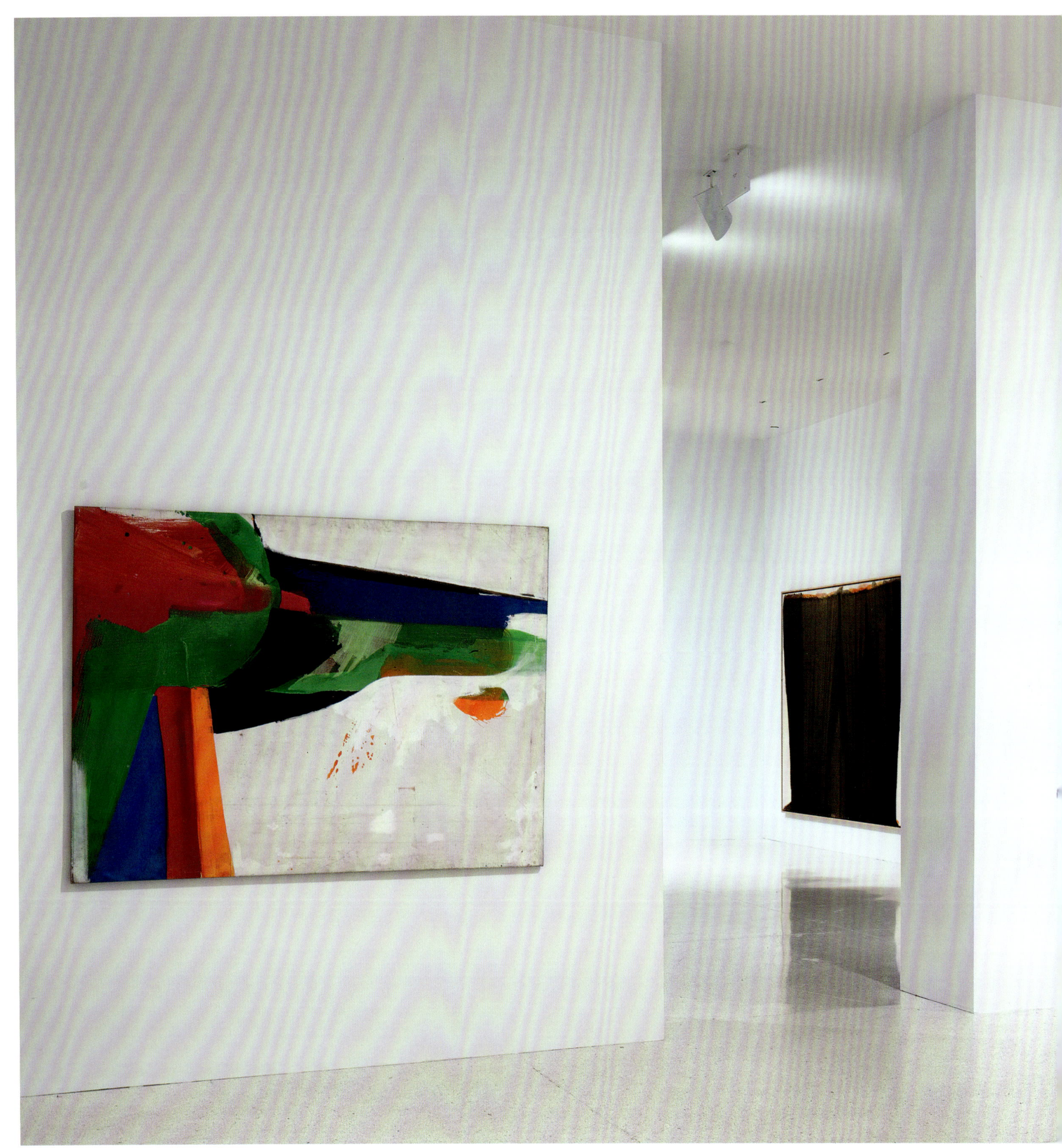

Fig. 18 Left to right:
Edward Clark, *Paris series*, 1966
Morris Louis, *Beth Peh*, 1958
Jack Bush, *Red Column #2*, 1963
Frank Bowling, *Yonder II*, 1972

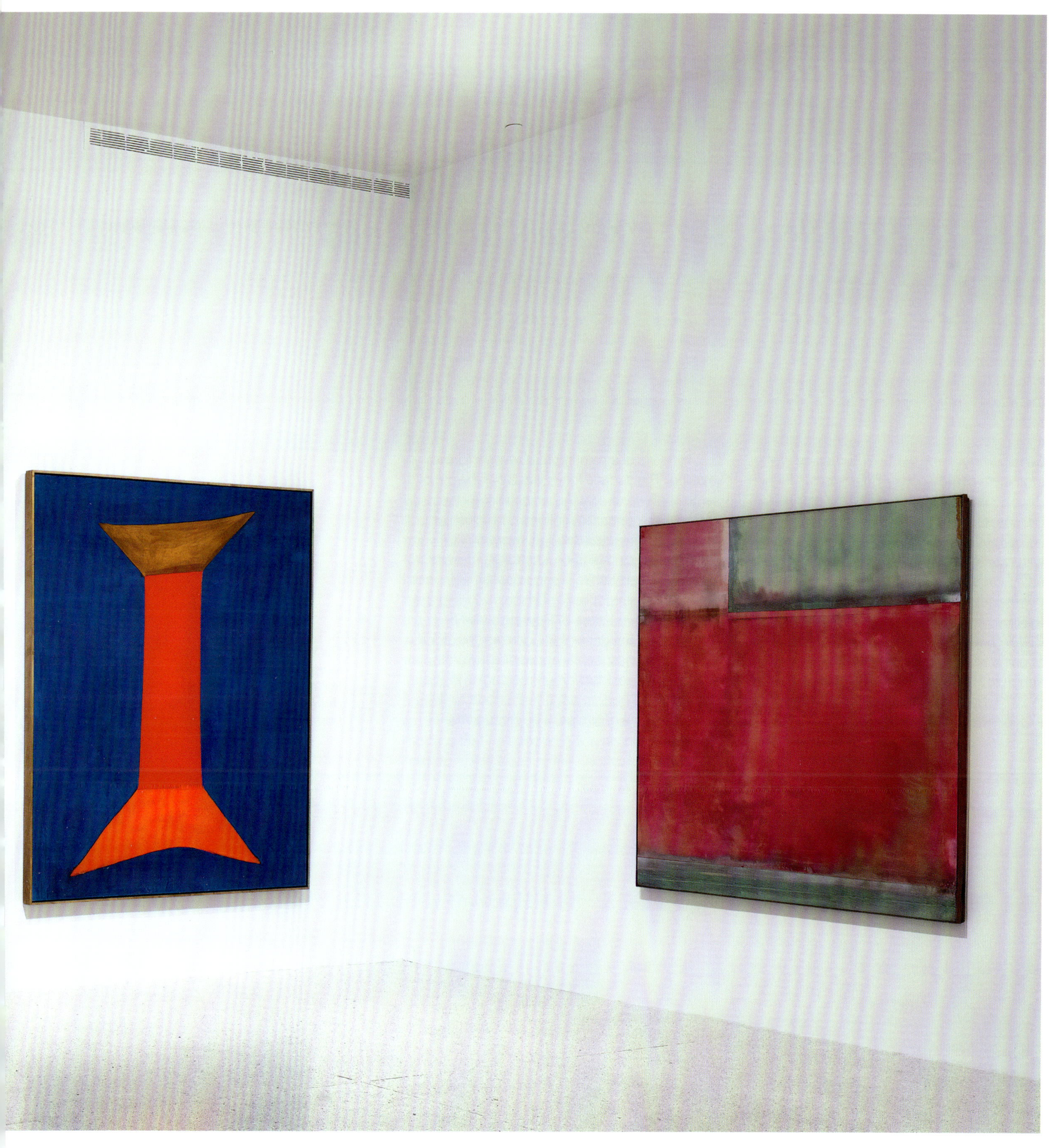

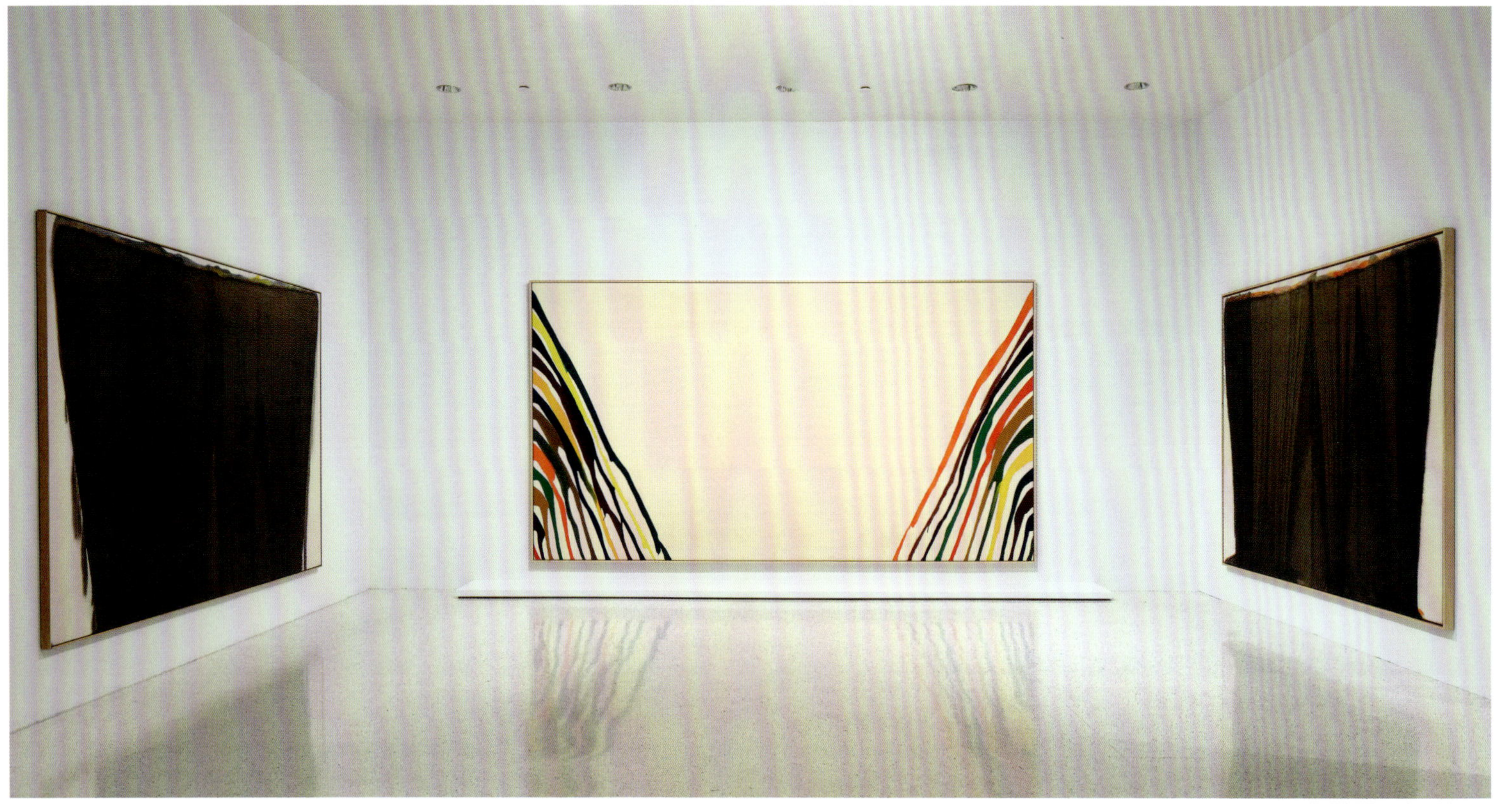

Immersed in Paris' postwar modern art scene, Clark had the ambition to paint on a large scale. In 1956, he found that painting with a push broom especially allowed him to create effects he could not achieve by manipulating a paintbrush with his hand. He continued to innovate this technique, which he called "the big sweep," after moving to New York in 1966 at the height of the city's global ascent in the art world. He found the push broom a particularly effective painting devise as it enabled him to cut through space with great velocity.

Clark allowed the everyday world to enter his work. Rather than paint on pristine canvas, he typically used canvas marred with grime. The result was dynamic swaths of startling color that course right across the bare surface, as in the painting *Paris series* (1966; pl. 31, p. 75). Clark is credited as one of the first contemporary American artists to break away from the confines of the rectangular format. Clark's first shape painting was not planned, rather it was the result of decisions he made while painting a picture on paper. During the process of painting this work, he added elements that extended beyond the edge. Clark consequently built up the stretcher to conform to the shape of the painting. Other artists immediately recognized Clark's innovation when it was shown at the Barta Gallery in December 1957.[26] By 1968, he came to the realization that the human eye does not see rectangles, noting, "I'm interested in the expanding image, and the best way to expand an image is an ellipse."[27] His oblong compositions created a new abstract dynamic that tested the furthest-most limits of the viewer's peripheral vision.

Morris Louis
b. 1912, Baltimore, MD; d. 1962, Washington, D.C.

Morris Louis was already a practicing artist with a significant career when he and Noland encountered Frankenthaler's stain painting *Mountains and Sea* in 1953. Louis found work during the Great Depression, while living in New York from 1936 to 1940, through the easel division of the Works Progress Administration (WPA). He had already begun experimenting with the newly produced Magna paint when he returned to Baltimore in 1948. He subsequently moved to Washington, D.C., where he lived for the remainder of his life.

While *Mountains and Sea* had an immediate impact on Louis, who recognized that Frankenthaler had unlocked the possibilities of Pollock's paintings, it took several years of experimentation both collaboratively with Noland and on his own until he achieved a breakthrough with an unprecedented series of paintings known as the Veils. Louis created these paintings by controlling the spontaneous pours and streams of his diluted paint onto

Fig. 21 Left to right:
Morris Louis, *Lamed Gimel*, 1958
Morris Louis, *Beta Psi*, 1960–61
Morris Louis, *Beth Peh*, 1958

Fig. 22 Left to right:
Helen Frankenthaler, *Wine Dark*, 1965
Morris Louis, *Curtain*, 1959
Morris Louis, *Lamed Gimel*, 1958

Fig. 23 Left to right:
Morris Louis, *Beth Peh*, 1958
Lawrence Poons, *Regulus*, 1985
Morris Louis, *Gothic*, 1958

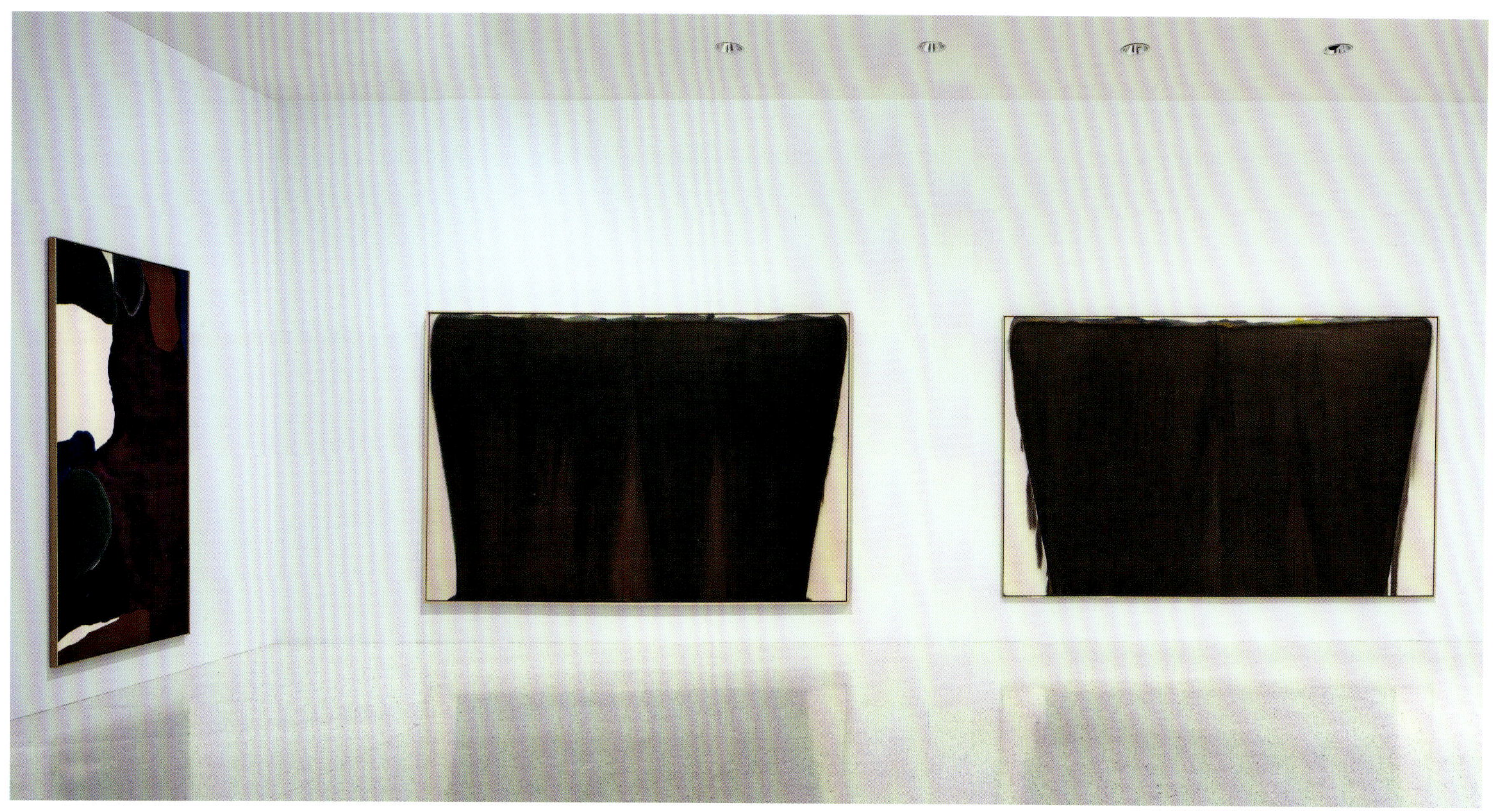

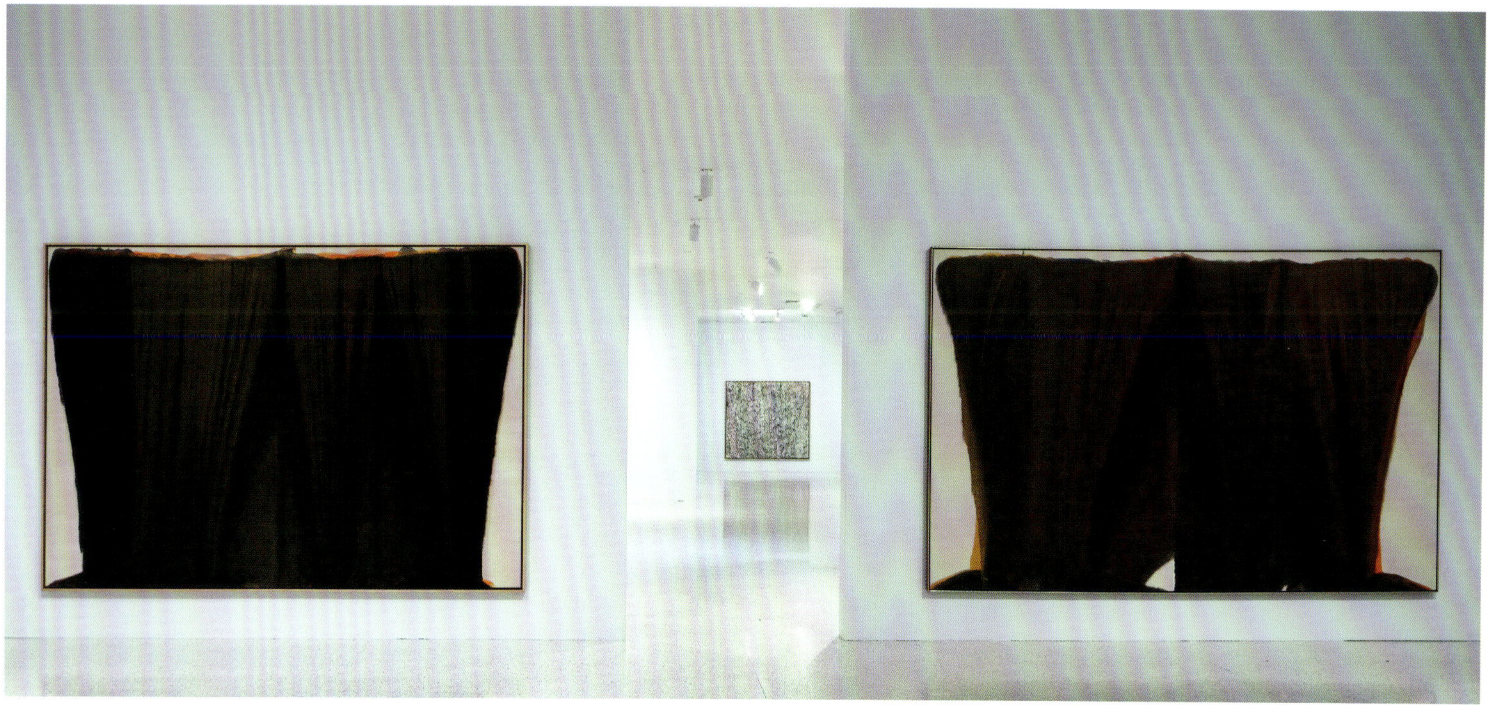

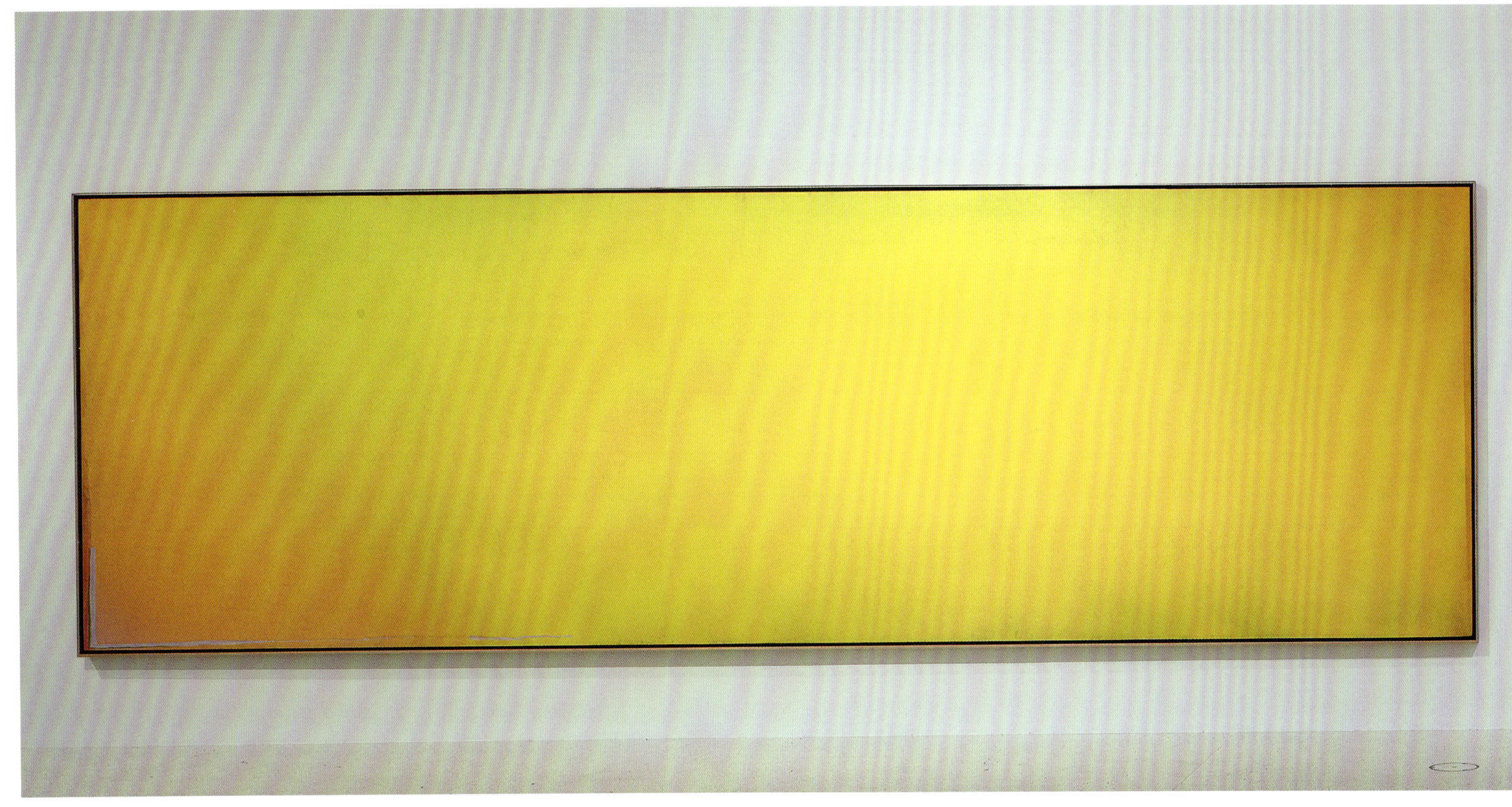

Fig. 24 Left to right:
Jules Olitski, *Yellow Looshe*, 1968
Helen Frankenthaler, *Hint from Bassano*, 1973

unstretched raw canvas. The nearly symmetrical compositions and enormous scale fix viewers in the center of his paintings, where they are confronted with the mysterious, nebulous space produced by the thinly layered pigments. Although the paint soaks directly into the raw canvas, their stratification produces the sensation that viewers could penetrate these paintings. In the Bronze Veils that were included in the exhibition *Glory of the World*, pours of diluted brown and black pigment create a sheer curtain over brighter and more intense colors, some of which radiate through the layers and produce an inner light that becomes more pronounced with prolonged viewing. The monolithic forms stop short of these paintings' sides as well as the top edge, bestowing a density and presence that defies the weightlessness of the watery pigment. Although Greenberg extolled Louis for reducing the tactile quality of painting by using the stain technique, these paintings actually take on the texture of the color saturated canvas and generate perceptible depth through the layering of pigment.

Besides the Veils, Louis produced several series of paintings between 1954 and his untimely death in 1962 at the age of 49, including the Florals, Unfurleds and Stripes.

The Unfurleds were radical in their framing of an unpainted center by multi-colored rivulets of paint flowing from the extremities (pl. 20, pp. 56–57). Unlike the Veils, in which it is difficult to identify the sequence of the colored layers, the viewer can trace the flow of each color as it traverses the canvas and soaks into the weave. The occasional overlaps of color suggest the order of the pours, which contributes to a sensation of depth.

While the viewer encounters Louis' finished works as two-dimensional paintings stretched on a rigid support, the artist experienced them as occupying three-dimensional space as he worked; draping, folding, and pleating the canvas as the thinned pigment soaked into the surface. Louis' studio was so small that he could only see a section of the canvas at a time as he painted. Consequently, the finished painting was as much a revelation to him as it is to the viewer. Oftentimes Louis discovered the composition within the spontaneous paint spills by deciding where to crop the edges of the canvas before stretching it.[28]

Jules Olitski
b. 1922, Snovsk, Russia [now Ukraine];
d. 2007, New York

Jules Olitski emigrated to the United States with his mother in 1923, where they settled in Brooklyn. His early interest in art was stoked by the old master paintings he saw at the New York World's Fair in 1939. With financial aid provided by scholarships and the G.I. Bill,

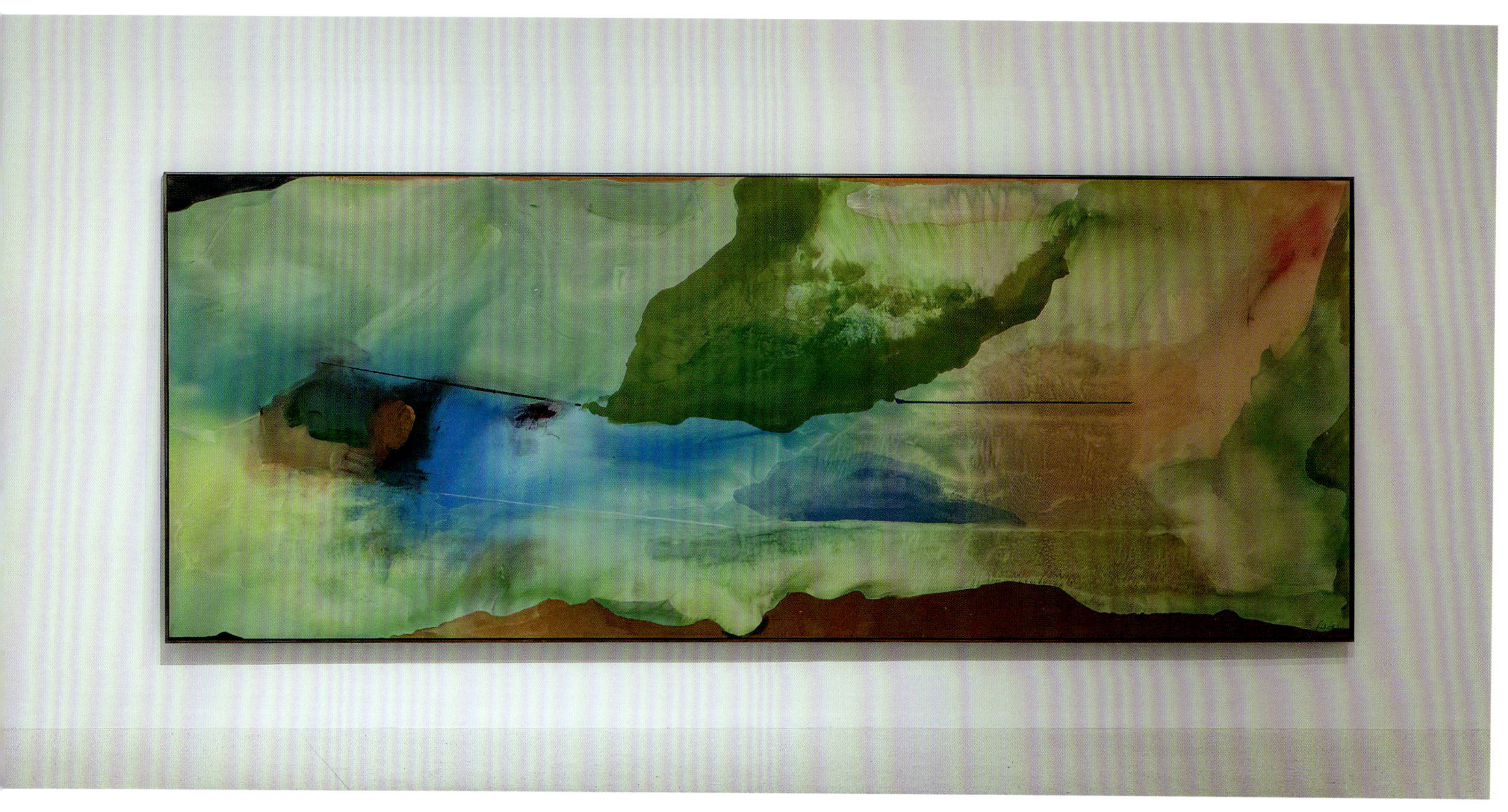

FOLLOWING PAGES

Fig. 25 Left to right:
Jules Olitski, *Yellow Looshe*, 1968
Helen Frankenthaler, *Hint from Bassano*, 1973
Frank Stella, *Waskwaiu II [Variations on a Circle]*, 1968
Morris Louis, *Lamed Gimel*, 1958
Jules Olitski, *Polly La Touche*, 1964
Jules Olitski, *Zem Zem*, 1964
Jules Olitski, *Prince Patutsky Diary*, 1965

Olitski was able to study art in New York and Paris. He realized early that he had to unlearn the habits he acquired in art school in order to move his painting forward. One such method was to blindfold himself as he painted.[29]

By the late 1950s, Olitski's thickly encrusted abstractions garnered him gallery shows in New York and Greenberg's advocacy. Despite this early success, he was already seeking new ways to paint by 1960, including dying pigment directly into the canvas and using paint rollers to layer one color over another, as in *Polly La Touche* (1964; pl. 26, p. 68) and *Zem Zem* (1964; pl. 27, p. 69). These paintings blend one pigment into another and transpose the light-and-dark chiaroscuro effects in the paintings of Caravaggio, El Greco and other old masters that thrilled Olitski.[30]

He subsequently innovated the use of an industrial air compressor spray gun to apply atomized pigment directly onto unprimed, unstretched canvas on the floor. The spray gun made it possible to achieve the desired effect of color that looks like it is suspended in air.[31] The result is an indescribable presence of color that is at once physical and diaphanous. The colors produce a unique density of space that is unrelated to the principles of Hofmann's push-and-pull color theory.

While the scale of these paintings directly addresses the viewer's presence, it is hard to identify exactly where one exists in relation to this pictorial space. *Prince Patutsky Diary* (pl. 29, p. 71) and *Comprehensive Dream* (pl. 28, p. 70), both dated 1965, are among Olitski's first spray paintings. Upon close inspection of *Prince Patutsky Diary*, one can spot areas in the painting where Olitski applied pastel, which added density to the surface. From a distance this treatment produces an effect of the depth-of-field associated with photography, in that the more opaque masses of pigment appear sharper and more defined, and consequently closer to the front of the picture plane, whereas the sprayed areas retreat into a blurry distance. In the panoramic spray painting *Yellow Looshe* (1968; pl. 30, pp. 72–73), defined marks on the lower left corner gently coax viewers' eyes back towards the center, where they can continue to explore the subtly modulated glowing yellow field.

The elimination of expressive brushwork does not mean these paintings are devoid of the artist's touch or are lacking emotional or conceptual content. For Olitski and other American artists of his generation, including Stella and such Pop artists as Warhol and Lichtenstein, the gestural brushstrokes of Abstract Expressionist painting had become an empty gesture, with little personal meaning. Using mechanical means such as the spray gun process produced effects in ways that Olitski could not have achieved with a paint brush.

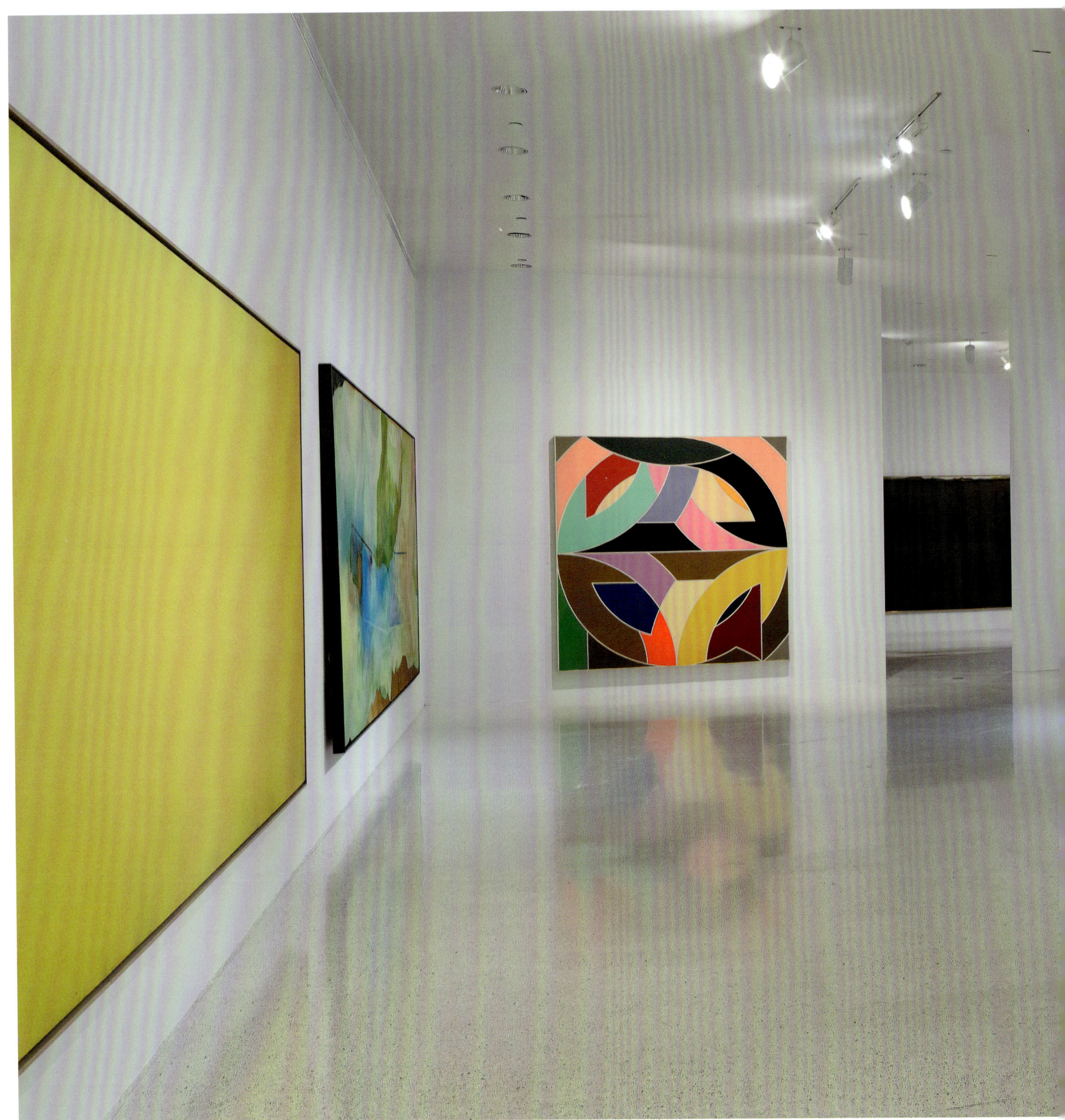

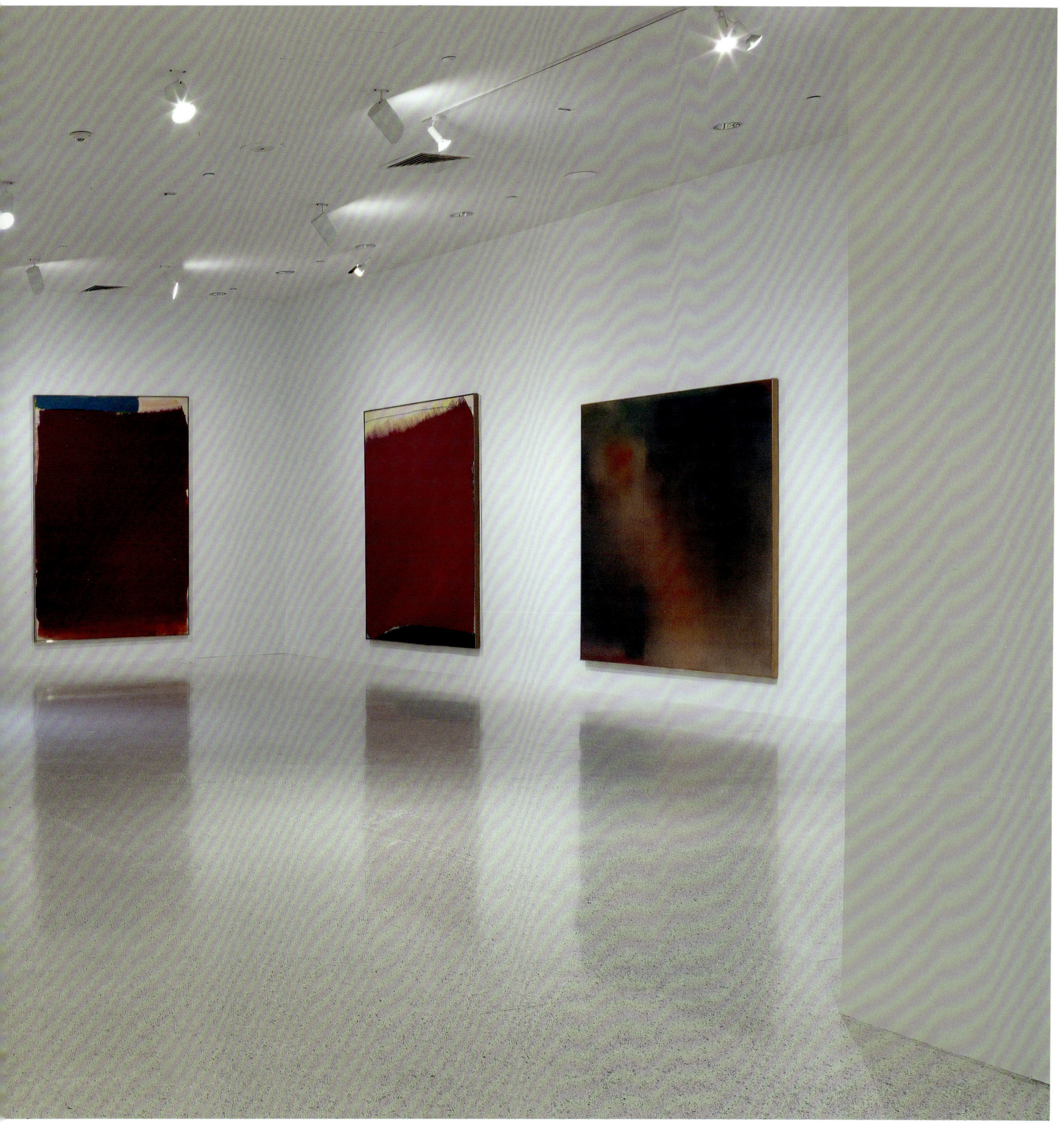

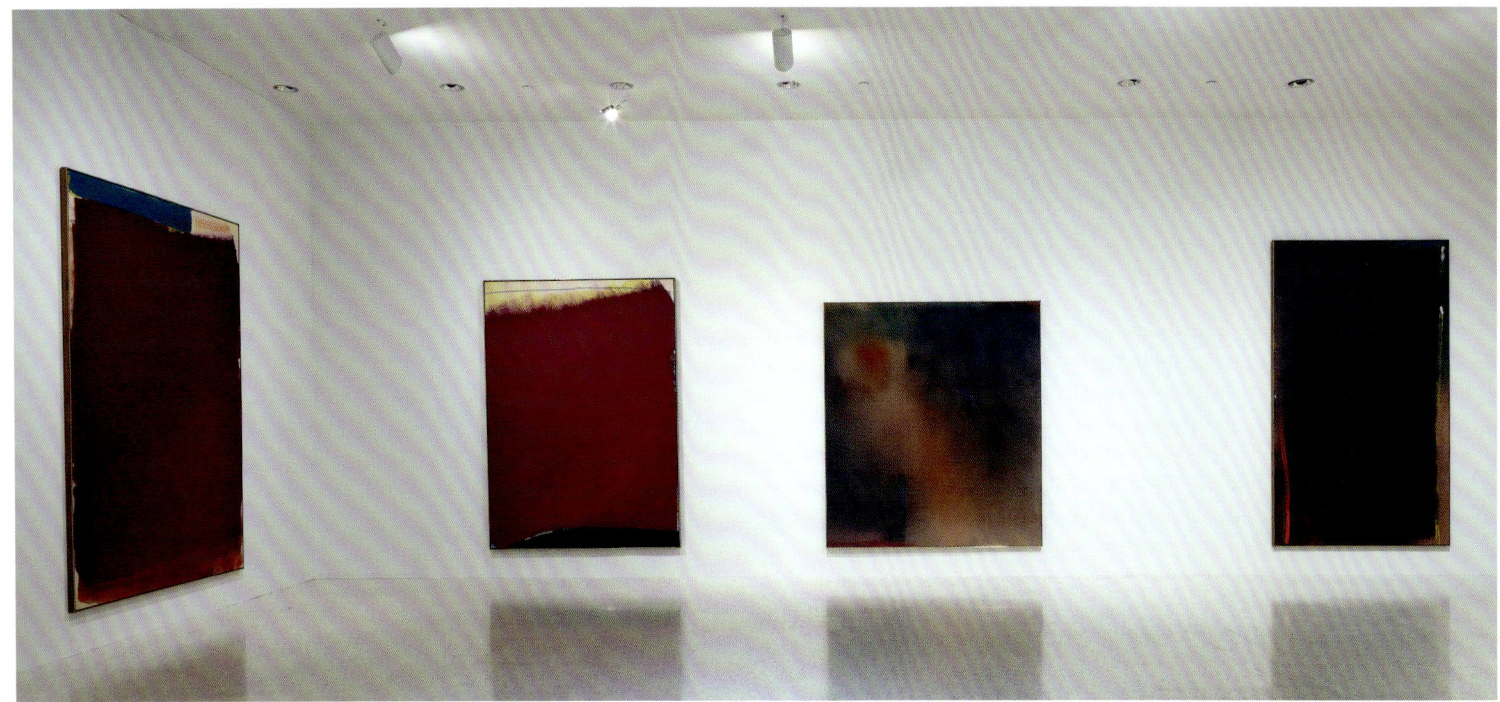

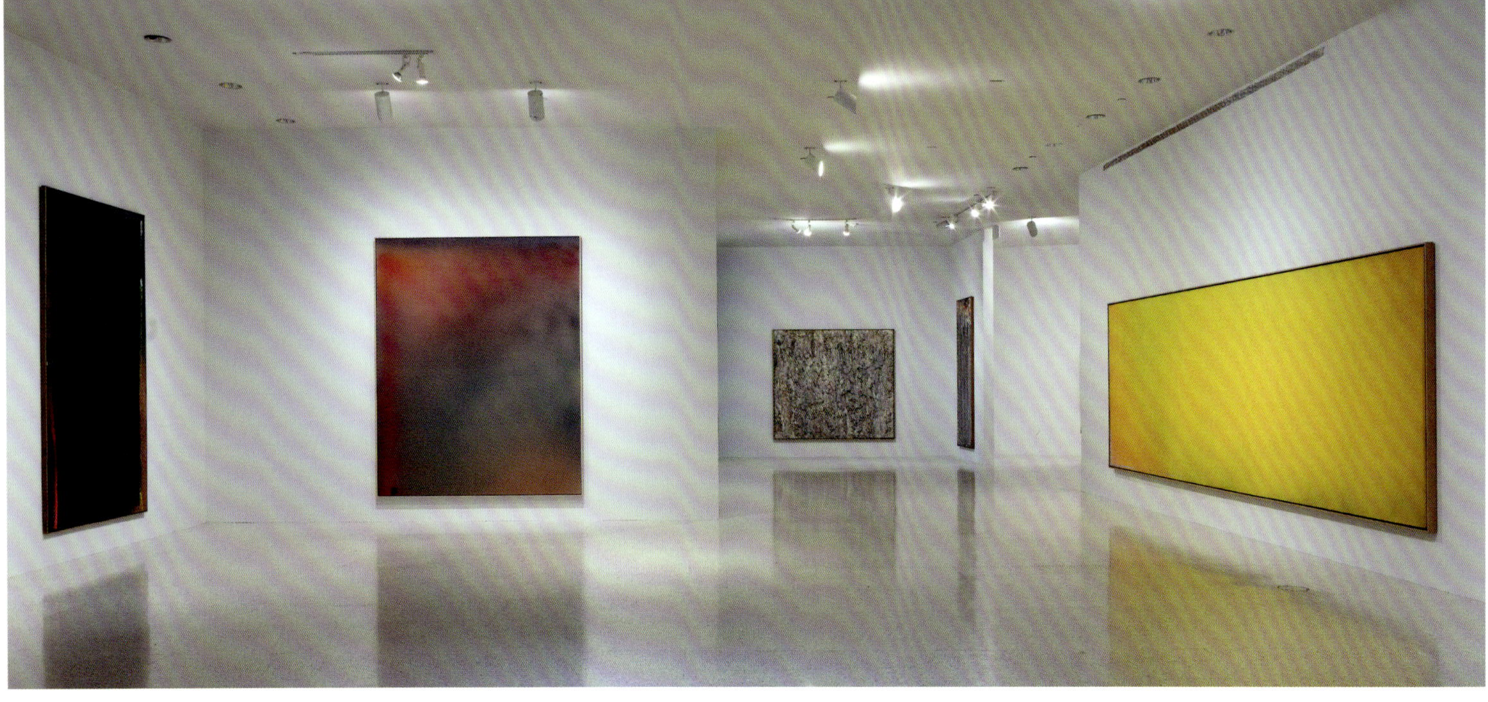

Fig. 26 Left to right:
Jules Olitski, *Polly La Touche*, 1964
Jules Olitski, *Zem Zem*, 1964
Jules Olitski, *Prince Patutsky Diary*, 1965
Jules Olitski, *Eighth Loosha*, 1970

Fig. 27 Left to right:
Jules Olitski, *Eighth Loosha*, 1970
Jules Olitski, *Comprehensive Dream*, 1965
Lawrence Poons, *Regulus*, 1985
Lawrence Poons, *Lady Accessorie*, 1976
Jules Olitski, *Yellow Looshe*, 1968

Larry Poons
b. 1937, Tokyo, Japan; lives and works in New York

Larry Poons was on track for a career as a professional musician and composer after studying at the New England Conservatory of Music (1955–57), but changed course after seeing a survey exhibition of Barnett Newman's abstract paintings at the French & Company gallery in New York, in 1959. Although reviews of Newman's show were generally negative, Poons, Stella, and other young artists were impressed by the radical expression of space in his paintings of broad fields of color that were interrupted by the vertical lines dissecting his canvas. The scale and magnitude of Newman's paintings moved Poons emotionally about painting (fig. 28).[32]

Seeing Stella's shaped paintings of the early 1960s also made an immediate impact on Poons. He became conscious of paring his paintings down to their essence with small circles and ellipses that optically float across a monochromatic background. His paintings were never about achieving purity in painting. Even his dot and ellipse paintings were a way to expand "the limited space that a canvas affords you."[33] Poons' selection of the ellipses contributed to the complexity of his pictorial space as these shapes could be perceived as circles drawn in perspective, which suggests illusionistic depth. These minimal early paintings brought Poons early success and were included in the group exhibition *The Responsive Eye* at the Museum of Modern Art in New York (1965). In 1969, he was the youngest artist included in the landmark survey exhibition *New York Painting and Sculpture, 1940–1970* at the Metropolitan Museum of Art, New York.

Poons' paintings took a dramatic turn in the early 1970s, when he began throwing, hurling, and splashing paint onto his canvases, resulting in tangled cascades of viscous, multi-hued medium. Poons' unprecedented painting technique employed gravity as a partner in creation. The evidence of the weight and speed of these paint throws is tracked as a frozen gesture in the completed work, while the uncanny play of light and dark, emerging both from the illusionistic effect of graduated hues and from the real shadows cast by the thick protrusions of paint across the surface, lessens its density. The experience of these paintings changes as viewers shift position. From a distance the paint flows move with a delicate rhythm as light-and-dark patterns traverse the surface. Up close paintings like *Pine Plains* (1983; pl. 38, pp. 86–87) and *Regulus* (1985; pl. 39, p. 89), become forceful. The resulting craggy fields of color look about as far away from Frankenthaler, Louis, and Noland's stained canvases as one could get, yet they were created with a shared desire to innovate ways of working that would harness the power of the sheer manipulation of paint.

Poons painted on single expansive lengths of canvas rolled out on three studio walls. A rhythmic pattern emerged as he threw one bucket of paint after another onto the canvas. Freed from the confines of a rigid rectangular stretcher, Poons would subsequently edit the roll to mark where he would cut the canvas to form individual paintings. *Lady Accessorie* (pl. 35, p. 84), *"To Clara from Robert"* (pl. 37, p. 85 right), and *The Morning Lies in the Afternoon Sun* (pl. 36, p. 85 left) were all cut from the same roll of canvas painted in 1976. The surfaces of Poons' Throw paintings grew thicker in the early 1980s, with paintings such as *Pine Plains* and *Regulus*. The addition of polyurethane pellets, corn kernels, and other elements beneath the paint propped up each layer so that they physically intrude into the viewer's space.

Stella, a long-time friend and admirer, called Poons "Mr. Natural" in an essay written in 1999. At the time Poons created his first Throw painting, the *Railroad Horse* in 1971 (collection

Fig. 28 Barnett Newman
Vir Heroicus Sublimis, 1950 + '51
Oil on canvas
7' 11⅜ × 17' 9¼ in. (242.2 × 541.7 cm)
Museum of Modern Art,
gift of Mr. and Mrs. Ben Heller

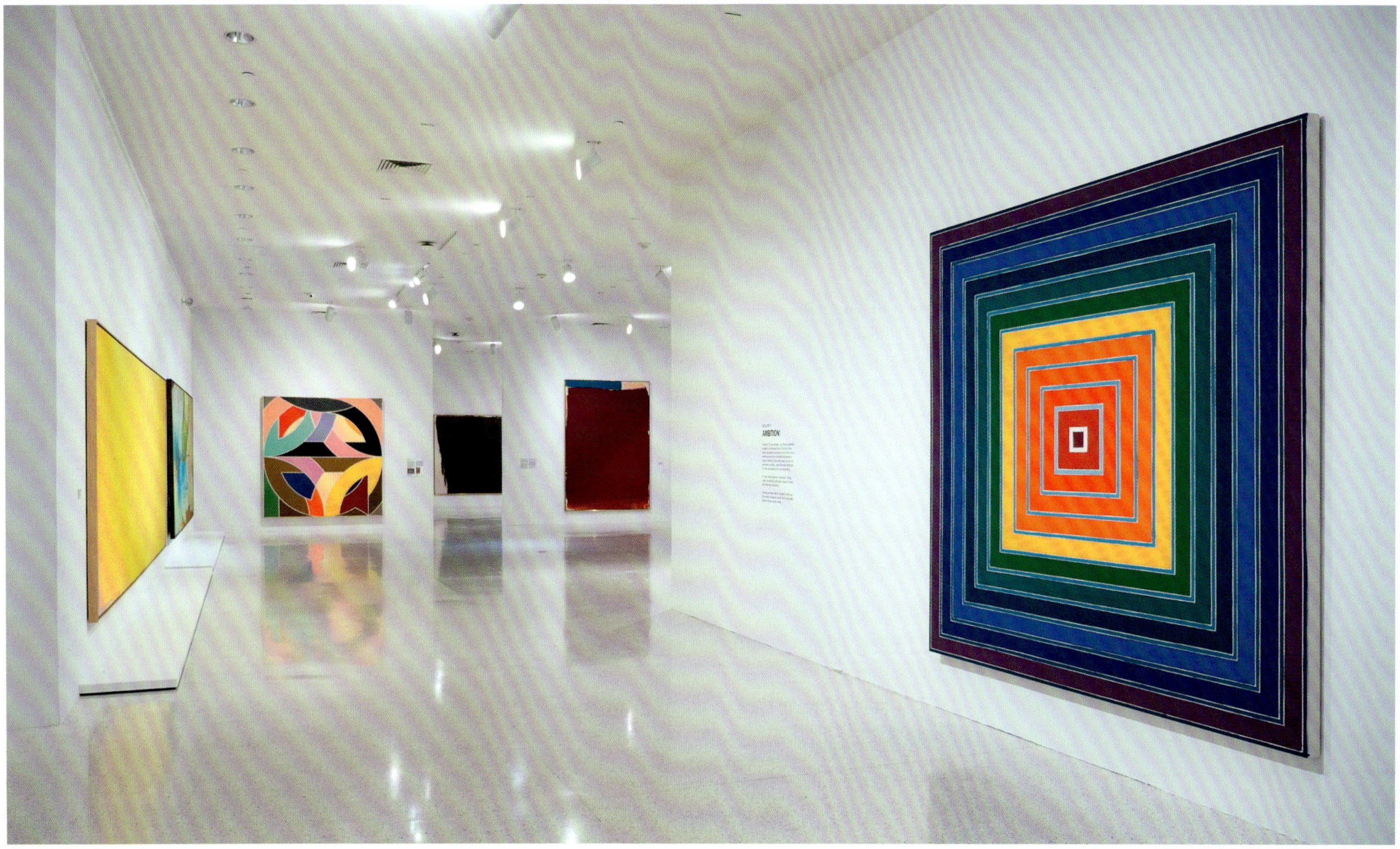

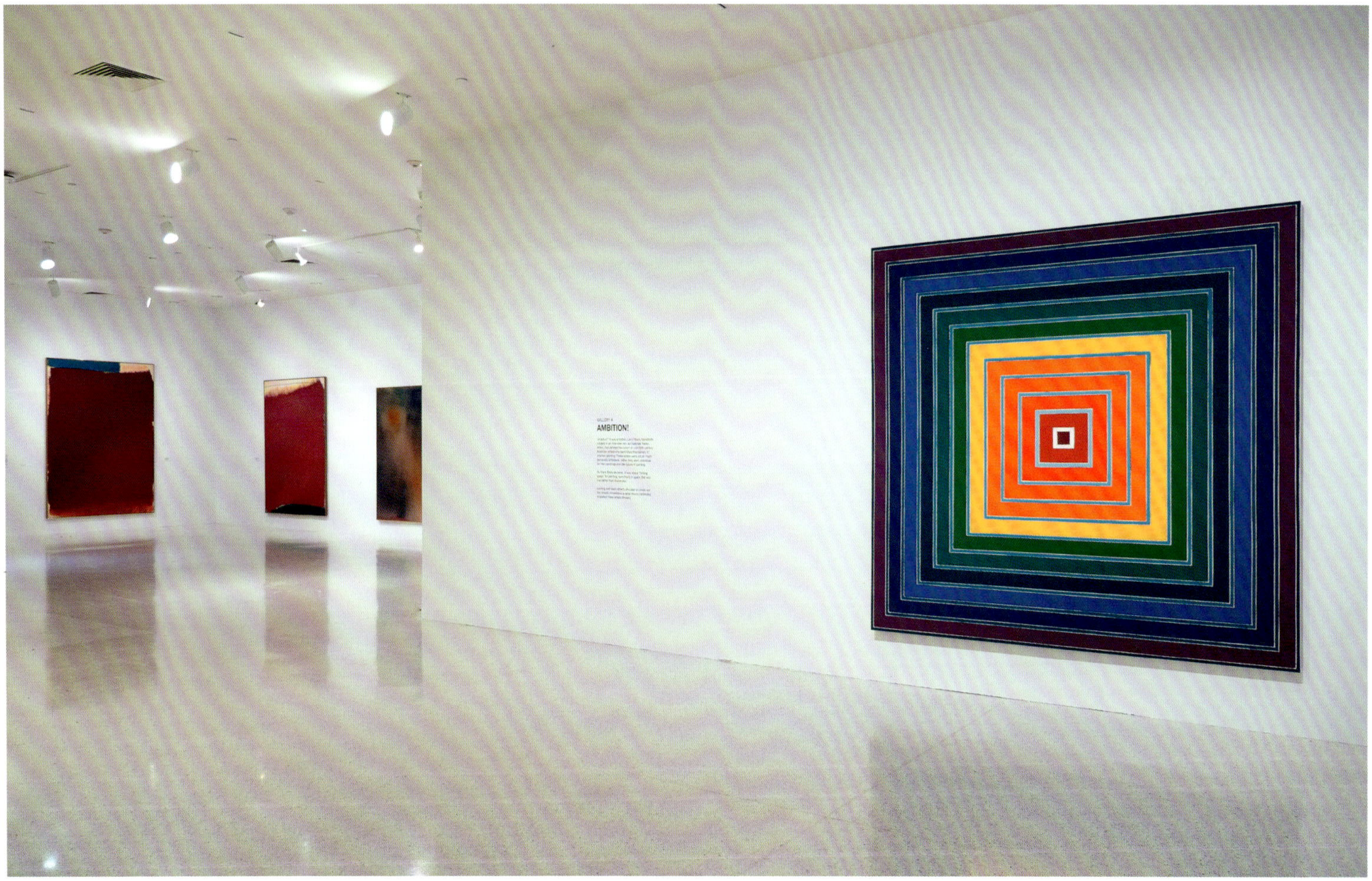

Museum of Fine Arts, Boston), Stella was certain it would "set painting on course for the 70s." This painting, according to Stella, seemingly had "everything going for it: size, scope, purpose, originality, and the ability to carry a kind of compelling conviction about the importance of art making." It was ambition personified, and it was "beautiful."[34]

Sam Gilliam
b. 1933, Tupelo, MS; d. 2022, Washington, D.C.

Sam Gilliam arrived in Washington, D.C., in 1962, after completing his master's degree in painting at the University of Louisville. He credited Thomas Downing, an abstract painter associated with the Washington Color School, for introducing him to the new line of thinking among Color Field painters. It was also through Downing that he became interested in Albers' color theory.[35] Gilliam found Pollock's way of working on unstretched and unprimed canvases on the floor liberating. He was attuned to how Pollock's repetitive movement around the canvas created a rhythm as he poured and flicked paint onto the surface that produced structure and space.[36]

While Greenberg was a driving force in New York, Walter Hopps played an important role in Washington, D.C., as director of the city's Corcoran Gallery of Art (1966–72) and curator of 20th Century American Art at the Smithsonian's National Collection of Fine Arts (1972–79). He encouraged artists to take risks and featured their works in exhibitions. Gilliam credited Hopps with providing him with a "sense of purpose."[37] In 1969, Hopps challenged Gilliam to work in spaces thirty-by-sixty feet for a solo exhibition at the Corcoran Art Gallery. The sheer magnitude of this project, as Hopps remarked to Gilliam, meant he would have to build a "hell of a lot of stretchers" for the paintings.[38] Gilliam came to the realization that, despite tradition, there was no rule that required paintings to be stretched. Instead, he worked in twenty-foot sections of canvas that he attached directly on the wall, creating his first Drape paintings. Although the origin of Gilliam's Drape paintings was a practical response to a challenging situation, he continued to display his unstretched paintings on the wall, as in the graceful *Idylls I* (1970; pl. 11, p. 39), with its scalloped bottom edge and flirty folds, throughout his career. Although the draping and folding of these paintings is deliberate, chance and gravity intervene with

Fig. 29 Left to right:
Jules Olitski, *Yellow Looshe*, 1968
Helen Frankenthaler, *Hint from Bassano*, 1973
Frank Stella, *Waskwaiu II [Variations on a Circle]*, 1968
Morris Louis, *Lamed Gimel*, 1958
Jules Olitski, *Polly La Touche*, 1964
Frank Stella, *Sacramento No. 6*, 1978

Fig. 30 Left to right:
Jules Olitski, *Polly La Touche*, 1964
Jules Olitski, *Zem Zem*, 1964
Jules Olitski, *Prince Patutsky Diary*, 1965
Frank Stella, *Sacramento No. 6*, 1978

Fig. 31 Left to right:
Lawrence Poons, *Regulus*, 1985
Lawrence Poons, *Lady Accessorie*, 1976
Sam Gilliam, *Cordial I*, 1972

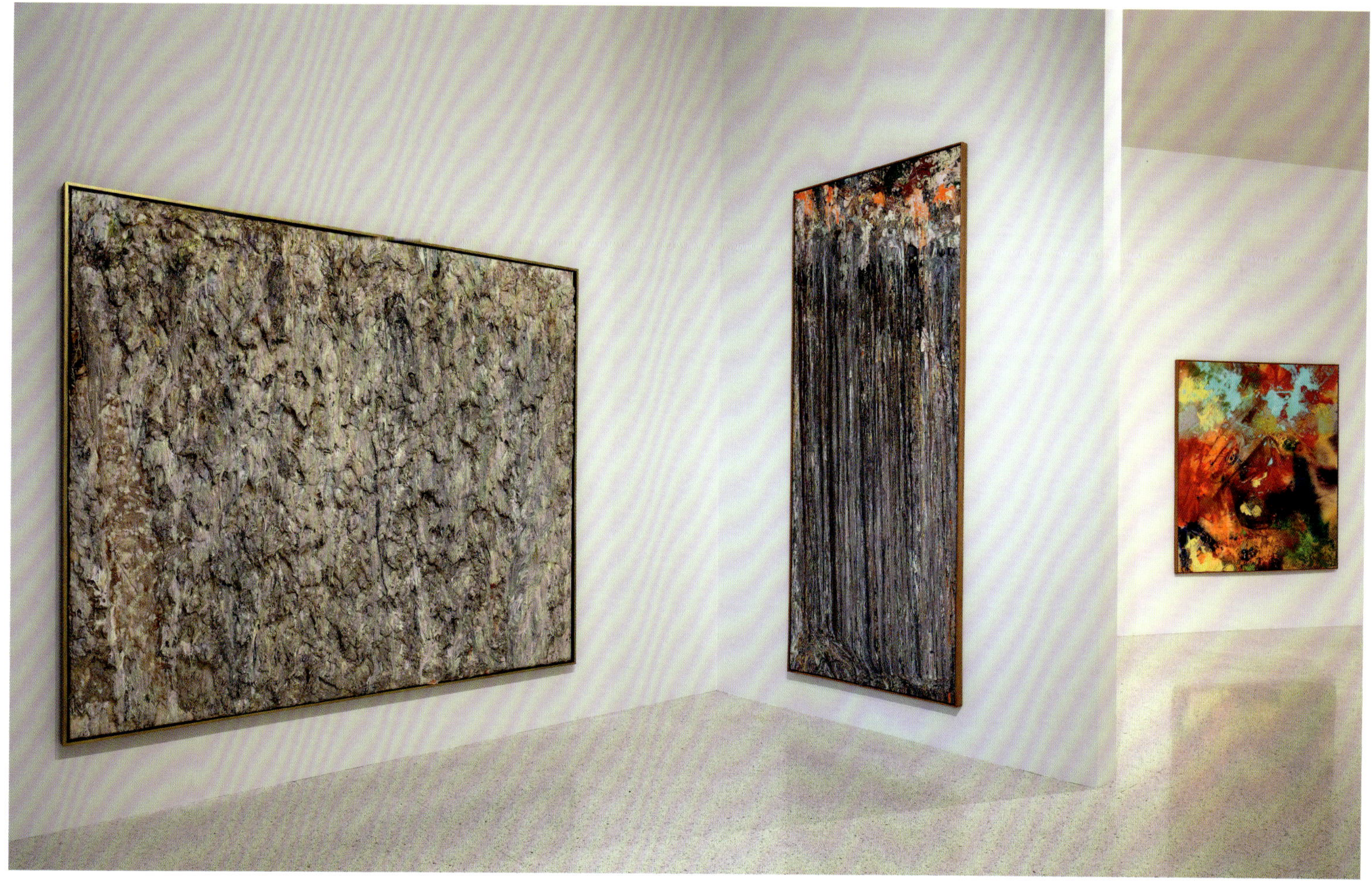

each installation of the work. Gilliam's Drape paintings also held other non-art associations for him, including the way laundry was clipped to a line or flags and banners are furled or unfurled.[39] His manipulation of the unstretched canvas was very physical. Attached to the wall, the canvases project forward and backward in space like low-relief sculpture. He amplified this effect in his paintings wrapped around beveled-edge stretchers, such as *Clear Around* (1973; pl. 13, p. 41), in which the stretcher slopes away from the front of the painting, creating the phenomenological sensation that the flat picture plane is hovering in space in front of the wall.

The titles of Gilliam's paintings contribute a poetic dimension. *Cordial I* (1972; pl. 12, p. 40), for instance, aptly describes the painting's palette infused with an array of rich cordial liqueur hues. The allusion to these heady and aromatic elixirs appeals to the sense of smell and taste, as well as the eye. The double meaning of the word also suggests the countenance of a politely pleasant personality, like a person or, perhaps, a painting that maintains its friendly distance from the viewer. The title *Idylls I* alludes to the genre of short poems known as idylls. It also is a term used to describe a type of music and painting, which like poetic idylls, conjure the intimate world of simple moments of rustic or everyday life, such as scenes of laundry hanging on a line to dry.

Alma Thomas
b. 1891, Columbus, GA; d. 1978, Washington, D.C.

A participant in the Washington Color School movement, Alma Thomas began experimenting with abstraction in the early 1920s as an art student at the city's Howard University, a historically Black institution (she graduated in 1924 as possibly the first African American woman to earn a Bachelor of Fine Arts degree).[40] She would remain in the nation's capital for the rest of her life, teaching at Shaw Junior High School (1925–60), while also taking courses at Columbia University in New York (MA in Art Education, 1934). She was active in the local art scene as founding vice-president of the Barnett-Aden Gallery, one of the first African American owned and operated galleries in the United States, which from 1943 to 1969 presented a racially-integrated program at a time when Washington itself was segregated.[41] Traveling through Europe in 1958, she was enthralled by the architecture of the Basilica of San Vitale, Ravenna, Italy, with its mosaic tiles depicting Biblical parables and its soaring octagonal basilica, which supported a glorious central dome surrounded by flowing images of religious scenes. The experience prompted her to seek abstract means that would match the ecstatic state of gazing into the Basilica's dome.[42] During this excursion she additionally encountered the work of the British abstract painter John Herron and the mystical calligraphic paintings of the American artist Mark Tobey. The impact of this trip was immediately evident in the paintings she created upon her return home in which she flattened the shapes and began applying brilliant colors in staccato brushstrokes.

Thomas' introduction to Color Field painting occurred after she retired from teaching and enrolled in American University, Washington, D.C., at the age of 59. Thereafter, color became her essential means of expression. Her luminous palette evolved from her extensive study of color theory and from observing natural phenomena. Thomas would typically start each work by drawing shapes lightly with a pencil across the canvas, which she would subsequently fill in with thinned paint. Unlike most of the Color Field artists, Thomas painted on canvas sealed with gesso. She opted to use a brush to apply thinned paint in regular strokes that minimized her touch.

In the exhibition *Glory of the World*, viewers could compare and contrast the glowing orb in Thomas' *A Fantastic Sunset* (1970; pl. 44, p. 101) with Stella's Protractor painting *Waskwaiu II* (1968; pl. 41, p. 94) and Concentric Square *Sacramento No. 6* (1978; pl. 42, p. 95), and Noland's Concentric Circle paintings *This* and *That* (1958–59; pls. 23 and 24, pp. 64–65). All three artists used a centralized circular pattern that pulsates with color and directs the eye outward and back towards the center; Stella in *Waskwaiu II* and Thomas in *A Fantastic Sunset* solve the problem of inserting a circular form into a square canvas by allowing it to continue beyond the painting's edge, while in Stella's *Sacramento No. 6* the circle is squared with mitered edges so that it could fit within the painting's border. Noland's pigments are intuitive and relational, whereas the color progression in both Stella's *Sacramento No. 6* and Thomas' painting follows the color spectrum. Thomas' title, *A Fantastic Sunset*, emphasizes the connection between the sun and her painting's spectral pattern. Her paintings are as abstract as Stella's and Noland's, but Thomas' are more likely to be discussed in terms of the natural world than her counterparts, even when Stella alludes to landscape or places in his titles, such as Lake Waskwaiu in Saskatchewan, Canada, the capital of California, Sacramento, and even well-known racetracks, such as the Circuit

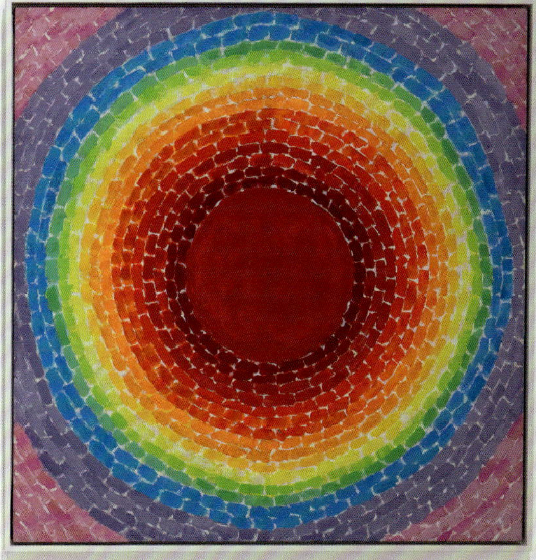

Fig. 32 Alma Thomas, *A Fantastic Sunset*, 1970

Zolder in Belgium that was the source of *Zolder—ONE ELEMENT*'s undulating cut-out shapes and title (1982; pl. 43, p. 97).[43] It is not that Thomas' paintings are any less abstract, rather, the landscape allusions in Stella's work have been less studied due to the long-held assumption that his paintings make no allusions to anything except painting itself.[44]

Thomas was active in the civil rights movement, and although her abstract paintings did not depict racial protest, they were indicative of Thomas' right to determine her individualistic way of painting and her optimistic view of humanity. As she noted, "The use of color in my paintings is of paramount importance to me. Through color I have sought to concentrate on beauty and happiness in my painting rather than man's inhumanity to man."[45] Art historian Erin Jenoa Gilbert drew attention to the artist's remarkable achievements. Not only was she the first African American woman to have a solo exhibition at the Whitney Museum of American Art in New York in 1973, but between 1970 and 1985, she had more solo exhibitions than nearly any other contemporary American woman artist.[46] Gilbert further commented that, considering Thomas was working during a time when African American artists were defining "Black Art," placing "herself in competition and comparison with white male Color Field painters of the Washington Color School," was in itself a radical act.[47]

Peter Bradley
b. 1940, Connellsville, PA; lives and works in Saugerties, NY

Peter Bradley committed himself to abstract painting when he discovered that photography could capture an image better than he ever could. He never retreated from this commitment, even in the face of criticism from writers of the Black Arts Movement, who contested its relevancy to the civil rights movement. As he saw it, formal abstraction was "clean and free and wide open." Its clarity and order could "go all the way back to early Egyptian and African art."[48] He refused to allow his work to be shown in exhibitions that were exclusive to Black artists, and insisted on curating an integrated exhibition of contemporary American abstract painting when Houston collector and philanthropist John de Menil invited him to organize an exhibition in Houston, in 1971. The exhibition, titled *The De Luxe Show*, after the defunct DeLuxe movie theater where it was presented in Houston's Fifth Ward, a predominately

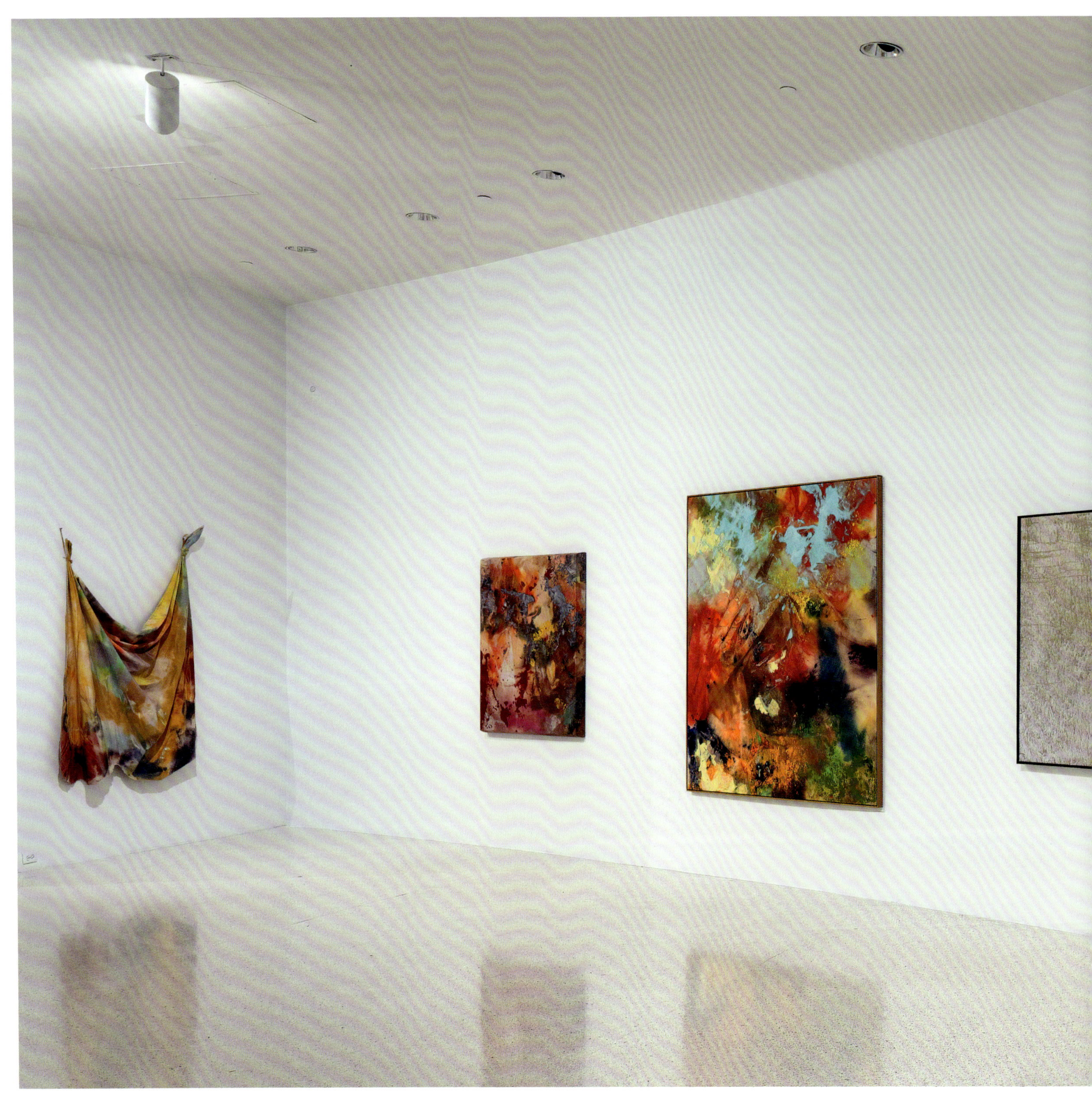

Fig. 33 Left to right:
Sam Gilliam, *Idylls I*, 1970
Sam Gilliam, *Clear Around*, 1973
Sam Gilliam, *Cordial I*, 1972
Peter Bradley, *Belle Coast*, 1973
Peter Bradley, *Stormy Weather III*, 1975

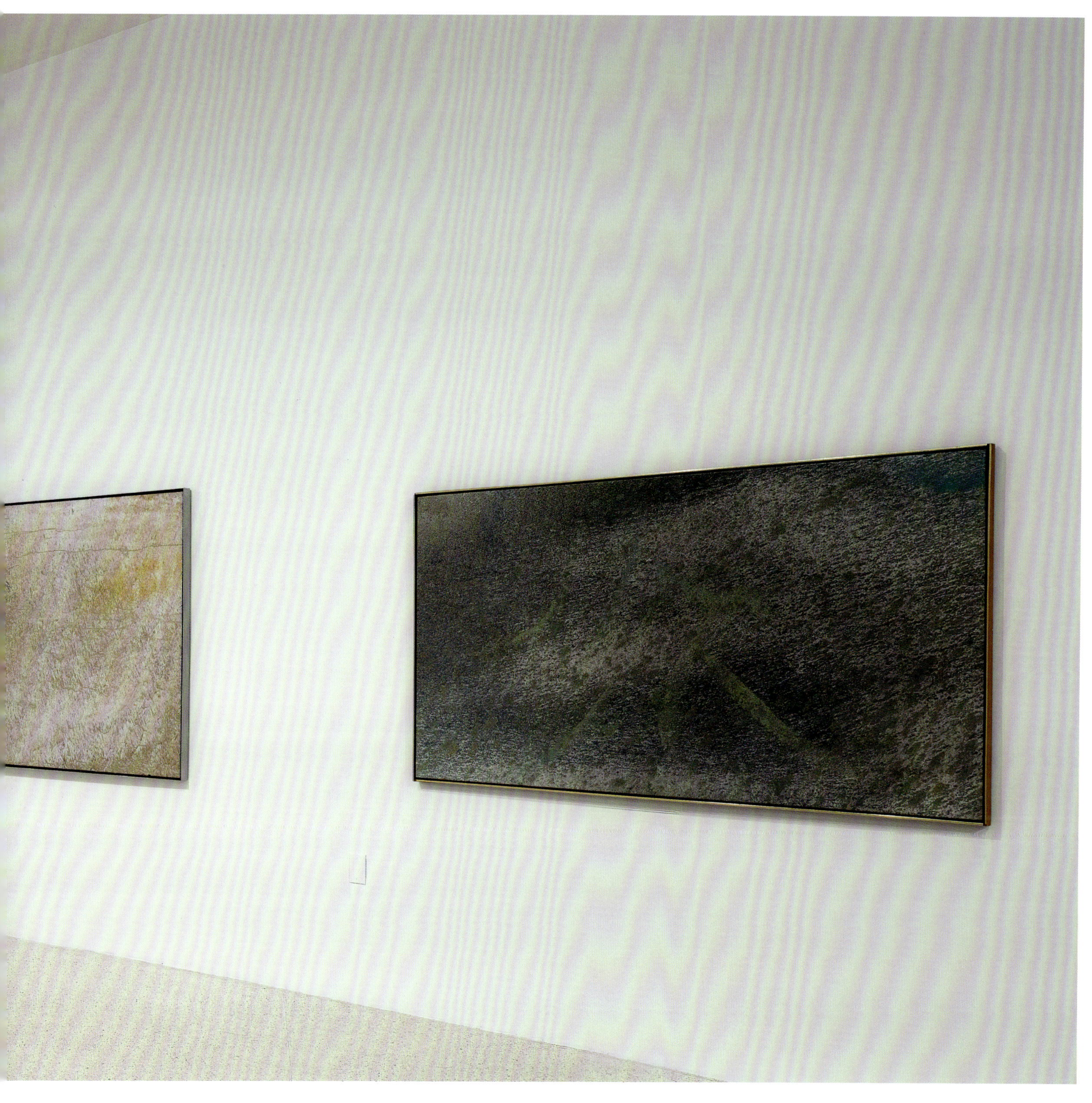

Black, low-income neighborhood, is considered one of the first integrated exhibitions of art in America.

Younger than the other Color Field artists, Bradley admired how Noland, Olitski, and the British sculptor Anthony Caro were risk-takers. At the same time, he was faced with the dilemma of creating paintings with colors that had no precedent in Western art and producing surfaces that dealt with a feeling of the unknown and the unknowable.[49] Speed was essential to Bradley's innovations; and so was getting as much color onto the surface as possible. Observing how Olitski effectively used a mechanical spray gun to paint, he began using this device to dispense paint out as fast as possible.[50] Unlike the predictability of working with a paint brush, the spray gun paintings surprised him. Using a moveable board to direct the gushing paint as it flowed, Bradley produced worlds of shimmering hues as in *Stormy Weather III* (1975; pl. 3, pp. 20–21), or subtle lights and darks as in *Belle Coast* (1973; pl. 2, pp. 18–19). As he worked, he moved around the canvas on the floor to get different perspectives of the painting's dynamics and reflected light. The resulting craggy surfaces fluctuated between micro and macrocosm. Their luminosity, scale, texture and physical and optical depth are exhilarating.

Al Loving
b. 1935, Detroit, MI; d. 2005, New York

The De Luxe Show, which opened in August 1971, included one of Al Loving's geometric paintings of 1969–71. These early paintings were composed of hard-edged polyhedron shaped canvases that Loving connected in complex arrangements on the wall. These shapes' shared edges seemed to flip position in space depending on where viewers chose to direct their focus. Soon after moving to New York with an MFA from the University of Michigan in tow, Loving received significant recognition for his geometric paintings, which led to a solo exhibition at the Whitney Museum of American in 1969. Not only did this exhibition launch a new series of exhibitions of Black artists at the museum, but it was the first solo show for a Black artist at the Whitney.

Loving's career abrubtly changed when his participation in the Whitney Museum's controversial exhibition *Contemporary Black Artists in America* (April 6 – May 16, 1971) sparked writers associated with the Black Arts Movement to criticize his abstract paintings for being devoid of empowering images for Black people.[51] This reproval moved him to reject his hard-edged works, which he saw as in conflict with the civil rights movement.[52] Bowling countered this criticism of Loving's geometric paintings in his article "It's Not Enough to Say 'Black Is Beautiful'" (see Appendix, pp. 154–58), noting that these works are "discomforting like any new kind of art, however much of it may operate within the context of the already accepted, and hence be fliply *understood*. And it demands attention if the black shared experience and heritage are not to go wasted."[53]

Loving soon found an alternate approach to abstraction in the geometric designs of the vintage American quilts he saw on view at the Whitney Museum in the summer of 1971. This exhibition, presented in one of New York's most prestigious art museums, elevated quotidian

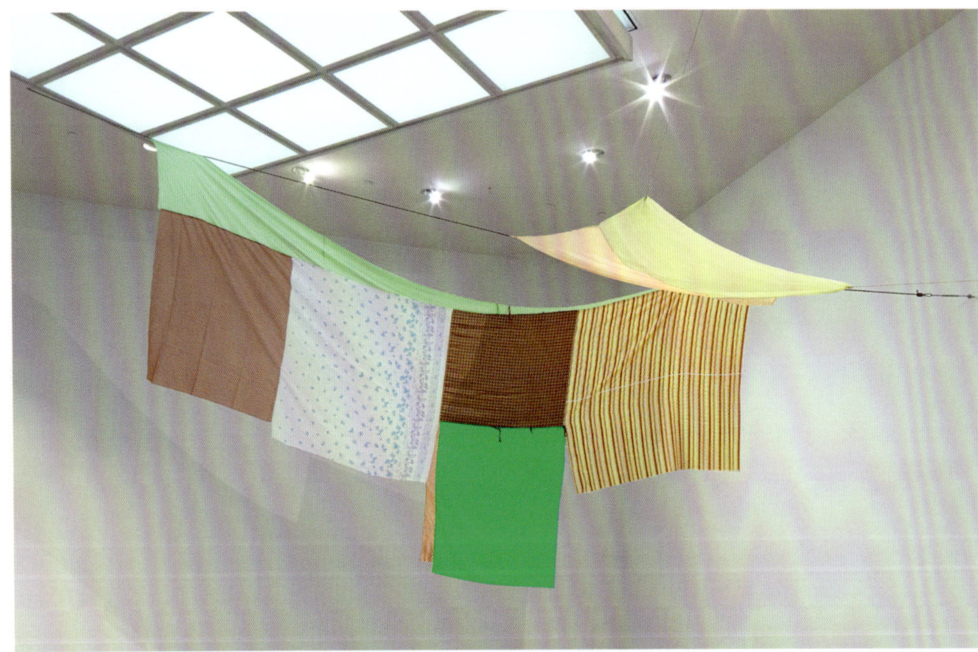

Fig. 34 Eric N. Mack
Tessuti Raponi (Ciao Milano), 2018
Fabric
193 × 322½ × 87 in. (490.2 × 819.2 × 221 cm)
NSU Art Museum Fort Lauderdale; purchased with funds provided by Michael and Dianne Bienes, by exchange

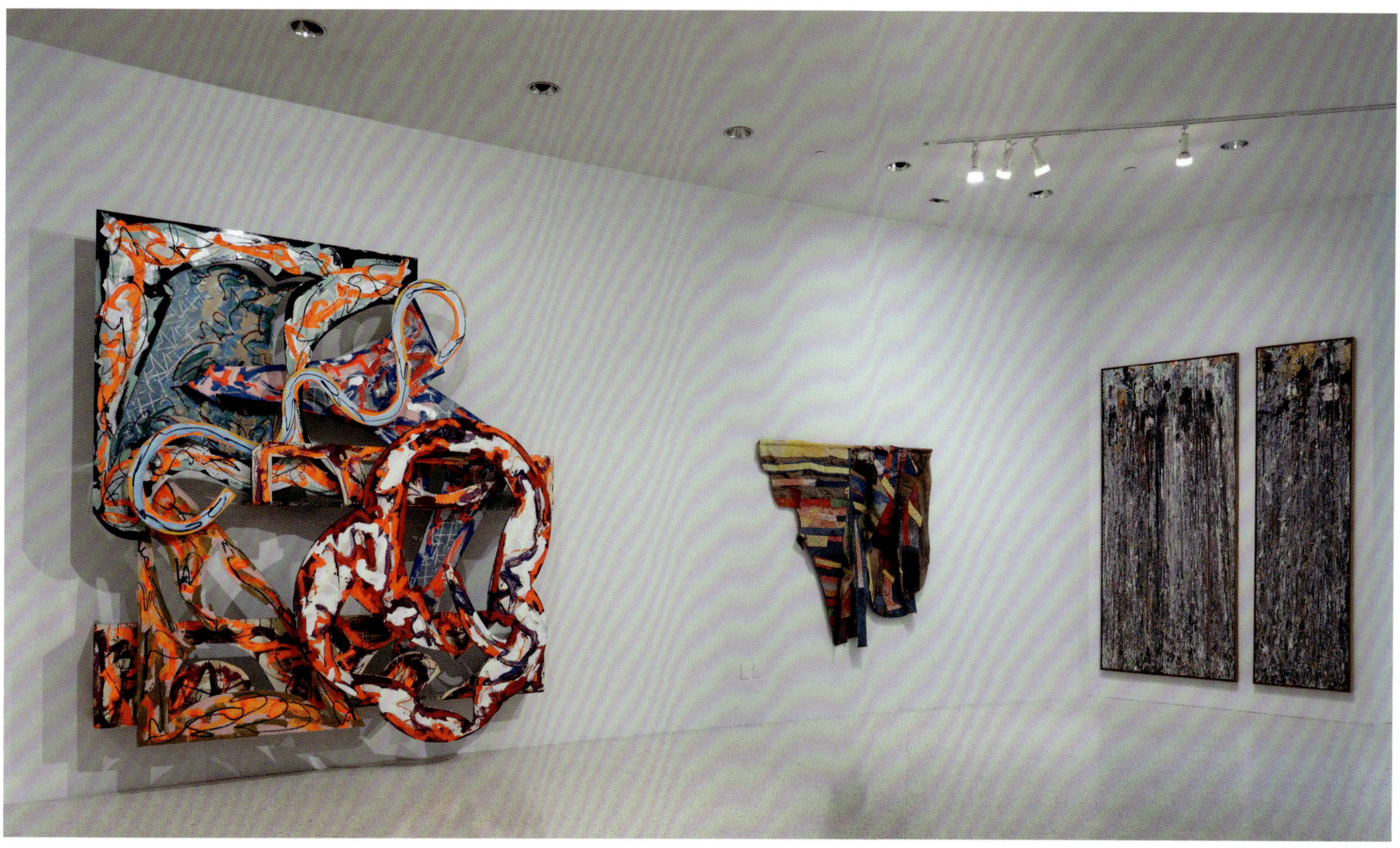

Fig. 35 Left to right:
Frank Stella, *Zolder—ONE ELEMENT*, 1982
Al Loving, *Untitled*, 1975
Lawrence Poons, *The Morning Lies in the Afternoon Sun*, 1976
Lawrence Poons, *"To Clara from Robert,"* 1976

bed coverings to art displayed like paintings on the walls. They were at once utilitarian—providing warmth and comfort—as well as visually exciting. Loving and other artists recognized the similarities of the geometric quilt patterns to the allover compositions of Color Field and formal abstraction. While both delivered a visual punch, abstract painting tended to put off viewers, whereas the familiarity of these common household quilts, with their technical mastery, was alluring. Likewise, Loving was attracted to the collages of the eminent Black American artist Romare Bearden, which were exhibited at New York's Museum of Modern Art the same summer. Bearden began collaging figurative scenes and narratives in the 1960s by cutting up his own abstract paintings of the 1950s among other elements. The experience of the two exhibitions inspired Loving to start anew by making works comprised of paint-less paintings. Like Bearden, Loving made a clean break with his past by cutting up his old abstract paintings and dying strips of canvas, which he layered, collaged, and stitched together (pl. 21, p. 59). The process itself was liberating for Loving, who remarked, "It just blew my mind. There were no boxes; just this dyed fabric sewn up. I didn't know what that was. It thrilled me to death."[54] These works built on the achievements of Bearden's collage work and commitment to presenting the struggle for civil liberties, as well as the artistry and abstract designs of American quilters (many of whom were Black women), which predated European abstraction. As art historian Mark Godfrey noted, Loving considered his new works in a distinct category of Black abstraction that combined elements of modern formal abstraction with vernacular materials and a visual expression that resonated within the Black American community.[55] Instead of supporting his textile paintings on a rectangular stretcher, Loving suspended them from a rod. Both Gilliam's Drape paintings and Loving's cut, torn, and stitched abstractions are soft and mutable and infiltrate the third-dimension like Stella's constructions. Loving's unprecedented works are essentially stain paintings in the tradition of Frankenthaler, Louis, and Noland, but their tactile qualities and association with the intimate use of quilts appeals to the viewer's sense of touch. The accumulation of multiple strata of canvas scraps also adds a sense of mystery as they conceal the many layers below from view. Loving's works continue to resonate with a new generation of artists, such as Eric N. Mack, whose textile-based painting, *Tessuti Raponi (Ciao Milano)* (2018; fig. 34), was suspended above NSU Art Museum Fort Lauderdale's atrium for the duration of the *Glory of the World* exhibition.

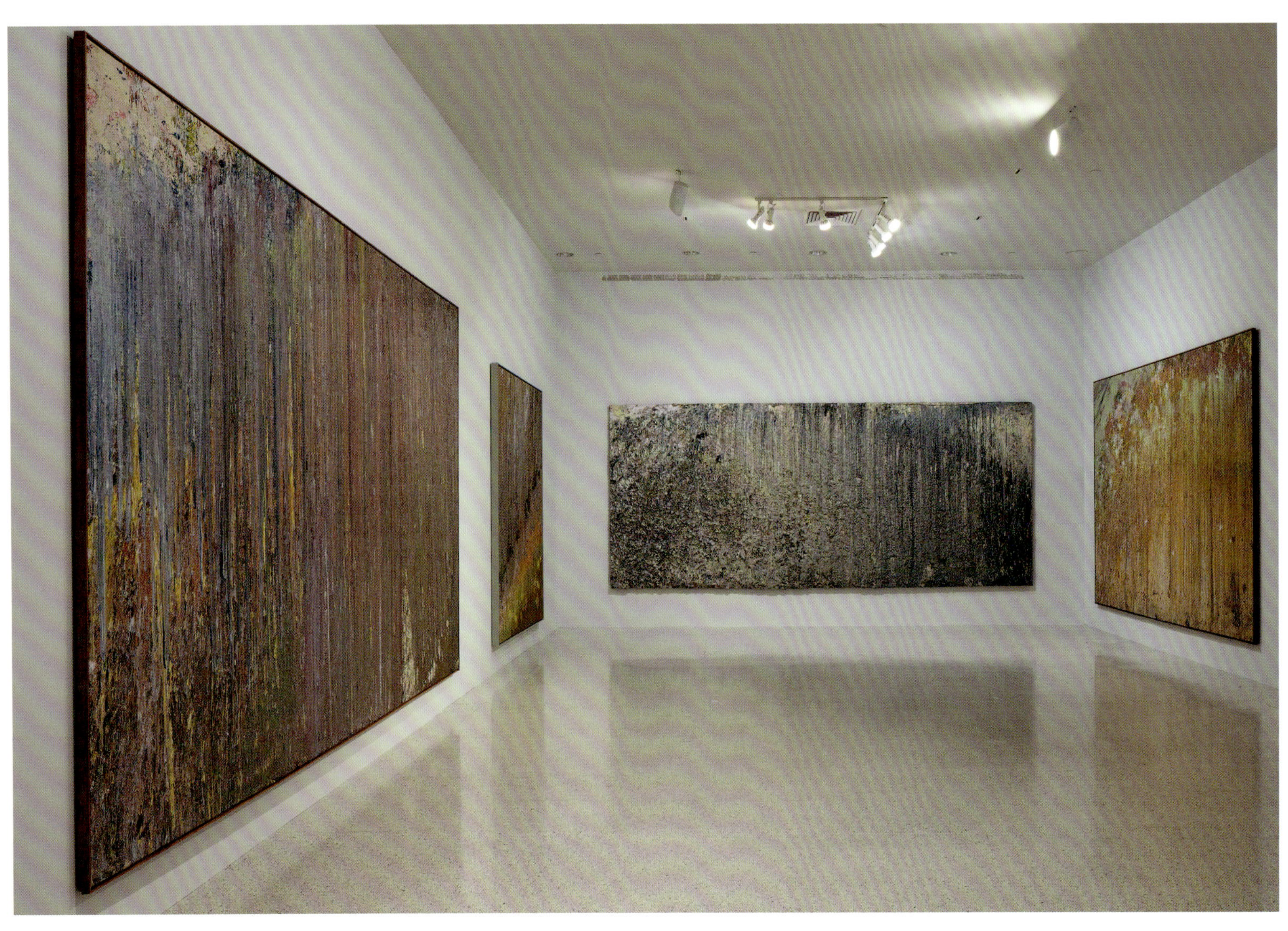

Fig. 36 Left to right:
Lawrence Poons, *"The Call,"* 1973
Lawrence Poons, *Big Purple*, 1972
Lawrence Poons, *Pine Plains*, 1983
Lawrence Poons, *Rain Race*, 1972

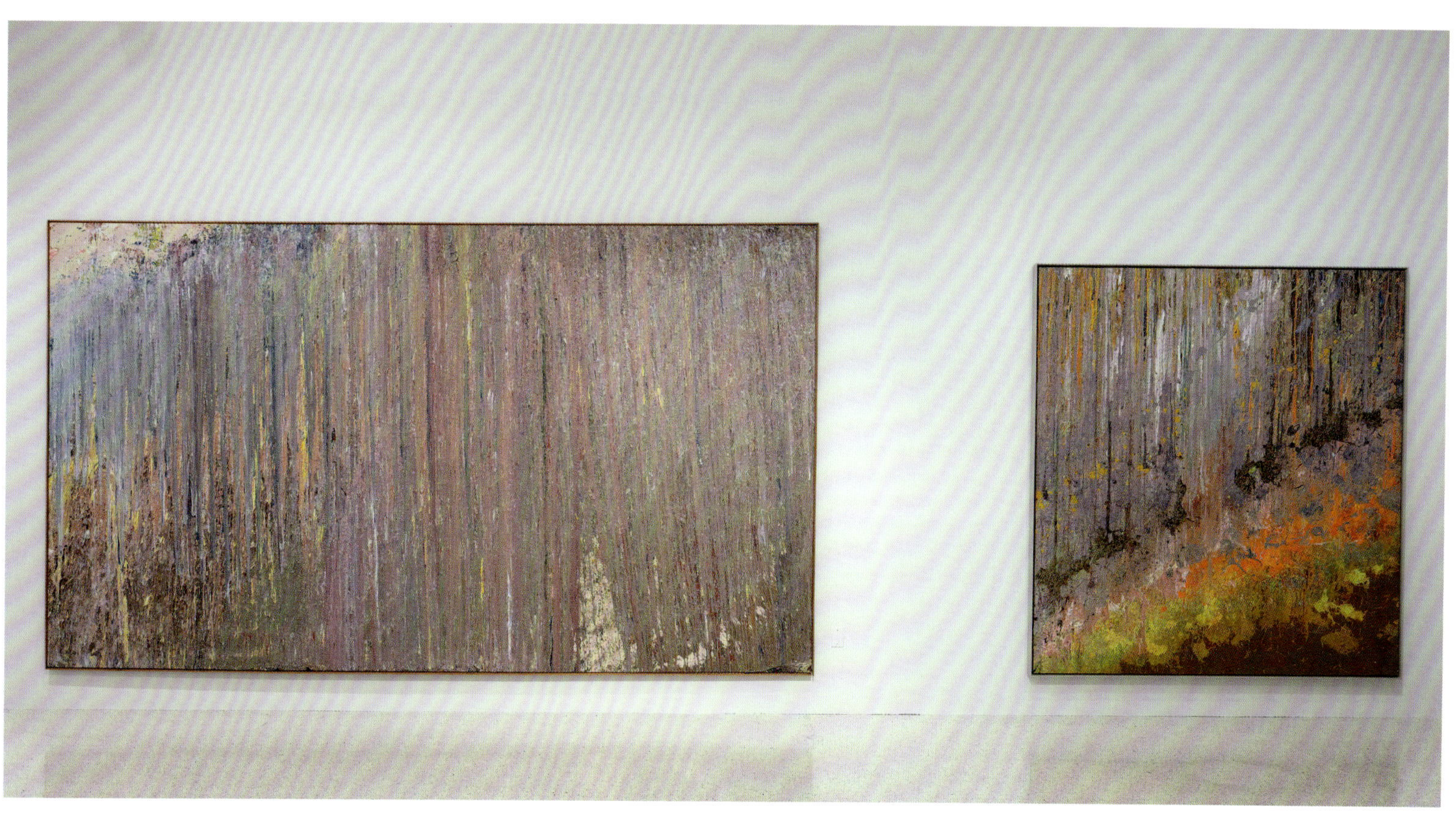

Fig. 37 Left to right:
Lawrence Poons, *"The Call,"* 1973
Lawrence Poons, *Big Purple*, 1972

[1] Frank Stella, "Bombs Away: Hans Hofmann at 2000," in Bonnie Clearwater, *Frank Stella at Two Thousand: Changing the Rules* (North Miami, FL: Museum of Contemporary Art North Miami, 1999), p. 105. See Appendix p. 159.
[2] In "Artists' Sessions at Studio 35," ed. Robert Goodough, in *Modern Artists in America*, eds. Robert Motherwell and Ad Reinhardt (New York: Wittenborn Schultz, 1951), pp. 12–13.
[3] In Bonnie Clearwater, *Frankenthaler: Paintings on Paper* (North Miami, FL: Museum of Contemporary Art North Miami, 2003), p. 23. Quote is from a discussion with the author, 2001.
[4] Motherwell and Rothko's friendship dates to the 1940s. The two artists, along with Clyfford Still, William Baziotes, and David Hare, established the short-lived experimental art school, the Subject of the Artist, in New York in 1948. The school's curriculum promoted a complex new method of image-making without using figures or symbols. In 1958, Rothko was commissioned to produce large paintings for the Four Seasons restaurant in the Seagram Building in New York (he subsequently withdrew from the commission). For this project, Rothko introduced a new image of rectangular shapes surrounding an open area. These mural-size paintings were displayed in Rothko's solo exhibition at the Museum of Modern Art, New York, in 1961. In both Rothko's Seagram murals and Motherwell's Open series the rectangular shapes frame and contain a pictorial space that looks simultaneously opaque and infinite.
[5] In Karen Wilkin, *Kenneth Noland* (New York: Rizzoli, 1990), p. 8.
[6] William Rubin, "Younger American Painters," *Art International*, January 1960, p. 28. See Appendix p. 150.
[7] Ibid., p. 26.
[8] Noland sold the two paintings *This* and *That* separately, but they were reunited by the current collectors, Audrey and David Mirvish. During Noland's lifetime the paintings were published with the date, 1958–59.
[9] Stella described his working process in *The New York Tapes: Alan Solomon's Interviews for Television, 1965-66*, ed. Matthew Simms (New York–Washington, D.C.: Circle and Archives of American Art, 2022), p. 428.
[10] During the installation of the exhibition, *Frank Stella: Experiment and Change* (2017), I remarked that Stella's Concentric Square paintings appeared to separate into triangular sections and a large central diamond, which projected and receded in space. Stella responded "That's what you see, it's not what I see."
[11] Stella in conversation with the author in 2017, described the impact of the van der Weyden diptych on him. Figure 13 is reproduced here for comparison rather than to suggest Stella used the diagram as a scheme for his paintings.
[12] Stella majored in medieval history at Princeton University (class of 1958). His junior-year paper on 8th–9th century Celtic interlace patterns in illuminated manuscripts and their similarities to Pollock's paintings reveals his early interest in the formation of indeterminate space of overlapping forms. This concept was "in the air" at Princeton while Stella was enrolled there (as he noted in conversation with the author in 1999), most likely because his instructor, the painter and art historian William C. Seitz, previously used a similar comparison in his doctoral dissertation, the first scholarly study on Abstract Expressionism, completed in 1955. Seitz observed in Pollock's drip paintings: "The linear maze elicits the ancient annunciations which men have felt for the labyrinth. It is easy to see three-dimensional structure in Pollock's pictures; and as one's conscious moves, in the explaining his endless space of cellular division, time is involved as well. Finally, allowing the perceptual jolt by which one's impressions of a usual field shifts, hollow space becomes flat surface. What was open structure is seen as a network of lines that weave above and below each other across the canvas, and the spectator is excluded. The picture, still vital, becomes a wall decoration." William C. Seitz, *Abstract Expressionist Painting in America* (Cambridge, MA, and London: Harvard University Press, 1983), p. 26. (It is unfortunate that Seitz's dissertation was not more widely available until its publication in 1983, as it is based on essential interviews he conducted with the artists at a time when they were defining their own philosophy and approach to their paintings.) Stella described his junior year paper in 1969 (by which time he had begun his Protractor series): "I wrote my thesis on Celtic, Carolingian and Ottonian manuscript illumination. And it was ostensibly involved with historical problems about problems in kingship and political issues, and how the ideas of the political leaders of the time were presented by the representations of the God or king figures in the manuscript illustration. But more than a third of it is devoted to a kind of pseudo-aesthetic appreciation of the problems of sort of interweave and interlace mainly in Celtic work, with a long aside which should have been in a footnote. But since I had to pad my thesis to make it acceptable I actually included the thing on Pollock and the basic problem of decoration and what actually constitutes decoration. And my argument was that both Pollock and Celtic illumination was art. One happened to be painting and one was manuscript illumination but they both reached the category of art and left the lower category of simple repetitive design or pedestrian decoration far behind. What I saw in this thing, was the possibilities of a kind of space that was not illusionistic in the customary landscape or horizon or horizontal atmospheric space." Frank Stella interview with Sidney Tillim, Archives of American Art, Smithsonian Institution, Washington, D.C., transcript, 1969, pp. 25–26.
[13] The effect of transparency and interpenetrating planes was demonstrated in popular instructional art books circulating during this period. Chief among these was György Kepes' book, *Language of Vision*, "if one sees two or more figures partly overlapping one another, and each of them claims for itself the common overlapped part, then one is confronted with a contradiction of spatial dimensions…." Kepes further stated, "Transparency means a simultaneous perception of different spatial locations. Space not only recedes but fluctuates in a continuous activity" (in György Kepes, *Language of Vision*, intro. S. Giedion and S. I. Hayakawa, Chicago: Paul Theobald, 1967 [first published 1944], p. 77). Lichtenstein, who was well versed in these phenomenological studies, made direct reference to Stella's Protractor paintings (as well as his Irregular Polygons series, 1965–67) by depicting overlapping transparent drafting tools in his paintings as in *Mural with Blue Brushstroke* (1985) that was commissioned for The Equitable Life Assurance Society of the United States, see Bonnie Clearwater, *Roy Lichtenstein: Inside/Outside* (North Miami, FL: Museum of Contemporary Art North Miami, 2001), pp. 36–37.
[14] Stella began conceiving his paintings within series in 1969 (the Black Stripe paintings, 1958–60, only became a series after they were created). A curious small painting on sandpaper from 1960 provides insight into the significance of this development. This painting's pattern of dark blue parallel lines—whole and broken—is based on one of the 64 hexagrams of the ancient Chinese *I Ching* or *Book of Change.* Although *I Ching* was traditionally used as a form of divination (or by experimental musician John Cage and dancer Merce Cunningham to use chance in the creation of their work), Stella was intrigued by how it calculated all the sequences that could be formed by combining these two opposing broken and unbroken lines (the Yin

and Yang respectively). By working within series, Stella likewise could predetermine the compositional permutations, whereby he generally knew in advance how many works would constitute a series and what each painting would look like before painting it.

[15] In Little, "Jack Bush's Stripes and Solids."

[16] Ibid. This and other paintings in Bush's Sash series were inspired by seeing a mannequin in a store window wearing a 1960s shift dress with a sash around the waist.

[17] In Caroline Harris, Alexxa Gotthardt, and Christina Chan, "Mapping a Life in Paint: An Interview with Frank Bowling," *SFMOMA.org*, July 2023.

[18] Ibid

[19] Ibid.

[20] Ibid.

[21] In Zachary Small, "Historical Memory Haunts Frank Bowling's New Paintings," *Hyperallergic*, October 1, 2018.

[22] In Courtney J. Martin, "The Middle of the Day," *Frieze.com*, May 1, 2012.

[23] During a visit to the exhibition *Glory of the World*, art historian David Moos noted that Bowling would sometimes attach the molding strips he used to aid in his formation of horizontal and vertical areas in his paintings to the sides of the stretched canvas.

[24] "Oral History Project: An Oral History with Edward Clark and Jack Whitten," *Bomb,* June 2, 2014.

[25] Ibid.

[26] In interview with Quincy Troupe, *Ed Clark: The Big Sweep* (New York: Hauser and Wirth, 2023), p. 54.

[27] In Corrine Robins, "Push-Broom and Canvas," *Art International* 17, no. 8 (October 1973), reprinted in *Ed Clark: The Big Sweep*, p. 94.

[28] For issues concerning Louis' compositions and posthumous stretching of his canvases, see Kenzie Kajiya, "Non-Composition in Color Field Painting," *Color Fields from the Collection of Audrey and David Mirvish* (Kawamura Memorial DIC Museum of Art, 2022), pp. 180–82.

[29] In Kenneth Moffett, *Jules Olitski* (Boston: Museum of Fine Art, 1973), p. 34.

[30] Alex Grimley, "An Expression of Order: Jules Olitski's Traditional Painting,'" in *Jules Olitski: 100 Paintings, 100 Years* (New York: Yares Art, 2022), pp. 19–21.

[31] In "An Interview with Jules Olitski," by Louise Gauthier, *Perspectives* 0 (Spring 1990), p. 8.

[32] In *The New York Tapes*, p. 400. The two artists struck up a friendship, and Newman even encouraged Poons' father to let him pursue his artistic career (John Zinser, "The Long Ride of Larry Poons," *The Brooklyn Rail*, December 2005 – January 2006).

[33] In *The New York Tapes*, p. 407.

[34] Frank Stella, "Mr. Natural: Larry Poons," in Clearwater, *Frank Stella at Two Thousand*, p. 112.

[35] "A Conversation with Sam Gilliam" with Hans Ulrich Obrist, in *Sam Gilliam: Existed, Existing* (New York: Pace, 2020), p. 53.

[36] Ibid., pp. 45–46.

[37] Ibid., p. 47.

[38] Ibid.

[39] Gilliam also associated Louis' Unfurled series with the unfurling of banners, see, "An Interview with Sam Gilliam," *ARTnews*, 1973.

[40] Erin Jenoa Gilbert, "Seeing Red: Romance, Rage, and Resurrection," *Alma Thomas: Resurrection* (New York: Mnuchin Gallery, 2019), p. 10.

[41] Ibid., pp. 10–11.

[42] Ibid., p. 13.

[43] Ibid.

[44] Stella described his two elliptical Race Track paintings of 1970—*Deauville* (based on the circuit of the horse track in Deauville, France) and *Agua Caliente* (based on the racetrack in Tijuana, Baja, Mexico)—as a "kind of landscape." He referenced French Impressionist Raoul Dufy's many Race Track paintings, such as *Race Track at Deauville, the Start*, 1929 (Fogg Museum, Harvard University) as a source (conversation with the author, 2017). His Imaginary Landscape series of the 1990s, translates the effect of the three-dimensional site plan he designed for his proposed architectural design for the Dresden Kunsthalle, with its serpentine pathways, sculptural mounds and clusters of buildings and pavilions, to the two-dimensional picture plane. Stella sees "landscape as motion and landscape in motion" (Frank Stella, "Melrose Place," in Clearwater, *Frank Stella at Two Thousand*, p. 84).

[45] In Katherine Markoski, "Alma Thomas, American Women's History Initiative," *Americanart.si.edu*, 2024.

[46] Gilbert, "Seeing Red: Romance, Rage, and Resurrection," p. 21.

[47] Ibid., p. 18.

[48] In "Conversation with Peter Bradley, Curator of The De Luxe Show," Simone Bradley, *The De Luxe Show*, exh. cat., Houston, TX, 1971, p. 67.

[49] Ibid., p. 68.

[50] Ibid.

[51] For the history of the exhibition *Contemporary Black Artists in America*, Whitney Museum of American Art, New York (1971), and the response by the Black Emergency Cultural Coalition (BECC) and the featured artists, see *Soul of a Nation*, p. 106.

[52] Ibid., p. 148.

[53] Frank Bowling, "It's Not Enough to Say 'Black is Beautiful,'" *ARTnews* 70, no. 2, April 1971. See Appendix, p. 57.

[54] Mark Godfrey, "Notes on Black Abstraction," in *Soul of a Nation: Art in the Age of Black Power* (London: Tate, 2017), p. 148.

[55] Ibid., p. 150.

APPENDIX

Now, the notion of an "American style" seems to me preposterous. How can de Kooning be said to share a style with Still, Rothko, or Newman? Among the younger painters, how can Kelly, Parker, Mitchell, and Johns be regarded as sharing a style? There is no more an American style than there is a French style. Barrett's notion of a collective style is not only foreign to the nature and historical development of modern painting, but suggests a profound misunderstanding of what is really happening on the American scene. The collective character of style in older painting ceases with Manet. Since then every great painter has been to some extent the creator of a new style. And even when the style encompasses more than one painter (Renoir, Monet, and Sisley in Impressionism; Picasso and Braque in Analytical Cubism), only those artists who participated in the creation of the style ever practised it meaningfully.

The degree to which the de Kooning style has pervaded American painting during recent years has given rise to the idea that a new academy has been born. "Is there a new academy?" was the topic of an "Art News" roundtable recently. The question itself, as was observed by some at the time, betrays a rather shallow awareness of what the old academies really were. There is, of course, no modern academy. But that the question should even arise is symptomatic of the hegemony of the de Kooning style, at least in New York. It seems to me not without significance that this should come about at a time when de Kooning himself is faltering. His last show, though it established a new high in prices for living American painters and received much attention in the national press (partly on that account), was something less than a critical success. In fact, to some critics, myself included, it appeared more like a failure. Even de Kooning's ardent admirers admitted that the paintings in that show did not measure up to the black pictures and the work of the early fifties. That Kline, too, should be working in a tentative manner, not simply by colouring his big bars (as was the case in his earlier colour pictures), but by moving in a direction as much related to that of Guston as to that of de Kooning, seems further evidence of the enfeebling of the older style.

These developments bring into relief the argument put forth increasingly since the early 1950's by the dean of post-war American critics, Clement Greenberg. He has contended that by 1951 the de Kooning style began to be a losing proposition for de Kooning himself. Even if Greenberg's sense of the faltering of this style was slightly premature, his preference for the directions pointed by Still and Newman showed extraordinary prophetic insight in terms of where the younger painters of quality find themselves today. It may also be true, as Greenberg holds, that the fact that a new major painter has failed to emerge on the New York scene during the last seven or eight years is not unrelated to the domination of the de Kooning style. If this is so, then the work of the younger painters I shall discuss below is heartening, if only for the sense of new departures it communicates.

Of course, there are still some large talents directly committed to the de Kooning style, and one of these, Al Leslie, was represented in both the Museum of Modern Art and the Stable exhibitions. But while Leslie successfully sidesteps the pitfall of decorativness by borrowing some of de Kooning's acidulous colour and leaning heavily on a slashing, paint-splattering attack, his work strikes me more as an exercise in virtuosity than a statement of artistic content.

The only really refreshing painter working in this vein (and one certainly not nearly so close as Leslie to what de Kooning and Kline do) Is Joan Mitchell, and It may be significant that this exception is a painter who for some years has lived in Paris. When this style was most alive—around 1950 and for a few years thereafter—it was an insurgent direction, in competition with other modes of painting. The more common it became on the New York scene, the less it seemed to have to say. In Paris, on the contrary, even today it is but one direction in a situation of great ferment. I rather suspect that this has been to Mitchell's advantage. In any event, her work retains a freshness that one misses in her near-counterparts in New York.

While participating In the de Kooning tradition in terms of a slashing attack and a "salting'" of the work with drip, Mitchell's style is much more personal than that of Carone or Leslie. Behind the Abstract-Expressionist appearance of her recent work is something more akin to Cézanne and Cubism. Her characteristic long narrow stroke of colour does not constitute (as in the big-brush painters) a flat shape on the surface, but rather defines the edge of a plane which we feel emerging slightly from the grey-white core to which all her colour is attached. A narrow frontal space is created by these implied planes, a space articulated with extraordinary decision and clarity by the slicing stroke that "dices" the surface. (I see an affinity here for Mondrian's semi-abstract "Tree" series of 1911.) In pictures like "Lady Bug" at the Stable, the closeness of the coloured edges creates an almost impressionist flicker of light across the surface which tends to give the work an outdoors, pleine-air look. As a woman painter, Mitchell is untainted by the usual cosmeticism, yet she is able to endow her work with real finesse and refinement–a welcome contrast to the blustering, heavy-handed stance of much Abstract-Expressionism.

Robert Rauschenberg has also used the de Kooning style as a point of departure for something highly personal. He has been mistakenly called a Neo-Dadaist because of the jolt of the apparently unrelated real objects he juxtaposes in "combine" sculptures and reliefs. But there is nothing nihilistic in Rauschenberg's attitude toward the making of the work. He has the same affection for the traditional materials of the painter as he has for the studio scraps and junk he uses. One aspect of post-war art and particularly of the de Kooning style is the replacement of the finessed, painterly approach (modelling, etc.) with a pushing or manipulation of the paint. Manipulation in this spirit leads Rauschenberg to the manipulation of objects and materials with which he structures his combines, cementing them in place with bursts of pigment. The boxiness of his compositions, however, reveals an attachment to the cubist grid, on which de Kooning has depended since the early fifties, and this seems to me his main limitation as a composer. Within this larger compositional framework he is insured against the repetitious forms and mannered brushwork patterns of de Kooning's followers by the great variety of edges and surfaces of the collage elements.

In comparison with the art of the past, Abstract-Expressionism is an inherently autobiographical style. Rauschenberg has developed this dimension through the application of figurative collage elements within the framework of an abstract style of painting, rendering it even more personal, more particular, and sometimes almost embarrassingly private. Everything the eye delights in is eligible to enter into the autobiographical poem. The iconography of the Rauschenberg pictures seems to reach back through time and consciousness, memory by memory. The juxtaposed coke bottles, mirrors, snapshots, stuffed animals, and kitchen utensils do not join in the Symbolist-Surrealist manner of Lautréamont's umbrella and sewing-machine on the dissecting table. Not that they fail to evoke Freudian associations, but they are particular rather than archetypical in their interrelationships, and they never relinquish their autobiographical intimacy.

The role of figuration—fragmented and subordinated in Rauschenberg to the abstract division of surfaces—is more obvious in the work of Jasper Johns, but ultimately no more central. For him the image is meaningful in its meaninglessness. I quite agree with Ben Heller (in the Grove Press essays mentioned above) that Johns' favorite subjects are, in their very commonplaceness, "a means of forcing the viewer to focus upon the canvas itself, to react to it as an immediate and direct painting experience". By making his subjects completely identical with the pictorial field, Johns mockingly accepts as given the general contours of his composition, having thus available the centralized (targets), the "all-over" (letter and number grids), and the asymmetrical (flags). The real drama is local—minute variations and adjustments of edges, richness, refinement in surface textures; these make the surface vibrate and give to the commonplace flag, target, or letter a disconcerting liveness. John's genius is essentially miniaturist, and the finesse of his hand compares with the finest in the French tradition (with which tradition he has a basic affinity of "facture").

The strangeness of subject in Johns is not like that of the Surrealists. His flags and targets are not familiar objects in an unfamiliar context (à la Lautréamont), but objects deprived of context. We do not "associate" to them, but respond to their enigma. This enigma stems, first, from the paradoxical-oneness of the picture as painting and image. Such a peculiar ambiguity cannot be achieved with just any subject. As far as I know, no one has pointed out that all Johns' favorite subjects share an emblematic or "sign" character. We do not think of targets, flags, letters, and numbers as objects in the sense that we think of still-life, figures, or even the illusionistically "real" phenomena that might turn up in a Dali or Magritte painting. Thus, to be correct we would have to say that Johns represents, not objects, but signs. Now, signs are two dimensional; letters and numbers have no tactility, and though targets and flags enjoy a greater degree of actuality, they, too, are experienced as flat. Thus, the paradox lies in Johns' reversal of the usual process of representation, by which a three-dimensional object from the real world is represented as a two-dimensional illusion. Johns gives his two-dimensional signs greater substance, weight, and texture than they have in reality; in other words, he turns them into objects. This came home to me particularly on viewing the magnificent "Large White Flag" in the Museum show. The thickly textured canvas, enclosing a deep stretcher projecting markedly from the wall, had more solidity, hardness, in short, 'objectness', than a real flag. Johns thus participates directly in the predominant trend of contemporary painting, which has turned the picture from illusion to object, and his particular incorporation of figuration curiously enhances rather than contradicts this development.

Helen Frankenthaler, whose large "Madrid Scape" dominated the installation at the Stable, is the only painter in either of the exhibitions who represents what I should like to call "inductive" or indirect painting. In the various forms of this method the direct, assertive mark of the brush, central to the de Kooning style, is largely replaced by less controlled, more accidental techniques, such as spilling. The picture is "provoked" as much as it is "painted". These paintings relate to Pollock, but to his post-1950 work rather than to his classical drip pictures where the matrix is linear and the fabric is closely determined and willfully controlled. In the more Rorschach-like, blotty pictures of 1951 and particularly the Rockefeller picture (No.12, 1952) and "Blue Poles" (completed 1953), the spilling of the pigment was freer and the resultant com positions more loose and informal, the paint being allowed to "find" its form.[2]

The beauty of Frankenthaler's unassertive canvases lies for me in their breadth and airiness. The patterns of her pictures show a refreshing variation, there being no repetitious "signature" shape or gesture. But in her dialogue with the empty spaces of her canvas, a dialogue in which she appreciates the strategy of silence, the pleasure of hearing the language often fails to be accompanied by a sense of deep meaning in what is said.

Paul Jenkins practices inductive painting, taking the maximum of risks and suffering many failures (unevenness is, of course, inherent in this style), but when he does hit it, as he does frequently enough, the results are really exciting. His pictures seem to paint them selves, with Jenkins as a witness, and the relationship of his hand to the surface appears charismatic. My main objection to his work in the past has been a too frequent oiliness or fatness in the paint. Aside from making what I consider to be an unpleasant surface, this luminosity tends to magnify an illusionism inherent in the way he works. In recent pictures, however, Jenkins has gone a long way toward matting his surface and giving his pictures a flatter, more frank character. I look to him as one of those who may provide the radical solutions in the painting of the 1960's.

Within the ambit of this inductive approach lies the work of Morris Louis, whose show last year at French & Company seemed to me one of the most significant in years. Louis stains his canvas, spilling diaphanous veils of liquid colour one over the other. The virtuosity with which these extraordinary feats are managed is reflected in the effortlessness and delicacy of the results. My objection to many of the pictures in his last show stems from the isolation of his large stained areas in immense stretches of unpainted canvas, placed in such a way that, though themselves flat, they are silhouetted like sculpture against an unshaped background surface. Louis has transcended this limitation in a number of pictures I saw recently in his studio, pictures that reinforce my feeling that he may be emerging with a painterly profile comparable in stature to those of the "first wave" pioneers. In his forties and living in Washington, D. C., Louis was not a candidate for the Stable show of younger artists of the New York School. The Museum of Modern Art, however, missed an excellent opportunity when it omitted him from "Sixteen Americans".

Also from Washington, D. C., and a friend of Louis, is Kenneth Noland, whose recent show at French & Company represented a radical departure from what he had shown previously at Tibor de Nagy. A few of his pictures, in which tentacles of diluted pigment were flung out from a central core, seemed to recall Louis' method. But in the majority of his paintings, the centrifugal motif appeared in the form of what have been called targets. These targets have image-object tension. They should be called simply concentric circle compositions. The optical punch of these pictures is phenomenal, but it does not prevent the spectator from savoring their delicacy. Their simplicity of means, their absolute disengagement from the seductive possibilities of texture and brushwork, seem at first more Spartan than they really are, for it is by this directness that we are brought to focus on the beautiful colour chords. The application of the colour bands is flat but, like Newman's surfaces, luminous.

In the realm of the bold, flat composition, no painter is more impressive than Ellsworth Kelly, whose room in the "Sixteen Americans" exhibition was even more brilliant than his recent show at Betty Parsons. Kelly has been wrongly related to Mondrian (on the basis of the flat, pristine surfaces and the hard edge) and Arp (flat curvilinear shapes). But being very much a colourist, Kelly is opposed to both, particularly to Mondrian, against whose intellectual attitude he sets a thoroughgoing sensuous approach. Though certain devices (such as the "anchor" shape in "Wave Motif") recall Arp, Kelly's sense of form does not emerge, as does Arp's, from the vocabulary of the organic. And he is further distinguished from the latter by a monumentality which, owing to his extraordinary sense of scale, is communicated in canvases of relatively modest dimensions (e.g., "Rebound" in the Museum show).

Kelly's work comes as a refreshing contrast to the fatiguing exploitation of impasto and brushwork typical of New York painting. He reminds us, as did Newman earlier, that more personality can be projected with less means. Kelly is a marvelous creator of shapes, bold shapes that seem very summary at first but that are really complex and elusive, full of subtle local decisions and un assimilable to formula and geometry. This last fact, plus the sensuousness of his coloured surface, separates him completely from the geometricians of the Nouvelles Réalités and the still-born local followers of Mondrian. (I recall how his picture at last year's Carnegie International stood out both in kind and quality from those of the "geometricians" with which he had been sequestered.)

As an inventor of forms Jack Youngerman, whose work I have come to know only recently, is a painter of great accomplishment and extraordinary promise. Unlike Kelly, he retains a textural viscosity of paint and a decisive marking of the brush. One is struck by a tremendous sense of authority in his painting, even in the less interesting pictures, an authority stemming from a direct, no-nonsense approach to the surface, so different from the self-conscious, ejaculatory brushwork to which we have become accustomed. If Youngerman has an affinity for a painter of the "first wave", it is Still, whose influence seems to be present in the surfaces, the jagged edges of the forms and in the "fingers" of colour that move in from the frame. But this relationship is very indirect at most, and the burgeoning shapes of most of Youngerman's canvases constitute an independent image. The pictures are fairly large, but many (like "Coenties Slip") seem even larger than they really are owing to the way in which Youngerman truncates his expanding shapes with the frame. One picture, "Big Black", disturbed me quite a bit—a good sign, I am sure. This picture breaks away somewhat from the superimposed blossomings of coloured shapes, and though it does not yet make full sense to me, I feel in it intimations of future possibilities. Miss Miller and her associates at the Museum of Modern Art deserve a vote of thanks for bringing Kelly and Youngerman to the attention of the Museum's large audience. The omission of these two painters from the Stable show certainly gave nothing in common with Johns' and are uninvolved in the latter's the latter a more predictable, parochial look.

The situation is reversed with respect to Ray Parker, whose pictures were the most fresh looking in the Stable show, and who might well have figured in "Sixteen Americans". I first saw Parker's work a few years ago in a show at the Widdifield Gallery, at which time he was painting juxtaposed rectangles of colour fanned out over the entire surface on the basis of an implicit cubist grid. During the following year his compositions became more and more elemental, the shapes of colour condensing, becoming fewer, and freeing themselves from the grid. By the time of his exhibition last spring he had distilled from this process a highly personal image. He now uses but a few shapes which combine a primordial gravity reminiscent of Stonehenge with a balloon-like airiness as they float in suspension against the unpainted white ground. The edges of these tenderly coloured flat monoliths are irregular, being constantly discovered afresh and revealing a searching painterliness that calls Motherwell to mind. Clement Greenberg finds an affinity to Gottlieb in the isolation of pure colour shapes against the white ground, but whether or not this is so, Parker's present work stands defined in a wholly independent way, all the more so because it does not rely on exotic innovations of method or image-making. In the context of the Stable show his pictures stood out in their concentrated simplicity and purity, a purity that carries with it an indefinable moral imperative rare in the painting of the second generation.

Where does all this leave us with respect to younger American painters as a whole? Certainly, we are not now, and have not been for almost a decade, in a situation characterized by major contributions, statements capable of redirecting the history of art. The younger painters have achieved nothing comparable to the revolution wrought by their predecessors, particularly in the period 1947–51, the intensity and variety of those years being in turn comparable io the period 1908–13. The best work in America is still being done by the first generation, men now (with the exception of Motherwell) over fifty. However, there are more first-rate painters among the men now in their thirties and early forties than could have been counted among the first generation at the same age. The base of good painting has been broadened even as the stature of individual accomplishment has shrunk. I rather like B. H. Friedman's characterization of the younger men as "colonizers" rather than "explorers". He might have added that in the last decade the first generation have also become colonizers, except that in their cases they have been cultivating their own gardens. The fact that so many of the painters I have discussed have come into their own only in the last two or three years seems to me a good sign. Prospects look brighter now than at any time since the early fifties.

[1] The term Abstract-Expressionist has been mistakenly applied to all recent advanced American painting. It is a misnomer when used to describe the work of Pollock, Still, Rothko, Gottlieb, Motherwell, or Newman. Abstract-Surrealist and Abstract-Impressionist are a bit clumsy but would be a bit closer to the truth for these painters. New American Painting is a handy term which I prefer for the group as a whole, reserving Abstract-Expressionist for de Kooning, Kline, and their followers. However, since Abstract-Expressionism, often used in conjunction with the term "Action Painting", has been rendered ambiguous in usage, I shall refer to such art simply as de Kooning style painting.

[2] While the classical drip Pollocks became symbols of liberation for younger painters, they constituted such a perfect, closed system that they could not offer a viable methodology or "handle" on which to take hold (as could de Kooning). The influence of Pollock was exerted only marginally to his main contribution and by pictures in which he had become a painter of the hovering colour spot rather than the line.

Louis and Noland
by Clement Greenberg
***Art International* IV, no. 5, May 1960**

The arrival of American painting has been demonstrated more tellingly by a younger generation of good second-rate artists than by an older generation of major ones. The latter may have made American painting exportable in the first place, but the former prove that it is. We used to have first-rate artists, like Eakins, Ryder, and Homer, or Maurer and Hartley, who filled a provincial situation to Its limits but could never quite break out of these, and who therefore remained unexportable. Now we have artists who get shown and known abroad while still relatively young, and though none of them has yet done anything that warrants his being mentioned in the same breath with Eakins, Eakins still has to be rated a provincial artist and they manifestly do not. The paradox is one which the future may resolve, but for the time being it has to be endured.

What this paradox has already taught us in America is that the fact of not being provincial has an effect all its own. A certain vehemence, a certain confidence, and even authority, make themselves felt in hollow as well as resounding works of art. The pitch of everything gets heightened. Artists are buoyed up by a sense of vast possibilities of attention and reputation, by the feeling that the eyes of art history are focused not too far away from the place they happen to be in. But this situation has its handicaps as well as advantages, and in the last ten years the former have increasingly outweighed the latter in New York. Kinds of art that would otherwise have faded into the background, or never even come to be, acquire a destructive virulence and set a bad example. Never before in New York has there been so much false and inflated painting and sculpture, never before so many false and inflated reputations.

In a previous number of this magazine William Rubin dealt with some of the brighter as well as darker aspects of the present situation of New York art. While agreeing with much of what he said, I still found him a little too kind toward many of the artists he discussed. They may have set their faces against the loose-brushed, dry-bristled, scumbled, and lathered surfaces of the de Kooning and Kline school, with its Cubist hangover, but not one among the New York painters Mr. Rubin mentioned has quite succeeded in breaking out of the cycle of virtuosity which began with that school. Virtuosity implies performance, and performance implies conformity with received tastes. There is a little too much of the received and the performed in even the best of the New York painters Mr. Rubin wrote about. I myself admire, or at least enjoy, the works of Raymond Parker, Ellsworth Kelly, Jack Youngerman, and Jasper Johns, but find them a little too easy to enjoy. They can't challenge or expand taste. This may not condemn their art, but it has made it, so far, less than major in its promise. And I do not see any reason why we, in America, should go back to celebrating what is less than major.

It is no coincidence that among all the painters Mr. Rubin discussed, neither of the two I consider serious candidates for major status (leaving Helen Frankenthaler and Paul Jenkins to one side as special cases) works in New York. I mean Morris Louis and Kenneth Noland, who both live in Washington, D. C., which fact is not unrelated to the quality of their work. From Washington you can keep in steady contact with the New York art scene without being subjected as constantly to its pressures to conform as you would be if you lived and worked in New York. This circumstance, both Louis and Noland have known how to exploit—there are other artists living at a similar distance from New York, whether in Washington or elsewhere, who have not benefited from it at all. Louis and Noland are curious about what goes on in New York; they show there, and have learned a lot there. But what they have learned mostly is what they do not want to do, and how to recognize what they do not want to do. When they return to Washington to paint it is to challenge the fashions and successes of New York, and also its worldly machinery. (No New York museum has yet shown or bought the work of either.) Mr. Rubin says, rightly, that Raymond Parker's new painting carries with it a moral decision; so, I think, does the painting of Louis and Noland—a decision not eased in their case by the fact that 250 miles separate them from the new Babylon of art. Those miles also isolate them, and insofar as they accept the consequences of their isolation they make all the more of a moral decision.

Louis, who is now in his late forties, found himself only some seven or eight years ago. Until then he had been doing abstract pictures in a late Cubist vein that belonged more to the 1930's than the 1940's; the enormous accomplishedness of these pictures did not make them any the less provincial. His first sight of the middleperiod Pollocks and of a large and extraordinary painting done in 1952 by Helen Frankenthaler, called "Mountains and Sea", led Louis to change his direction abruptly. Abandoning Cubism with a completeness for which there was no precedent in either influence, he began to feel, think, and conceive almost exclusively in terms of open colour. The revelation he received became an Impressionist revelation, and before he so much as caught a glimpse of anything by Still, Newman, or Rothko, he had aligned his art with theirs. His revulsion against Cubism was a revulsion against the sculptural. Cubism meant shapes, and shapes meant armatures of light and dark. Colour meant areas and zones, and the interpenetration of these, which could be achieved better by variations of hue than by variations of value. Recognitions like these liberated Louis's originality along with his hitherto dormant gift for colour.

The crucial revelation he got from Pollock and Frankenthaler had to do with facture as much as anything else. The more closely colour could be identified with its ground, the freer would it be from the interference of tactile associations; the way to achieve this closer identification was by adapting watercolour technique to oil and using thin paint on an absorbent surface. Louis spills his paint on unsized and unprimed cotton duck canvas, leaving the pigment almost everywhere thin enough, no matter how many different veils of it are superimposed, for the eye to sense the threadedness and wovenness of the fabric underneath. But "underneath" Is the wrong word. The fabric, being soaked in paint rather than merely covered by it, becomes paint in itself, colour in itself, like dyed cloth: the threadedness and wovenness are in the colour. Louis usually contrives to leave certain areas of the canvas bare, and whether or not he whitens these afterwards with a thin gesso—as he has taken to doing lately—the aspect of bareness is retained. It is a gray-white or white-gray bareness that functions as a colour in its own right and on a parity with other colours; by this parity the other colours are leveled down as it were, to become identified with the raw cotton surface as much as the bareness is. The effect conveys a sense not only of colour as somehow disembodied, and therefore more purely optical, but also of colour as a thing that opens and expands the picture plane. The suppression of the difference between painted and unpainted surfaces causes pictorial space to leak through—or rather, to seem about to leak through—the framing edges of the picture into the space beyond them.

This kind of painting requires a large format. Abstract painting in general has begun to require it, and abstract "colour" painting in particular requires it. Even Monet, toward the end of his life, required It. Louis is "confined" to the huge canvas as inevitably as Clyfford Still is. This is not the place to go into all the intefral reasons involved in this necessity of largeness, but one of them is, most definitely, the need to have the picture occupy so much of one's visual field that it loses its character as a discrete tactile object and thereby becomes that much more purely a picture, a strictly visual entity. As it seems to me, the "esthetic" of post-Cubist painting—by which I mean painting after Kline, after Dubuffet, and even after Hans Hofmann—consists mostly in this renewal of the Impressionist emphasis on the exclusively visual.

The logic of Kenneth Noland's art does not demand an out-size format, but only because that logic in itself is so purely visual. Noland, who is now in his middle thirties, came under the same influences as Louis at the same time that Louis did, and was then influenced, on top of that, by Louis himself. Only within the last two years has he been able to break free and begin speaking with his own voice. However, just as the predominantly vertical movement of Louis's later paintings was already apparent in his earlier ones, so the centered movement of Noland's most recent pictures had already entered many of those he painted before. And he, too, was a highly accomplished artist before he was ever an original one.

With Noland, the denial of the picture's orientation to gravity, thus of its weight as well as of its palpability, amounts to an obsession. But it is an inspiring obsession, and only when he was at last able to act upon it without qualms did Noland become a mature painter. It was then that he began to let the centered, revolving movement of his earlier pictures crystallize out into compass-drawn concentric bands of flat colour, or into ruled lozenge shapes, or into wavering cruciform patterns. The picture, composed of a single motif, was "planted" in an almost absolute symmetry, with the difference between top and bottom as well as between right and left indicated in only the smallest ways and the canvas itself always square. As Mr. Rubin pointed out, Noland's motifs do not possess the quality of images; they are present solely in an abstract capacity, as means solely of organizing and galvanizing the picture field. Thanks to their centeredness and their symmetry, the discs, the diamonds, and the crossed arms create a revolving movement that spins out over unpainted surfaces and beyond the four sides of the picture to evoke, once again, limitless space, weightlessness, air. But just as in Louis's case—and the middle-period Pollock's—the picture succeeds, when it does succeed, by re-affirming in the end (like any other picture that succeeds), the limitedness of pictorial space as such, with all its rectangularity and flatness and opacity. The insistence on the purely visual and the denial of the tactile and ponderable remain in tradition—and would not result in convincing art did they not.

Facture plays as essential a role for Noland as for Louis. He too works on unsized and unprimed cotton duck, [but] he usually leaves much more of the surface unpainted (seldom going so far even as to whiten it with gesso). The naked fabric acts as a generalizing and unifying field; and at the same time its confessed wovenness and porousness suggest a penetrable, ambiguous plane, opening up the picture from the back so to speak. And given that Noland uses "hard-edged", trued and faired forms, both the bare wovenness and the colour-stained wovenness act further to suppress associations with geometrical painting—which implies, traditionally, a smooth, hard surface. Often Noland garnishes his discs and lozenges with painterly flicks and splashes, but whether he does so or not, the effects of geometrical art remain foreign to his purposes. But so too do those of painterly abstraction, especially now that painterliness in abstract art has degenerated almost everywhere into a thing of mannered and aggressive surfaces (or else has evolved into bas-relief). Noland's art owes much of its truly phenomenal originality to the way in which it transcends the alternative between the painterly and the geometrical. Perhaps Louis (and Frankenthaler) have set the precedent here, but Noland has confronted the issue more squarely, and I think that his solution has had an

call up the spirit or the situation or event; what remains are peculiarities, in a journalistic sense, of an event. What is missing is the feeling, the complicated response, not as history, even instant history, not now as television or radio, but as direct "inherited" experience.

A work of art with the power of making actual or implicit the nature of the species immediately apprehensible to sense perception and *more*, must also stand up to a rigorous analysis consistent with that which is "inside" the given discipline. The essence of the articulated experience may belong solely to the species; it constitutes its essence, and not what was contrived by politics, fashion or mannerisms. Thus it might be discovered that the species Black may have a *face* as part of its essence, whereas its *color* is merely an accident. Color does not in any way define *black*. It is not enough to say "black is beautiful."

The traditional esthetic of black art, often considered pragmatic, uncluttered and direct, really hinges on secrecy and disguise. The understanding is there, but the overwhelming drive is to make it complicated, hidden, acute. Being *up front* is so often given a double edge, often turning such things as language inside out. What was overlooked in Mel Edwards' barbed wire and chains show at the Whitney was its wit, in the tradition of Duchamp, kept afloat by Robert Morris and Les Levine. The elegance and deliberately loose-hanging serial geometry were a sure cover for painful implications. The fact that so many critics missed the point is a lesson in the separation of white from black. Inherent in this delivery is the bondage neurosis in top hat and kid gloves. This particular museum exhibition was not a game, but controlled criticism gone beyond anything Minimal or anti-form art had achieved. In terms consistent with the convention of dropping hints, Edwards "drew" a linear pyramid directly in a material whose identification is with agony; it is not the same activity as Morris or Olitski invoking the state of Fallen-on-the-floor. And Edwards' unforced delivery is the opposite of political-realist art. He reroutes fashion and current art convention to "signify" something different to someone who grew up in Watts rather than to "signify" only in the meaning of Jack Burnham and his colleagues. Never mind the implication of the "free *drawing*" of a pyramid as opposed to *building* one. The work was like taking the Classical tradition and Humanism by the ear and making them face reality from the inside. The trouble is if your gaze is elsewhere, only an act of violence will redirect you, and, as I've pointed out elsewhere, *don't burn the museum down*; this will only bar you from the art experience. Watching the museum burn is *a spectator sport*. Tangling with barbed wire hurts.

William Williams' work is like Frank Stella's in not being about memory. It's about discovery. There is almost no apparent residue, only amazed recognition as these bright abstractions register their charge to the eye and brain. The flow of energy is astonishing. But before I discuss Williams' work specifically, I want to establish a clear and to me obvious distinction between what Williams does and what Stella has done. Criticism, none the less influential for being word-of-mouth, seems to want to penalize the former. But I contend that this is what we are about: Self-evident change!

Stella and Williams don't share an educational background. One went to Abstract-Expressionist Princeton, the other to Bauhaus Yale. This simple fact is not only important, it's explicit. The influence on Williams' work, for very special reasons (social reasons, if you lie, but it is self-evident from the nature of white American art, that he, like so many others before him who also happened to be black, couldn't identify with it) was *not* Abstract-Expressionism. Instead it appears to have been European abstraction of the hard-won sort, represented by people like Albers, or even Johannes Itten. There is something (an attitude, a drive in so much of this energy) recalling the force of the Bauhaus, the inconsistencies of proletarian ambition; the implied, if not actual *kitsch*, of knowing too much and understanding too little, except in the larger societal sense. It is a kind of style and energy which glitters like a newly manufactured brass button.

Much of Williams' early work was close in spirit and execution to Lissitzky. The posture and the placing of forms recalled Russian Suprematism and re-enacted in an uptown situation things one had read about that kind of revolutionary drive. More important however, compare Williams' jazzy, jagged 1968–69 works (when they settle into the format of the dominant rectangle, after the confused burst of first encounter) with Lissitzky or Malevich and one gets a near equivalent of that circle-and-square tyranny dominating the intentful works of the Russians. One begins to appreciate that the content of this work is not about abstract decorative high art, but aggressive hammer blows in the uptight geometry of color and line. Everything in those paintings—colors as line, line as in between the colors—clashes wherever the elements meet in a confused surge of passion. The work is virtually irresistible, hallucinatingly original, when it should be pathetic and disastrous.

In the end there is a reason for this attention toward European abstract revolutionary art, not unlike the late Bob Thompson's absorption in European old masters. Over and above Williams' Yale schooling—in the sense of a talisman—the brother is standing on the corner winning a round of "the dozens," hands down, against all odds.

The mood has begun to change in his recent work. In a four-part picture like *Overkill*, 28 feet long, what seem like leftovers of Cubist faceting have crept in, creating concave and convex drives, flattering and asserting equivalents or challenges to the surface geometry; but they seem on closer scrutiny more a flirtation with what has come down to us from the flattening of certain spherical forms in the sculptures of Baluba art (with its distinctly spaced out and incised hemispheric curves) than with any of Cézanne's discoveries. The picture switches from positive to negative, which intellectually implies cancellation. This is not such a new idea, in fact it is common currency. The astonishing thing is that just the opposite of the expected response is received. Looking at the painting top to bottom, left to right, the forced diagonal drifts both ways from the pink to the white panel through to the black and the off-blue into green at the end. You begin to want to hold on to *something*.

What is delivered through this hectic drive—a kind of circus go-cart sensation—is the idea that these pockets of space begin to exhaust one (they "giddy" the blood or whatever it is) because the exposed channels of the raw duck support, left like trails of tortured passage, have little to do with flatness, but build almost to relief. Kinesthetically the works begin to collapse in a confusion between painting and such sculpture objects as pyramids—pyramids which keep appearing in a tactile way, more sneaking up than appearing. It's as if a confusion of forms that once had to do with face masks and the psychological implications of the pyramid have come together to produce something completely original. Most of Williams' work is like this I have difficulty convincing myself that they are paintings, even though painted. *Doctor Buzzard Meets Saddle Head* is almost completely red and green painting. The saturated green field seems to accommodate the busy lines and swirls on the left panel allowing an illusory pyramid of green on the right to assert itself with a kind of no-nonsense dignity.

In a sense (not our sense, but painting and sculpture), the subtlety of black experience, as articulated by behavior, is amply demonstrated in several examples from the recent heated past. What however is never fully taken into account, hardly ever acknowledged, is born in the new world. Since time immemorial blacks have had to content themselves with the "sneaky" approach. It is a tradition of subtle, driven awkwardness, now stretched to the breaking point, now suddenly a moment not of release, but of explosion of voluptuous, cynical amusement. Irony and sudden change, complete many-leveled contradiction are stock-in-trade and automatic. This is part genesis of the species and the finely wrought articulation of the sensitive. Many completely successful works by black artists can be viewed as direct, arrogant spoofs generated from a complete understanding of the issues involved in the disciplines. The game of white-face is not the same as black-face. Desperation takes on the image of survival and makes for grim touching irony in the face of extinction.

Robert Farris Thompson in an essay in *Black Studies in the University* points out that Anglo-Saxon America missed "an entire dimension of New World Creativity" and suggests that Afro-Carolinian potters made vessels "as a deliberate gallery of tormented faces in order to vent response to a slave environment." Further in the same essay he quotes a South Carolinian "Strut Gal" (accomplished dancer) of the 1840s: "Us slaves watched the white folks' parties where guests danced a minuet and then paraded in a Grand March. Then we'd do it too. But we used to mock 'em, every step. Sometimes the white folks noticed it but they seemed to like it. I guess they thought we couldn't dance any better."

Several black artists work in certain genres which I take to be pretty awful attempts at this spirit of "jive" (a word black people rarely use to mean dancing).

The work of Al Loving is a different story. Loving's educational background consists of undergraduate work at the University of Illinois and graduate work at Michigan. He also taught for five years in the Middle West. In fact Loving is very much a Mid-West middle-class or professional-class entity. Loving began as an Expressionist, and he still regards himself as one. However much of his early work (portraits of his first wife konking her hair, putting on make-up, etc., in front of a mirror) also implied the geometry it *grew out of*. Rectangular windows, mirrors, etc., echo the fact of the framing edge in a way that convinces through its consistency and persistence. Objectifying impressed itself on Loving through this earlier work *into* geometry to the discovery that "even a box can be a self-portrait." The emphasis in Loving's earlier boxes, apart from self-discovery, is on composition. Then he moved to change the shape of the supports of his canvases from the rectangular to other "viable structures." It was as though such perspectives could clear the confused or confusing Surreal imagery of the work of such an artist as M.C. Escher (whom Loving admires) and declare painting's distinct expressive content through structuring.

This observing through discovery of rules and instant drive towards order, evident in Loving, is consistent with his background; it cannot be fully explained without a full dissertation on this gifted artist's development. His "activated branding," "small fine lines," which seemed so imperative in the segments, the individual hexagonal pieces recently dominant in Loving's work (like being boxed-in, incarcerated) have now given way to color mixing. In this sense one can say that Loving's earlier Expressionist color is changing: "I'm thinking about color as viable structure." Instead of "not being conscious [of color] except whether I like it or not." The interesting thing here is, much as Loving is convinced by his "natural" colorist sensibility, as one follows the progress of his work, the lines keep creeping back. That I could be fooled by an apparent elimination of lines in the big pieces is heartening. But the lines are still there as function in the pure sense. Loving says: "If I could get that's strong enough, the lines would go…but anyway I like what the lines do."

For lots of rarely mentioned reasons, Loving's work denies sedate enjoyment, if less so than Williams'. It is discomfiting like any new kind of art, however much of it may operate within the context of the already accepted, and hence be fliply *understood*. And it demands maximum attention if the black shared experience and heritage are not to go wasted.

Loving's *Timetrip One*, 25 by 12 1/4 feet, consists of 11 hexagonal pieces, painted on primed or in some instances unprimed cotton duck, in totally artificial colors, held together by cunning as well as by experiments with chemical formulas. It is an important work. Even the dense brushing and priming do not let the colors operate as anything more than tints. The opacity pushes the artificial light (under which most of this work is seen) back into one's eyes, to the extent that one can't *see* the color. It's ever too bright and dazzling, like bad, bad neon glitter.

A weakness in Loving's work, and it is reflected in his attitude, is rather like what went wrong with Neo-Impressionist painting. He seems to neglect the fact that color activants are not color expressions. His response, both intellectual and physical, is not essentially expressive (as was so much what was done by the Pollock, Kline, de Kooning generation), but an ego trip into ways of excess or extravagance. Enormous paintings are more literal signifiers to a better way of life than those which illustrate freedom in realist or Expressionist styles.

Loving's painting intelligence is beyond question. After his early pictures, he decided that "just to go to other imagery made little sense…I could repeat *any* imagery and still come up with the same…I chose the cube or the box simply because it was a foundation to intellectualism…a sort of mundane form that could be very very dull unless a great deal was done with it." He was impressed by "Frank Stella's first pieces where had dropped the Expressionist vocabulary about composition."

Even though painting is still dealing with the wall and the floor, its expressive content relates to how one responds to the object as a specific. Painting is so complicated that it really doesn't bear explaining except as to what it decidedly is not—i.e., not architecture or sculpture. In this sense, Jack Whitten's work gives off a sunny, glowing, natural response from somewhere in the spots of paint pushed up from orange to that kind of rich grey one only gets from an instinctive and natural response to color. The color is not greyed-out. On first confrontation one may be confused until one realizes that this grey has a richness which must have something to do with weathered Southern sensibility exactly in tune with itself. Whitten makes "fine" paintings which his new technique of pushing the randomly selected color through a fabric screen of various dots on already wet and receptive *other* fabric (in this case cotton duck) makes for a kind of tough choosing that only such a sensibility can pull off. The pictures are so new and mysterious that only intuition tells me this *down home brother* has it in his hands, his mind, his psyche. His mind reading back to me is laughter. His very body action makes every mark without a mistake, even though painting is full of mistakes.

Dan Johnson's work is, he says, in transition. He is under no illusion as to what it is he is doing. His sculpture may be a spectator sport, but his commitment is without question. His position in the community is easily consistent with his status as a kind of *Ebony* magazine STAR, emerging into a larger society. It's more than Bill Bojangles Robinson tapping out and shuffling the *Star Spangled Banner* at a party for President Nixon…or Larry Rivers' arrogant remark about "a better life for black people with the emergence of people like William Williams…" If River's remark has any truth or meaning, it is only true in my opinion for Dan Johnson, who is a magic man and should be Mayor of Soho, at least.

Bombs Away: Hans Hofmann at 2000
by Frank Stella
In Bonnie Clearwater, *Frank Stella at Two Thousand: Changing the Rules* (North Miami, FL: Museum of Contemporary Art North Miami, 1999), pp. 105–07

"Now on the left and then coming from right you'll see the bombs .... " Of course, we can't lift our eyes off the crosshairs on the middle of our TV screens quickly enough to see anything but the explosion billowing up at us. Given the patience to watch repeated NATO briefings, eventually we will begin to catch the gray blurs that ignite large fiery clouds of smoke. Perhaps, if the allied campaign continues long enough, we can hope to see the speeding bombs and their consequent matter-of-fact black and white explosions presented in full color. Transmitting a wider palette would show that in the information age military victory guarantees us not spoils but better, more colorful media entertainment.

Such entertaining bursts of color have been around the art world since the 1940s, although the precedents for colored gesture occupying the whole pictorial surface, and hence the whole

TV monitor, were set with Impressionism in the latter part of the nineteenth century. In our century Hans Hofmann has produced more successful colored explosions on canvas than any other artist. Although not as familiar as they should be, many of his paintings are overwhelmingly beautiful and most of them are obvious sources of the best painting of the second half of this century. Notice how the path of Pollock's headlong return to the womb seen in *The Deep,* 1953, had been traced out early on in Hofmann's pursuit of nature in such examples as *The Wind,* 1944 and *The Conjurer,* 1959. Similarly, Rauschenberg's incredible sendup of Abstract Expressionism, *Monogram,* 1955-59, with its stuffed goat savagely defaced by oil paint, had its antecedents embedded in the equally ferocious paint smears of Hofmann's *Bacchanale,* 1946.

We revere Hofmann, as Pollock did and Rauschenberg does, for proving that the straightforward manipulation of pigment can create exalted art. Simply put, Hofmann's ability to handle paint, to fuse the action of painting and drawing into a single, immediate gesture carried colored pigment into the viewer's presence with the force of a bomb. The force of this visual explosion catalyzed the bond between European and American art, irreparably cementing the first half of twentieth-century art to the second half.

The trajectory of Hofmann's career was beautifully described at the Addison Gallery of American Art (Andover, Massachusetts) in an exhibition entitled *Hans Hofmann: Continuing the Search For the Real,* and although this exhibition has recently closed, there is a similar exhibition now on view in New York until October 13, 1999, *Hans Hofmann in the Metropolitan Museum of Art*, which is, of course, at the Met. At the Addison there were twenty-two works spanning four decades. The exhibition checklist divided the work into three groups, "The '30's and '40's: Moving Beyond Realism," "The '40"s: Fluid Abstraction," and "The '50's and '60's: Compositional Explorations." The last grouping, "Compositional Explorations," provided a title of mind-blowing modesty. All of the five paintings in this group were magnificent and original. They were without precedent except in Hofmann's own work. More amazingly, they were without equal in quality when they were painted and are without equal in quality since they were painted. David Hockney used to get a rise out of collectors who were trying to pump him for information about 60s artists when he replied that the best was "Picasso, of course." Of course, late-Picasso ranged from O.K. to great. They certainly spawned a lot of late Picasso shows and considerable market activity (here Hockney was on the mark). Still, Hofmann was more legitimately the best artist of the 1960s and, at least, as surprising a choice as Hockney's Picasso was in the face of the boom for color-field painting, pop art, and minimalism which dominated the decade. Two titles of paintings from the University of California, Berkeley Art Museum, *Goliath,* 1960, and *Gloriamundi,* 1963, effectively tell the story of Hofmann's relation to the art of his time, which, by the way, included all of the twentieth century. The Goliath so convincingly slain in the 1960 painting of that name is Cubism, and with its demise the armies following Picasso and Matisse are put to rout. Color defeats planar structure. The rectangles of red, yellow, blue and green are knifed and brushed onto the pictorial surface in such a way that the color is clearly experienced as a volume, even though the colored rectangles are delineated as two-dimensional figures. The color has recessional and projective depth but its shape is not experienced as a three-dimensional solid but rather as a resonance and vibration of color that creates a feeling of in-exact dimensionality, a thickness that is less than an added dimension but more than the existing delineated dimensions, in this case, two. So, for the sake of convenience, we could say that the volumetric sense of a Hofmann color slab is experienced as something like a fractional dimension, somewhere between two and three dimensions, something like 2.5 or 2 1/2 dimensions.

Following this line of thought reveals that Hofmann's genius lay in his ability to expand our dimensional experience of the pictorial surface, in this case brilliantly enlarging the clean, liberated and open planar surface made available to abstraction after the abandonment of conventional recessional space. He believed that color alone could activate a flat shape on a flat surface, making it appear as if the colored shape had enough substance to both create its own space within that surface and occupy a space in front of that surface. Moreover, he seems to have grasped almost immediately that this notion (nondelineated pictorial positioning) could also work in the opposite direction; that color, in fact, could give the impression of receding and dissolving into the space behind the surface plane. In this sense, the colored washes which appear behind Hofmann's rectangles might also be seen as acting in a fractionally dimensional manner, so that the washes and diluted splashes recede from a two-dimensional surface toward a one-dimensional point, creating spirited pictorial activity in a space of 1.5 or 1 1/2 dimensions. I don't want to belabor the speculation, but the creation, with properly inflected color, of a vital, vibrant pictorial space for real, abstract gesture in an area bounded by fractional measures between 1 and 3 dimensions is really a nice way to appreciate how special Hofmann's touch was and to understand how, by fleshing out the modernist rephrasing of pictorial space, he helped make it possible to go beyond Cubism.

So much for *Goliath*; on to *Gloriamundi.* Glory of the world this painting surely is, and glory of the world his painting surely was and is. This straightforward personification of painting as the glory of the world and himself as the glory of painting counteracts the modesty of the Addison Gallery's characterization of Hofmann's late work as mere "Compositional Explorations," although it may be that I missed the grandeur hidden in the notion of explorations. Great discoveries are often the offspring of successful explorations, and any viewer in the presence of the inventive as well as explorative *Gloriamundi* will feel a sense of discovery. Viewers will, in fact, discover how to be at one with painting. Following the path of American Zen of the 40s and 50s, they will see Hofmann reach back to the painting of the past with the act of painting, watch as Hofmann pushes his painting to engage with all the painting of his time and, finally, recognize how, by example, Hofmann thrusts painting into the future.

In addition, *Gloriamundi* looks out over a cyclorama of past painting that winds back to Hofmann's birth. It can hardly be a coincidence that Van Gogh's presence is so strongly felt in this painting. From Van Gogh it's easy to engage the early Pollock and the midcareer de Kooning. As well as celebrating the achievement of his abstract expressionist compatriots and linking his and their accomplishment to the cadmium yellow splendor of Van Gogh, Hofmann somehow recognized the advanced process-driven art of the early 60s. There is plenty of Hofmann to be seen in the likes of Smithson, Serra, and Heizer. Their bulldozed topography, splattered surfaces, and defining minimalist geometries are well represented in Hofmann's spectacular pictorial surfaces. It's no surprise that his successors should try so hard to emulate his illusionistic success with their own literalist efforts. His painting, backed up by his explicit titling, seemed to lay it on the line — gloriamundi for him, perhaps gloriamundi for them.

Goliath and *Gloriamundi* have shown how Hofmann helped make the greatest change in twentieth-century art both possible and successful. He just stepped up and painted abstract paintings to match the achievements of the best representational paintings of the past. His essay "Search for the Real" explains how his pictorial thought process evolved. The trick that made the transition from realism to abstraction possible turned on the idea of making abstraction real. It's really very simple: to understand art is to be able to grasp in some meaningful way its vitality. The vitality, what Hofmann calls its "spirit," is always there and reprehensible in great paintings. We just have to give a little, we have to admit that we can feel the vitality and experience the reality. In Hofmann's hands abstract art becomes just as real as representational art, or any other kind of art, for that matter.

But being real is not good enough. We want to know who was the best. Wasn't Pollock America's greatest artist? Wasn't Hans Hofmann just a teacher? In 1963 when *Gloriamundi* was painted, weren't Jasper Johns and Bob Rauschenberg the most famous artists in the world? The answer to these three questions is "Yes." But the yes doesn't in any way diminish the splendor of *Gloriamundi;* it actually enhances it. Yes, Pollock, at this moment, riding deservedly high after his recent retrospective, can be hailed as America's greatest painter. However, could this be mostly the enthusiasm of the moment? Remember, this recent show was nearly identical to the 1967 Museum of Modern Art retrospective. At that time the museum was willing to risk only one color reproduction, *Lucifer*, 1947, in the otherwise completely black-and-white catalogue on America's greatest painter, who was not so incidentally described in a contemporaneous New York Times review as actually "a third-rate painter." Anyway, in the world of abstract painting there is plenty of room for greatness. Hofmann could easily remain the greatest abstract easel painter, leaving Pollock to be our greatest abstract mural painter.

Yes, Hofmann was the greatest art teacher of the twentieth century. Being the greatest art teacher of the century didn't, however, stop him from painting some of the century's greatest paintings. And, yes, in 1963 (the year of *Gloriamundi),* when Leo Castelli was king and Bob and Jasper were the most famous artists in the world, Hans Hofmann was showing the best painting painted in the world that year. He was in his eighties, well known, well loved, just not famous outside of the art world, but in that year, with that painting, he was far and away the best. He was typically at his best in your face, in color, in the painting *Magnum Opus*, 1962. When the allied war effort is updated, upgraded to color, the NATO monitors will try to replicate on our TV screens the force of the uplifted cadmium red monadnock which fills the surface of Hofmann's *Magnum Opus.* With *Goliath* behind us and *Gloriamundi* still pulsating in our ocular memory, it will not be as difficult for us (as it was at the beginning of the Strike against Yugoslavia) to pick up the barium yellow flare on the right and the cobalt blue bomb on the left. We won't need the briefing experts to guide our eyes to the big red explosion.

Artist Eric N. Mack on a 1971 Frank Bowling Essay About Black Art: 'He's Arguing for the Importance of Innovation'
by Alex Greenberger
***ARTnews*, April 23, 2021**

For more than 50 years, Frank Bowling, who turned 86 this past February, has been making abstract paintings that not only push the medium in new directions but also fold in nuanced statements about colonialism, racism, and xenophobia. In the '70s, Bowling was also known as a critic. For the April 1971 issue of *ARTnews*, he wrote "It's Not Enough to Say 'Black Is Beautiful,'" an essay that focused on the double standards to which black artists were regularly subjected. On the essay's 50th anniversary, *ARTnews* enlisted Eric N. Mack, an artist in his mid-30s who works with abstraction, to look at the essay anew. "I feel like we should all feel lucky that Frank Bowling is still with us and showing, and not forgotten," Mack said.

It is as though what is being said is that whatever black people do in the various areas labeled art is Art—hence Black Art. And various spokesmen make rules to govern this supposed new form of expression.

He's problematizing the space of Black art. He was able to afford that to his peers. There was a need for that. At that time, art criticism was so highly regarded. There was emotive argument around what it meant to make painting that has been lost on us a bit. He was trying to do things that critics at the time couldn't do, for this group of artists.

It is clear that modernism came into being with the contribution provided by European artists' discovery of and involvement with African works, and their development of an esthetic and a mythic subject from it. But the point I am trying to make concerns the total "inheritance" which constitutes the American experience and that aspect of it with which black people can now (perhaps they always have) fully identify, due to the politicization of blackness.

With the distance of reading this in 2021, you may not get the system of value at play and the ideological differences. You know, he's talking about this European understanding versus an American one. Bringing out those differences to give these artists dimension [due]. It's something that Bowling could do that would inform later critics and writers to look closer at the work of his peers.

William Williams' work is like Frank Stella's in not being about memory. It's about discovery. There is almost no apparent residue, only amazed recognition as these bright abstractions register their charge to the eye and brain.

I like the generosity in observing a little closer—almost a critical look at the past, the biography, the previous exhibitions that informed it. What he's doing is giving the work back to the artists, to politicize the labor of the time, as well as using the terms as they're set formally. I think that's important. It's important to have a Black artist talking about other Black artists. It's allowing them to possess themselves and hold their own space, especially in a space where people are devouring without taste.

We have not been able to detect in any kind of universal sense The Black Experience wedged-up in the flat bed between red and green: between say a red stripe and a green stripe.

It was clear he did a job, that this was a task that was important, to separate himself and the subjectivity of his studio. It gives a measure to his voice. He's arguing for the importance of innovation—that people were trying to make a new kind of art.

Sam Gilliam
Clear Around, 1973
Acrylic on canvas
52 × 48 in. (132.1 × 121.9 cm)
Collection of Beth Rudin DeWoody
plate 13, p. 41

Adolph Gottlieb
Green Turbulence, 1968
Acrylic on canvas
94 × 157 in. (238.8 × 398.8 cm)
Private Collection
plate 14, pp. 42–43

Hans Hofmann
Iris, 1964–65
Oil on canvas
72 × 84 in. (182.9 × 213.4 cm)
Private Collection
plate 15, p. 45

Morris Louis
Beth Peh, 1958
Acrylic resin (magna) on canvas
91¼ × 133 in. (231.8 × 337.8 cm)
Private Collection
plate 16, pp. 48–49

Morris Louis
Gothic, 1958
Acrylic resin (magna) on canvas
91¼ × 145½ in. (231.8 × 369.6 cm)
Private Collection
plate 17, pp. 50–51

Morris Louis
Lamed Gimel, 1958
Acrylic resin (magna) on canvas
89 × 146¾ in. (226 × 372.7 cm)
Private Collection
plate 18, pp. 52–53

Morris Louis
Curtain, 1959
Acrylic resin (magna) on canvas
91½ × 140¼ in. (232.4 × 356.2 cm)
Audrey and David Mirvish, Toronto
plate 19, pp. 54–55

Morris Louis
Beta Psi, 1960–61
Acrylic resin (magna) on canvas
102¾ × 194⅜ × 1½ in. (261 × 493.7 × 3.8 cm)
Audrey and David Mirvish, Toronto
plate 20, pp. 56–57

Al Loving
Untitled, 1975
Mixed media
66 × 74 in. (167.6 × 188 cm)
Collection of Beth Rudin DeWoody
plate 21, p. 59

Robert Motherwell
Open #149: In Ultramarine with Charcoal Line, 1970
Acrylic and charcoal on canvas
93 × 222 in. (236.2 × 563.9 cm)
Audrey and David Mirvish, Toronto
plate 22, pp. 62–63

Kenneth Noland
This, 1958–59
Acrylic on canvas
82 × 82 in. (208.3 × 208.3 cm)
Audrey and David Mirvish, Toronto
plate 23, p. 64

Kenneth Noland
That, 1958–59
Acrylic on canvas
82 × 82 in. (208.3 × 208.3 cm)
Audrey and David Mirvish, Toronto
plate 24, p. 65

Kenneth Noland
Carriage, 1964
Acrylic on canvas
70 × 70 in. (177.8 × 177.8 cm)
Audrey and David Mirvish, Toronto
plate 25, p. 67

Jules Olitski
Polly La Touche, 1964
Waterbased acrylic and magna on canvas
113½ × 81⅛ in. (288.3 × 206.1 cm; also horizontal orientation)
Private Collection
plate 26, p. 68

Jules Olitski
Zem Zem, 1964
Magna acrylic and pastel on canvas
104 × 75½ in. (264.2 × 191.8 cm)
Private Collection
plate 27, p. 69

Jules Olitski
Comprehensive Dream, 1965
Waterbased acrylic and pastel on canvas
112¾ × 92½ in. (286.4 × 235 cm)
Audrey and David Mirvish, Toronto
plate 28, p. 70

Jules Olitski
Prince Patutsky Diary, 1965
Waterbased acrylic and pastel on canvas
92 × 85 in. (233.7 × 215.9 cm)
Private Collection
plate 29, p. 71

Jules Olitski
Yellow Looshe, 1968
Waterbased acrylic on canvas
81 × 260 in. (205.7 × 660.4 cm)
Private Collection
plate 30, pp. 72–73

Jules Olitski
Eighth Loosha, 1970
Waterbased acrylic on canvas
115 × 68½ in. (292.1 × 174 cm)
Private Collection
plate 31, p. 75

Lawrence Poons
Big Purple, 1972
Acrylic on canvas
98 × 92 in. (248.9 × 233.7 cm)
Audrey and David Mirvish, Toronto
plate 32, p. 79

Lawrence Poons
Rain Race, 1972
Acrylic on canvas
103½ × 155½ in. (262.9 × 395 cm)
Audrey and David Mirvish, Toronto
plate 33, pp. 80–81

Lawrence Poons
"The Call," 1973
Acrylic on canvas
108½ × 192 in. (275.6 × 487.7 cm)
Private Collection
plate 34, pp. 82–83

Lawrence Poons
Lady Accessorie, 1976
Acrylic on canvas
115 × 47¼ in. (292.1 × 120 cm)
Private Collection
plate 35, p. 84

Lawrence Poons
"To Clara from Robert," 1976
Acrylic on canvas
115¼ × 28 in. (292.7 × 71.1 cm)
Private Collection
plate 36, p. 85 left

Lawrence Poons
The Morning Lies in the Afternoon Sun, 1976
Acrylic on canvas
114¼ × 48 in. (290.2 × 121.9 cm)
Private Collection
plate 37, p. 85 right

Lawrence Poons
Pine Plains, 1983
Acrylic on canvas
91 × 217 in. (231.1 × 551.2 cm)
Private Collection
plate 38, pp. 86–87

Lawrence Poons
Regulus, 1985
Acrylic on canvas
90 × 103 in. (228.6 × 261.6 cm)
Private Collection
plate 39, p. 89

Frank Stella
Fortín de las Flores, 1966
Synthetic polymer paint on canvas
77 × 154 in. (195.6 × 391.2 cm)
NSU Art Museum Fort Lauderdale,
gift of Mr. and Mrs. Thomas Scofield
plate 40, pp. 92–93

Frank Stella
Waskwaiu II [Variations on a Circle], 1968
Acrylic on canvas
96 × 96 × 4 in. (243.8 × 243.8 × 10.2 cm)
Private Collection
plate 41, p. 94

Frank Stella
Sacramento No. 6, 1978
Acrylic on canvas
103¼ × 103¼ in. (262.3 × 262.3 cm)
S. Donald Sussman
plate 42, p. 95

Frank Stella
Zolder—ONE ELEMENT, 1982
Painted aluminum
128 × 112 × 23 in. (325.1 × 284.5 × 58.4 cm)
Private Collection
plate 43, p. 97

Alma Thomas
A Fantastic Sunset, 1970
Acrylic on canvas
48 × 48 in. (121.9 × 121.9 cm)
Anonymous
plate 44, p. 101

Cover
Kenneth Noland
Carriage, 1964
Acrylic on canvas
70 × 70 in. (177.8 × 177.8 cm)
Audrey and David Mirvish, Toronto
Photo by Michael Visser

Art director
Luigi Fiore

Design
Anna Cattaneo

Editorial coordination
Emma Cavazzini

Copy editing
Carlotta Santuccio

Layout
Barbara Galotta

First published in Italy in 2024 by
Skira editore S.p. A.
Palazzo Casati Stampa
via Torino 61
20123 Milano
Italy

In association with
NSU Art Museum Fort Lauderdale

Printed and bound in Italy. First edition

ISBN: 978-88-572-5221-6

Distributed in USA, Canada, Central & South America by ARTBOOK | D.A.P. 75 Broad Street Suite 630, New York, NY 10004, USA.
Distributed elsewhere in the world by Thames and Hudson Ltd.
181A High Holborn, London WC1V 7QX, United Kingdom

www.skira.net

Museum Staff

Executive Office
Bonnie Clearwater, Director and Chief Curator
Tina Benedictsson, Executive Assistant

Communications and PR
David Guidi, PR and Communications Manager

Curatorial
Ariella Wolens, Bryant-Taylor Curator
Jordyn Newsome, Exhibition & Curatorial Project Manager
Rebecca Vaughn, Senior Registrar
Caroline McNabb, Assistant Registrar
Oliver Loaiza, Head Preparator

Development
Karen Oleet, Assistant Director of Development
Elisabeth de Lapresle-Wennberg, Major Gifts Officer
Ferida Mamatkazina, Development Associate

Education
Lisa Quinn, Lillian S. Wells Curator of Education
Michael Belcon, The Wege Foundation Assistant Education Curator
Sue Girardi-Sweeney, Education and Engagement Coordinator
Tristen Trivett, Education Assistant

Finance
Annette Cardoza, Business Administrator III
Marvin Rolle, Accountant III

Museum Store and Café
Sally Glenn, Store and Café Operations Manager
Smite Elize, Assistant Manager of Store and Café

Security
Leonard Rauch, Manager of Security

Special Events
Lisa Kasten, Event Manager

Visitor Services
Cindy Jo White, Visitor Services Manager, Volunteer & Intern Coordinator